WHITE BOLTS
BLACK LOCKS

WHITE BOLTS
BLACK LOCKS

Participation in the Inner City

David N. Thomas
National Institute for Social Work

London
ALLEN & UNWIN
Boston   Sydney

Allen & Unwin (Publishers) Ltd,
40 Museum Street, London WC1A 1LU, UK

Allen & Unwin (Publishers) Ltd,
Park Lane, Hemel Hempstead, Herts HP2 4TE, UK

Allen & Unwin Inc.,
8 Winchester Place, Winchester, Mass. 01890, USA

Allen & Unwin (Australia) Ltd,
8 Napier Street, North Sydney, NSW 2060, Australia

First published in 1986

British Library Cataloguing in Publication Data

Thomas, David, *1945–*
    White bolts, black locks: participation in the inner-city
    communities.
1. Cities and towns – Great Britain
2. Great Britain – Race relations
I. Title
305.8′00941   DA125.A1
ISBN 0-04-361066-8
ISBN 0-04-361067-6 Pbk

Library of Congress Cataloging in Publication Data

Thomas, David N.
    White bolts, black locks.
Bibliography: p.
Includes index.
1. Community development, Urban – Great Britain –
Citizen participation. 2. Great Britain – Race
relations. 3. Blacks – Great Britain. 4. Neighborhood –
Great Britain. I. Title.
HN400.Z9C67   1986   305.8′00941   86-1194
ISBN 0-04-361066-8 (alk. paper)
ISBN 0-04-361067-6 (pbk.: alk. paper)

Set in 11 on 12½ point Garamond by Paston Press, Norwich
and printed in Great Britain by Billings & Sons Ltd, London and Worcester

For Tabitha Thomas who has generously shared, and never lost, her fighting spirit; and

For Ted Bowman, Rupert Downing, Dolly Kiffin, Rene and Gus Krayer, Yvonne Maynard, Mary Owens and all the others who have not given up on the city.

Contents

Acknowledgements

This book has its origins in training events, consultations and discussions that go back several years. Some of the exploration of the idea of neighbourhood was made possible by the Calouste Gulbenkian Foundation's support of a previous study of the significance of community in social policy. Other parts of the book draw upon a six-month exploratory project that we undertook about the community participation of the black British. This project was funded by the Voluntary Services Unit at the Home Office, and we are grateful for permission to use Crown copyright material that was gathered in that project, and contained in our report on it. Further details of the project are given in the appendices. We are also indebted to the social services department of the London Borough of Southwark for allowing Hugh Morrison to contribute to the six-month project.

A number of people have supported us with ideas, hard work and administrative skills, including Ruth Page, Mavis Gordon, Dee and Bill Bourne, Poly Thrasivoulou, Triangle Translations, and Guistina Ryan and Jean Harding of the library of the National Institute for Social Work. It would not be unfair to single out Ruth Page and Bill Bourne as the mainstays of this and other pieces of work, without whose commitment and experience we would have floundered many times.

A first draft of this book was distributed to over 100 people; we are particularly grateful to the following colleagues and friends who have made substantial comments on the text, though for some of them there may be much they want to qualify or disagree with: Jim Cowan, Jan Dryden, Mark Gunning, David Jones, Stevie Krayer, Jenny Morrison, Tess Nind, Duncan Scott, Mary Sugden and Judy Weleminsky. We were also helped and encouraged by a number of group discussions, including those with Kate

Burger, John Hargreaves, Jean Houghton and Michael Jesse; and with some staff and committee members of ADVANCE, namely Michael Binns, Nadia Catouse, Rex Halliwell, David Jones, Tess Nind, Brian Pavitt, Jos Sheard and Chris Wood.

Stevie Krayer has made a number of important contributions to the book: to its editing and to discussions of some of the issues it raises about white racism; and her poetry. Paul Harrison was kind enough to let us use some material from his book, *Inside the Inner City*.

Finally, our thanks go to the local people and community workers who gave us their thoughts and time. The unattributed quotations in the text are taken from our interviews with local residents. While a good number of people have helped us, the opinions are our own and are not necessarily those of our colleagues and advisers. The views contained in this book are also the sole responsibility of the author and do not represent a Home Office view.

Pushpinder Chowdhry
Paul Henderson
Hugh Morrison
David Thomas

The Struggle Supports the Gap

In summer the loving was easy
Grew and slumbered like ears in fields
But now wind whispers in the corn –
I should have tried harder to listen.
Between one footfall and the next
I missed a harvest. Now broken stalks
Sigh underfoot. Between one footfall
And the next, I should have been
More attuned. Now underfoot
Tread carefully as I may,
Clumsy, I snap and crumble
Bones of unanswered questions.

Stevie Krayer

Introduction

This is an exploratory study of the relationship between black and white people as it affects participation in community groups in urban neighbourhoods. In essence, it is about the racism of white individuals, groups and institutions, but it is also an attempt to search for, and to ask for, more recognition of the complexity of black–white relationships.

The study explores some aspects of the community participation of black British citizens, both the generation who emigrated here, and their children who were born here and/or have spent the greater part of their lives in this country. We are primarily concerned with Afro-Caribbean and Asian people, though there are other groups, such as the Chinese and the Turkish, where there are special interests and issues associated with the intervention of community workers. The study does not look at community development with refugees, migrant workers, or black students from overseas.

There is a consideration of community development, the contribution of community workers and the practice theory for more effective intervention in multi-ethnic areas. The study is not a sociology of race relations, nor is it wholly about strategies for combating racism. It is about black participation in general community groups, although the experience of racism affects that participation and the adoption of anti-racist strategies by practitioners and groups is a pre-requisite for black people's membership of such groups. The study is not a sociology of the inner city or of ethnic participation in political parties, trade unions and voluntary agencies, so we have made only limited use of the extensive literature relating to these fields.

Our account explores some of the issues which white workers have to face in respect of black participation in community groups, though we do also examine briefly the employment of black community workers. Some 13 per cent of community workers in the UK are from ethnic minority groups, so in the short and medium term there is a major task to help white community workers in their work in multi-ethnic communities.

1

The study is not directly about participation in black groups, but more about participation in general (that is, non-sectional) community groups whose membership is open, at least in constitution if not in practice, to all those (black or white, men or women, young or old and so forth) living in the area with which the group is concerned. However, it is of interest to know whether involvement in ethnic or black groups is likely to be a precursor of involvement in general community groups, and what the relationship is between the two.

We were interested in groups with a neighbourhood focus that are open to and attended almost wholly by local residents, who have full responsibility for their management and direction. On this definition, we included general purpose groups (e.g. tenants' associations, residents' groups, community centre management committees); issue groups; service-giving groups (e.g. mother and child groups); and functional groups (e.g. pensioners' group, claimants' groups).

We were not directly concerned with:

(1) political parties, trade unions and political interest groups;
(2) the formal side of the voluntary sector (e.g. CVS);
(3) formal participation schemes (e.g. in planning proposals);
(4) official consultation arrangements initiated by local government (e.g. District Management Housing Committees).

The study has contained a fair measure of both intellectual and emotional challenges, not least because there are hazards to be negotiated when two white males initiate a proposal in this area. Some of these difficulties are discussed in the early chapters of the book.

What to Look For

It may help the reader to know that there are three major interests in the book.

The first is the issue of black participation in neighbourhood activities, and the nature of the interaction between white and black residents that affects their involvement together in such activities.

The second is the extent and quality of communication between black and white professionals (as we observed it through the project) and particularly its impact on the ability of institutions and structures to change.

The third is the development of the neighbourhood as a legitimate and meaningful part of our social structure.

In the book, we try to make clear the effect of material deprivation on social relations, particularly those between black and white. But in making the urgent and necessary demand for jobs, housing, services and so forth there is a double danger to be detected and avoided. First, what is needed are not just palliatives in the form of special projects or funding for the inner cities but a change in the priorities that guide the use of national resources – towards, for example, a new housing programme, public works and a decent programme of income maintenance. Secondly, this change of priorities is not to be construed simply as the outcome of political will, or a rational or technocratic mechanism of redistribution; what is implied is a programme of considerable change in institutions and structures – schools, social services, police, business and industry, the trade unions and so on – that currently fail the black British and, if we may add without clouding the issues, much of the white working class as well. But these long-awaited changes in the distribution of resources and the functioning of institutions must, we suggest, be paralleled by attempts at personal and inter-personal change; that is why we talk about the quality of communication between black and white professionals, and about the need to sponsor programmes that help black and white residents better to manage their livelihood together. The extent of resource distribution and the institutional changes needed to remove the disadvantage experienced by many black British will need to have legitimacy as part of our national purpose rather than being something that is pursued by courage-ous politicians in the face of white opposition or scepticism. This sense of legitimacy will be helped by a sustained programme of public discussion and learning that might bring about a reorienta-tion of the white consciousness in this country. This point was made by a reader of an early draft of the book:

My impression was that you just don't accept cultural racism as a powerful force in Britain and that racism, so far as a lot of white people live, is the reality and it performs powerful functions. Read Fanon on cultural racism to see its deep-rootedness in the order of things and that it has been created for very functional purposes; basically for money, power, international standing, etc. If the time has now come for white people (some of them anyway) to see that it is no longer functional or in our best interests to live in a culture which is endemically racist then we are going to have to do far more than create viable 'resources' by neighbour-to-neighbour 'transactions' between black and white. It's in orienting white people towards such programmes, and not just in neighbourhoods, that there is work to be done.

We try to place the issue of black participation squarely in the context of personal and institutional racism; and the failure of both social policy and of many community workers to elaborate strategies that acknowledge that the neighbourhood ought to be recognized as a proper part of our social structure.

The attention we give to how people themselves manage their livelihood at their place of residence means that this book may be read as much for the discussion of the significance of locality as for the specific interest in black and white participation in community activities. We have learned in doing the study that it is foolish (both in terms of analysis and policy implementation) to abstract relationships between particular groups (black–white, young–old etc.) from the quality of the general social framework in which these relationships occur at the local level. It is evident, too, that social relationships, and particularly those between black and white, will be adversely affected by the continuing impoverishment of the livelihood of those who are denied work and adequate housing. It is hard to envisage that Britain will be a stable and progressing society when the lives and aspirations of large numbers of its working class are blighted by unemployment, poor housing and the withdrawal or curtailment of services in education and health care; and when, in particular, black British people are so neglected or discriminated against[1] by a society that has the power and resources to ensure their access to levels of education, employment or housing that will make for a decent livelihood.

The stability of society is linked to the quality of the housing and environment of its people. Poor design and materials, inadequate maintenance and the lack of resources for improvements have helped to produce an impoverishment of human relationships and expectations in urban housing estates, and a despair and violence amongst those consigned to live in them. Many such estates have the atmosphere of terminal wards, where people are doing their best in exceptionally difficult circumstances, putting on a brave smile and contriving to be cheerful in the face of adversity and deprivation in managing their livelihood. Political leadership may not plead ignorance of what is happening: a report in 1980 from the Department of the Environment said of the Broadwater Farm Estate:

> little attention was paid to the suitability of the housing for likely occupants . . . At best, the local authority can hope to make it tolerable for the next decade or so but eventually . . . the possibility of demolition is one that will have to be considered.

The extent to which stability and progress have been put at risk by cuts in public spending on housing is indicated by the government review on the condition of the housing stock (Department of the Environment, 1985) and by the 1985 report of the Association of Metropolitan Authorities: some £20 billion is needed for urgent repairs to council housing.

It is not easy to watch the emergence of a black and white underclass in the inner cities, mostly young, toughened by the quality of their life and by their place in society, alternatively ignored or harassed by authorities, violent, aggressive, often immune to the pain they inflict on others, and celebrating in bouts of gang lawlessness.[2] They are usually outside the influences of family, school, community leaders and, above all, the routines of paid employment and the discipline imposed by the prospect of personal improvement and enhanced status, at work, in the community, and in society. The hooliganism observed on the streets of the rebelling inner city, the theft, the violence against person and property, the political discontent, the display of ethnic and class grievances, and the street-corner solidarity are part of the retribution meted out by those whom we have provocatively marginalized, denying them access to the basics of a decent livelihood, and depriving them of respect, dignity and a sense of worth and personal destiny as British people. After the riots of Handsworth, Brixton and Tottenham, there is talk of rubber bullets, tear gas and water-cannon; but the control technology which is failing in Northern Ireland and South Africa will not solve the inner cities' social and political problems. As Scarman observed: 'Good policing will be of no avail, unless we also tackle and eliminate basic flaws in our society' (HMSO, 1982).

We cannot even give proper consideration to these problems that we create because the very institutions which fail the black British continue to rigidify the white mind. In the hours of television given to inner-city riots, there are few interviews with young blacks; we miss their worried, serious faces, their caring, articulate accents, the burden of their grievances. In their place, we have long-range camera shots of gangs of Rastas looking menacing, followed by close-up shots of injured shopkeepers and beleaguered, white pensioners. Instead of bringing them to the forefront, in close-up interviews, long-range shots of black youngsters on a street corner mirror the way society pushes them to the edges, seeing only the threatening homogeneity of a group injured by racism, and never seeing in close-up the needs and aspirations of individuals. From behind the police lines, the camera gratifies the need for drama and danger; we observe with safety from the comfort of an armchair, looking but never heeding, observing but never listening, moved rightly by the plight of the injured in their hour of anguish, seldom touched by the lifelong anguish of those we as a society contrive to dispossess.

When the policy-maker and the politician, the affluent, the comfortable and the coping turn uneasily in their sleep after yet more news of inner-city rioting or hooliganism, or rising figures for crime or heroin addiction, then perhaps some force is at work to prick their awareness of being dependent members of a society that is a complex chain whose strength is only that of its weakest parts. The threat posed by an emerging urban underclass was noted by a leader writer in the *The Guardian* after the Handsworth riots:

> There is, though no politician of any major party cares to admit it, a link between the stabbings and stampedes on football's terraces and the bubbling mayhem of our inner cities. White or black, unemployed or fitfully employed, the rioters belong to the desolate, deprived under class of modern Britain's urban ghettos. They are not, in any real sense, part of the communities whose 'community leaders' bestride our television screens. (Ask yourself truthfully if you live in an inner city: what is your community? who is your leader?) They do not vote or join trade unions or write to the local MP. They are beyond the reach of conventionally organised politics. Their family life is a fractured nullity. Their homes, whether decrepit terraces or sixties' council estates, are run down hovels. Education has passed them by. They have no marketable skills. They are without immediate hope or immediate purpose in society. (*12 September 1985*)

A new deal for some is thus, in the best traditions of enlightened self-interest, a new deal for all, a reconstruction of the links in the chain without which things will fall apart, leaving no one untouched. For the young black British, this reconstruction is about the prospects for employment, decent housing and a radical change for the better in the way that the police force regards and deals with them. Such changes are dependent in large part on an improvement in the quality of political leadership in Britain.

An Outline of the Study

This book draws upon several years of work carried out on race and racism, public housing estates and on the significance of community. The book also makes use of a six-month exploratory project funded by the Voluntary Services Unit. This project was carried out full-time by David Thomas, and by Pushpinder Chowdhry, Paul Henderson and Hugh Morrison who contributed on a part-time basis. David and Paul worked on reviewing some of the British literature as well as some of the material from mainland Europe and America; interviewing a small number of community workers (Appendix 2); and organizing two one-day workshops for black and white community workers on the themes with which the study was concerned (see Appendix 3). They also obtained comparative material from Holland and France.

Pushpinder and Hugh were employed as project officers for one day a week to carry out a small number of reconnaissance interviews with black British residents, and to contribute to the design, implementation and analysis of the project. These interviews are described in Appendix 2, but we emphasize here that they were not intended to produce, nor have we used them to make, generalizations about minority ethnic groups. Not only the interviews but also the workshops were, or became, part of the project's fieldwork and helped us to form observations on black–white communication.

The project began in October 1984 and ended in the spring of 1985. The first draft of this book was completed by June 1985, and distributed for comments to over 100 people in the summer of that year.

We must stress that only so much can be achieved in a six-month project where only one worker was full-time. Research can be constrained and even distorted by the basis of funding, just as much as practice may be affected by the short-term nature of its resourcing. One of the limitations of the project was the small number of interviews with community workers – there was insufficient time to carry out more than a handful. This book, therefore, does not give an adequate account of the range of practice that is occurring and is an insufficient testimony to the skills and commitment of black and white community workers in our urban areas. We hope this publication will stimulate further writing and discussion of good practice.

The first two chapters indicate the main themes of the study, and consider available data on voluntary participation. In Chapter 3 we discuss some of the factors that seem to be present in the interpersonal relations of black and white, and attention is given to communication between black and white professionals. In Chapter 4 we ask the reader to reflect on matters to do with the neighbourhood, and in Chapters 5 and 6 we return to the more specific focus on black and white participation in community activities. The last chapter presents our conclusions from the study and indicates some opportunities for further work.

The three primary themes – participation, professional communication and the neighbourhood – are thus dealt with in particular chapters of the book; but it should be noted that in each chapter the discussion will often move from one theme to another, because in theory and practice they are connected. There is considerable emphasis in many parts of the book on the neighbourhood; this should not be taken as a message that institutional change is not necessary or important, but rather that such changes may be of limited value without programmes that try directly and immediately to mend the disrepair of relationships in the inner cities. Neither institutional nor neighbourhood programmes will be effective unless they are used to create, and to take advantage of, initiatives to remove the deficits experienced by black people in the employment, housing and education markets.

The Cross that Chris Bears

The form of the book is not conventional; part of it comprises a dialogue with a community worker whom we call Chris, who is a composite of some of the people and observations that we have encountered in the project. Chris is a device to allow different views within the study to be articulated rather than submerged, and to permit those who read the first draft of this book to enter the dialogue with their comments.

The first chapter begins with reference to Chris's 'journey of exploration'. This is a useful concept for the reader to retain, for what we have written is less a 'hard-and-fast' categorical research report and more an exploration of issues about which black and white professionals have, if only they were to share them with one another, numerous uncertainties and confusions. One of the readers of an early draft thus commented:

> The text . . . is not, as most academic reports are, partitioned to enable the reader to address it in a logical fashion. One cannot tell what comes from your literature review, what

from the interviews, and what represents your own perceptions. Instead we have this journey through states of
awareness, and a pretty bumpy journey at that. Chris's
consciousness is messy, it jumps from scene to scene, it is full
of surprises, there is not even a teleological pattern, and so
the only way to deal with it is to begin at the beginning and
end at the end.

As is the nature of such a journey, a great many matters impinge
on the main routes pursued; in trying to find the best way
forward, often in twilight or darkness, our torch reveals all kinds
of interesting diversions and detours, false trails, slippery paths
and slopes, and apparent culs-de-sac. All these must be negotiated
as the reader accompanies us, sometimes rafting precariously
down a stream of consciousness, at others plodding through the
mono-tonal landscape of survey data, sustained only by the will
to go forward, no matter how poor the equipment, difficult the
terrain, querulous our companions or hostile the white natives.

Notes

1   Those who require evidence on this point might refer to Brown's (1984)
book published by the Policy Studies Institute.
2   These behaviours cannot be dismissed simply by calling them 'criminal'.
Some kinds of crime are a social product and as such demand theories of
causation as much as do more explicit forms of social unrest and political
demonstration or riot.

As if the Sea Were But an Hour Wide

On 8 October 1985 Paul Stephenson wrote to *The Guardian*:

The recent events of inner city rioting and looting in Handsworth, Brixton and Liverpool pose a major threat and challenge to the future social stability and fabric of postwar British society . . .

No major English city with a sizeable black ethnic population can afford to be complacent to the dangers and lessons to be learned . . .

. . . the vast majority of white British people have no understanding of the deep psychological impact their racism has had on black British-born young people over the past two decades . . .

Britain's inner cities . . . are fast becoming firmly established black English townships policed by insensitive, racist, hostile, heavy-handed white law officers. The vast majority of Britain's blacks are trapped . . . by an invisible wall of white racism that denies them equal job opportunities, promotion . . . They are daily faced with having to live in poor housing . . . leading lives of despair, frustration and hopelessness.

Many of Britain's black youths now identify with the aspirations . . . of the black revolutionary struggle across South Africa. If England is to avoid the permanent establishment of black townships within its own cities as a feature of British society, then the Government and people of Britain must be jolted out of their complacency to the horrendous future it will face.

At the turn of this century, apartheid in South Africa will have been assigned to the rubbish bin of history. Will England have black townships still burning? It would be a bitter irony of history for the British people if this was to be the remaining legacy of the British Empire.

On 18 October, Benjamin Moloise was executed in Pretoria and the funeral of Cynthia Jarrett took place in Tottenham.

1

The Case of the Japanese Professor

> . . . the past is studded with sisters who, in their time, shone like gold. They give us hope, they have proved the splendour of our past, which should free us to lay just claim to the fullness of the future.
>
> *Alice Walker*

In a journey of exploration it is as difficult to say where the journey began as to predict where it will come to an end, if ever. Chris's determination to be more effective in working with black people in neighbourhood activities may have begun with reading Thomas Keneally's book, *Schindler's Ark*, a testimony to the case for resisting racism in the most extreme of circumstances. Chris took from it the message that each individual must do what he or she can (no matter how insignificant within the total picture) to assist those being oppressed. Victims do not usually have the energy to pull themselves up by their bootstraps (assuming they have some), and Chris believed that it would be as much a piece of inhuman nonsense to say that only blacks had a 'right' to look at issues affecting black people as it would be to say that only Jews had had a 'right' to help themselves escape from the genocide of the 1940s.

Chris was honest enough to reflect that those people who murdered over six million Jews, gypsies and disabled people over forty years ago were not remote or mythical figures of history but people of our parents' generation, from a nearby white, north European, Christian country with similar social and cultural traditions to those of Britain. Moreover, some of the most shameful acts of racism in British history were not distant moments of historical action but were events that belonged to our grandparents, our parents and ourselves. Chris belonged to the generation that was responsible for the 'nigger-hunting' riots that infected Britain in 1958 and 1959, for the election to Parliament in 1968 of Peter Griffiths on an openly racist platform ('If you want a nigger neighbour, vote Labour') and for a series of immigration and nationality Acts that discriminated against black people. Chris appreciated that racism was embedded in British culture and national life and wanted to find ways in which community workers could 'do something' not just in their personal lives but also in their professional work.

So that may have been one possible starting point for the journey of exploration. The other was the non-events of one winter night in a neighbourhood in north London in which Chris was employed as a community worker. After months of violence by white people against Asian residents, a number of tenants' associations and community groups had called an open meeting to discuss these attacks. Chris had persuaded the groups to make the issue a priority and, indeed, the small committee had worked hard to prepare for the meeting. It was called for 8 o'clock in the evening in a tenants' hall on an estate in the neighbourhood. Only one person turned up – a visiting Japanese professor who was renting the house of a linguistics don from London University who had gone to Japan on an exchange visit.

'Well, you wouldn't expect anything else, would you?' said the caretaker. 'What d'you expect when you call a meeting on a dark winter's evening? People won't come outdoors, d'you know, until the clocks change.'

Chris saw he had a point; but it missed the heart of the matter which was that the white residents did not seem to care about what was happening to their black neighbours. This was confirmed several weeks later when another meeting was called by local home-beat policemen to discuss robbery and break-ins on some estates; thirty people came to this meeting and a few had even gone to the trouble of arranging for mini-cabs to take them there and back home again. Some Asian people came and assented to the general swell of prejudice that the muggings and burglaries were the responsibility of 'black youths'.

This conjunction of events made Chris look more closely at the work of the community groups in the neighbourhood. There were two observations to be made: first, that black people were not participating in community groups in proportion to their numbers in the neighbourhood population; on some estates, for example, over half the tenants were black but none was on the tenants' associations. Were black people excluding themselves from these groups, or being excluded? In either case, were the black residents in the area part of black networks and organizations not known to white workers? Secondly, it might be necessary to seek help in understanding and working on these issues. Chris also guessed at how much fear white workers might have in their bellies – fear of what black activists would say to white workers interfering in their world, fear of knocking on the door of black residents and trying to win some communication and trust, fear of physical violence and threat from racists in the area, and fear that acceptability as a worker in supporting community groups would be jeopardized through confronting these groups with their racism.

Chris's starting question was this: what was the role, if any, for a white person working with black people, and with the white groups from which they were excluded? It was easier to pose the question than to find the time and energy to answer it. People working in the inner city in the inappropriately named 'soft' sector – in welfare, or education, for example – do not often have the opportunity to take a measured, reflective look at the issues they are dealing with: they are too busy using every trick they know to stretch impossibly limited resources to meet a barrage of human need and difficulties. This is a particular problem for the inner-city community worker operating, like Chris, alone and unsupported in a neighbourhood with chronic problems of housing, low income, inadequate play space, and traffic congestion, and depleted of a whole range of resources necessary for its healthy functioning. Expecting people and their activities to flourish in such an environment was tantamount to asking farmers to grow crops while every day their topsoil was being stolen or washed away. People, after all, are socio-degradable.

On the day Chris framed this starting question about the role of the white worker, the Association of Community Workers sent their final reminder to renew membership. It was expensive to be a member so Chris dithered, looking at the pros and cons yet again, doing a quick scan of the previous year's newsletters. They revealed most clearly that fighting racism and sexism was ACW's number one priority. So it was worth renewing membership because being a member of, and keeping alive, an organization so completely open about its views on racism was a small gesture that was important to make.

But making this gesture did not hide a real disappointment with ACW: true, the back numbers of its newsletter were replete with anti-racist statements and encouragement of anti-racist practice. But what *was* anti-racist practice? What were its principles and methods? What were workers to *do* when they came across prejudiced or racist practices in community groups? Why had no one written up their successes and failures so that others could learn from them? Chris was a willing subscriber to ACW's stand against racism but practitioners had a need to know how that particular stand was implemented on the streets, and in attempts to change institutions. A search of the agency library and that of the local university produced the same result: there was a vast literature on the sociology of race relations, on immigration and on the different social, political and cultural experiences of black British people, but there was virtually nothing on either the extent of the participation of black people in neighbourhood activities or the role, if any, of the white worker in supporting this participation.

Chris was chastened both by Juliet Cheetham's warning 'about the reluctance of most community workers to grasp the racial dimension of their activities' (1982), and by Robin Ward's conclusion that 'action by black and white designed to secure common political interests which go beyond the routine of the parliamentary and local government vote is not well documented' (1979). Such documentation that Chris did find in the libraries rarely focused on the community worker, and was based largely on groups which were organized in the early or mid-1970s.

So here was Chris, nervous and uncertain, waiting to start a journey of exploration about which there was much to be apprehensive, but neither ACW nor that fine, veneered shelf of researchers and sociologists could provide an orientation, let alone a set of maps and compass. And the one substantial article that was helpful was also very tantalizing. This was a paper by Basil Manning and Ashok Ohri (1982). It confirmed Chris's sense of legitimacy because it said quite powerfully that there *was* a role for white community workers in working with black people and black groups; it even offered guidelines for white workers which we shall look at in Chapter 6. Indeed, the purpose of the book was to 'show how little work is done by white community workers and groups to challenge racism, especially its institutional forms, both in relation to the power structure of the local authority and within the groups themselves'. It criticized white workers for rightly being concerned to remove racial prejudice and disadvantage in such areas as housing, employment and education but for failing to recognize how far racism (the economic and cultural subordination of one group for the benefit of another) has infected individuals and institutions in this society. Manning and Ohri came to a conclusion that re-enforced Chris's own evaluation of the literature:

> Addressing the issue of racial prejudice is a necessary task in white community groups, but should not be confused with addressing the issue of racism itself. Notwithstanding that reservation, it is difficult to determine how white community workers are breaking down stigmatisation in practical terms. *Nor can one recollect any guidance on possible methods emanating from academics or professional bodies . . . the issue of racial prejudice, let alone racism, is still treated as marginal by community workers.* (Emphasis added)

But there was in Chris's mind a seed of doubt that could hardly be acknowledged, let alone discussed openly with others. Would a white person ever take or be given the right to disagree with black writers and professionals, to question their judgements, and their use of reason and evidence? When Chris started talking with black residents in the neighbourhood would they share the analyses and goals of black activists? Would they, for example, validate or dispute the assertion (because it is only an assertion, Chris thought, waiting to be verified) that 'this process of political education, with the objective of development of political consciousness, could be the only way in which community work with the black community can develop at this stage' (Manning and Ohri 1982).

The only way? Who says so? And with what evidence? Chris

recalled occasions when white colleagues had lost faith in their own judgement, when they had ignored reason and evidence, only because the person disputing with them was black. The deference that liberal whites pay to blacks (and men to feminists) reminded Chris of student days when many classmates found it difficult to question what the professor said just because he was defined by his status as knowing the truth. Part of the price now being paid for the subordination of black people is the enslavement of many white liberals/radicals in their encounters with black peers to the principle that the colour of truth is black.

And now Chris felt isolated and vulnerable again, just as Manning and Ohri describe when they talk of the fear and uncertainty on the part of the white community worker about what to do.

> Fear and uncertainty is partly engendered by the racist context in which the community worker finds him/herself. That context is influenced by a number of current trends which are affecting both the community and the worker. These trends include a lack of positive leadership on the issue of racism in Britain. It is a sad reflection on this society that it can produce so many passionate racists like Enoch Powell and John Tyndale, or a Prime Minister who can whip up latent racism in the white community by claiming that 'white people in this country have legitimate fears of being swamped' by the black 3 per cent of the population.

Chris had some expectation that the context would be positively influenced by other national figures, or, at a local level, by the attitudes and practices of local authority departments. But on this point Manning and Ohri bring us up sharp:

> There is in this country no equivalent white 'leader' who will stake career, electoral prospects, popularity, on passionately speaking out for racial justice. Political, ecclesiastical, trade union or community leadership are astute enough to sense the racist mood within the country to be sufficiently careful to pay only occasional lip-service to the need for racial justice . . .

Chris recognized that when this lack of leadership was combined with the immigration debates, with immigration laws and procedures and with laws about nationality, 'the result will be a country in which licence, however subtle, is given to individuals and institutions to discriminate against those the like of whom, after all, every effort is being made to keep out'. And what were the effects of the lack of leadership, what were the 'messages' being given out by governments that initiate discriminatory laws and procedures? In what ways were ordinary people following the lead of national figures? Again, Manning and Ohri do not flinch from confronting us with the consequences of what we are creating:

> Those racist measures open the door for all the irrational blame and scapegoating of the black community, for bad housing and high unemployment, poor schools and lack of amenities in inner-city areas. It is into such areas and armed with the racist ammunition freely given by government leaders and others that the fascists move to play out their war drama, with the knowledge that other racists will join in the fray.

Leaving the Ivory Stockade

What happened next may seem peculiar to some people. Chris came to see the community work tutors at the National Institute for Social Work.

'I'm worried about how few black people are joining community groups in my area.'

'Join the club', we said.

'What club?'

'There's been a stream of white community workers with the same worry. And we don't know what to do about *that*.'

'But you should – you're supposed to be trainers and consultants in community work.'

'Two white, male trainers', we replied.

'You sound apprehensive.'

'We are; we don't want to be scalded.'

'What do you mean?'

'There's a lot of emotional heat in community work around race and racism'; and not much light either, murmured one of us incautiously.

'How d'you think *I* feel? I'm on the streets, not ensconced in a comfortable *art nouveau* building in Tavistock Place!'

'That's an illusion: you want to take some risks in your north London neighbourhood? Fine, nobody will notice. The streets are private. But if we do something – a project, or some training or some writing – that's exposure. That's quicksand.'

'That's funk.'

There was one of those long silences in which people tidily rearrange little bits of their world. So black people are not involved; is that really the case, and, if it is, why is it a problem and to whom? And *if* they are not involved, what else would you expect in a society contaminated by racism? The daily experience of it must sap people's motivation to participate, and make them expect racism in any groups they join – particularly groups of working-class people. And can you expect black people to come out to meetings when there is so much racial harassment? (There is a danger that 'harassment' will soon become a euphemism for murder, assault, arson, intimidation and robbery.) The threat or the anticipation of violence is a form of racism; the expectation of abuse or assault from young people drives deeper wedges between black and white neighbours.

'So can you help me?'

'You're opening up a can of worms.'

'Such as?'

'It's not a simple question about black participation; there's also the issue of the general level of participation in community affairs – especially that of the poor, both black and white. And it's not just an empirical question about who participates and who doesn't and why not, nor simply a practical question about how to improve participation. Don't you think there's a *moral* issue here about the balance in society between private lives and public roles? And isn't there a case for thinking about participation within the context of issues such as unemployment which have helped to make the neighbourhood a place where more people are having to spend more time? You've also got to be a bit brave and challenge some sacred cows in this field – and that is where you might get kicked.'

'What cows?'

'For example, a lot of activists will tell you that blacks don't get involved in general community groups because they're into black networks and organizations. Is that true? Are most black people as uninvolved in black groups as they are in other groups? We don't know, but it's the kind of question to be asking. And here's another: Manning and Ohri tell you that combating and confronting racism is the top priority of the black community. Leaving aside whether it is meaningful to talk about 'the black community', how would the black people in your neighbourhood describe their priorities?'

The question was not answered but was followed, perhaps unfairly, by another: 'And how willing are you and other white workers to discuss the whole of your feelings about black people?'

'Meaning what?'

'Our fears, for example, of black people, particularly Afro-Caribbeans . . . it's ironic really. Here we are, with many black people living in expectation of being harassed by the police or by white thugs when white people themselves . . .'

'You're not going to say something racist, are you, about white people's fear of being mugged by . . . ?'

'No, you're jumping to wrong conclusions. The point I'm trying to make is about the fears that Afro-Caribbeans inspire in many whites, and it's a fear that pervades and distorts their dealings with each other. That fear has to be named and confronted. And it's very complex; it's partly to do with the association of blackness with 'negatives' like death, evil, dirt, wrong-doing . . .'

'. . . And the stories from childhood of naughty children being carried off by black men', interrupted Chris, impatiently.

'. . . And partly to do with the fear of primitive, uncivilized man that has stained the white consciousness for generations.'

'But above all, it is the fear that is always in the heart and mind of the oppressor, the fear that the worm, if I might use that expression, will turn, and will exact revenge.'

'It's called the "Mau Mau phobia" and it's stimulated by the language and the imagery about black people in the media. It's the language of the black menace, of whites being "hacked to death with machetes", of assault, violation, rape. Whites were saturated with it in the 1950s and 1960s during the independence struggles, and more recently in the fight for emancipation in Zimbabwe and now in South Africa. And, of course, the fear in the white man that the pent-up fury of the black man will be unleashed against him (and, even worse, against his wife and daughter) is being richly primed by the way in which the events in Brixton and Tottenham are being reported.'[1]

'To be honest,' said Chris, 'I am apprehensive in the street, for example, about walking past a group of young black people. I feel they must hate me, and that makes me nervous. I don't really expect any goodwill or consideration from them – and I don't feel I'm *entitled* to any . . . but surely you can't argue that *all* whites feel these fears about *all* blacks?'

'That would be absurd. All we are suggesting is that white workers like yourself should explore and recognize these kinds of feelings, and how they affect relationships with black colleagues and residents out there.'

'Let's look at it another way. We could probably agree that there is a short-sighted tendency amongst some race equality workers to separate issues of race and racism from others to which they really are intimately connected – for example, class, age, sex, culture, religion and so on. It is similarly myopic to believe that the heat generated in the inner city by the discriminatory treatment of blacks is sufficient to boil down the ingredients in the relationship between white and black individuals in, say, a meeting or seminar, to those only about race and racism.'

'Yet, there is many a white professional who behaves and says things in the belief that a black person sees him only as a member of a racist group, and he thus gears his behaviour and language only to demonstrating to the black person that he is not a racist.'

'To respond to black people in this way is a crass form of racism because it denies their humanity by denying them the possibility of a whole range of differentiated reponses to you as a white colleague. And it does make that kind of white person vulnerable to "blackmail" and manipulation . . .'

'Would it be far wrong to guess that many middle-class professional white people, for instance, have worked out a system of threat management; a way of anticipating imagined physical, intellectual or emotional challenge from some blacks? Whether this system of threat management is conscious or unconscious, systematic or rudimentary will depend on factors like education, how much contact a person has with blacks, whether or not he was brought up together with black children from an early age, and so on.'

'And communication is based on perception which in turn is based on knowledge. But how many whites have learned to know and to "read" a black face? The lack of ability to do this reading, to make distinctions and categorizations, fuels the white fear. I mean, most whites still can't tell a South African black from a Nigerian (or a Hausa from a Yoruba), a Sudanese from a Kenyan, a Ghanaian from a Caribbean, a Bajan from a Jamaican.'

'I'd admit that in my own work I have a very crude system of threat management. In my contact with black people, I've come to the point of defining circumstances which look safe or threatening to me as a white person. The lowest form of perceived threat comes from women, rather than men, middle-class blacks rather than working-class, old and middle-aged rather than young, Africans rather than Caribbeans. I feel more threatened by groups (whether on the streets or in a meeting) than individuals, and the degree of threat varies with circumstances – for example, I expect more challenge and hostility in the atmosphere after a street rebellion or a heavy-handed police operation. Rightly or wrongly, I'm affected by people's clothes, hair-style and general presentation. and I'm just as nervous in a seminar of meeting a lean, close-shaven black with John Lennon glasses as I am by Rasta locks, tams and other insignia. Like you, Chris, I predict hostility and suspicion because I'm a member of a white group that has earned it.'

'That's quite a declaration', said Chris.

'It's very hard for a "non-racist" to convey to black people he meets in a seminar meeting (let alone on the streets) what his feelings and attitudes are; but it's even harder to be a non-racist *and* to express your anxieties, fears and doubts about engaging with black people.'

'I've often thought that the over-respectful attitudes of some whites to blacks is a perverted form of liberal politeness; but I think I'm wrong about that. It really is another tactic in managing expected threat and hostility. People don't argue, disagree and criticize because they don't want to provoke the black person to anger . . .'

'Better rather to let the beast slumber . . .'

'Well, people don't want to provoke an anger that will not just be about them as a person, or their judgements or points of view, but may largely be about them as whites. You can't cope with that kind of anger because it strikes at your very being, and thus forces you to acknowledge that this is what whites have done to blacks for generations.'

'Is there anything else?'

'Sex.'

'What's that got to do with it?'

'Just about everything. Wait until you do your first racism awareness training and then you'll find out. You've got to operate on at least three levels. First, the historical and the structural – understanding the roots and embedded nature of racism in this country. The second is its manifestations and abrasions in the neighbourhood – because that is where black and white people mostly interact. And the third level is the interpersonal – and particularly people's fears and fantasies about each other. And that's where sex comes in. Envy and anxiety about black sexuality torment the white psyche, and that is intimately connected to our economic and cultural subordination of black people.'

'I thought whites were upset by the noise from sound systems and ghetto blasters.'

There was another of those long silences; a clock clicked and whirred, the sound of prejudices ticking over, attitudes being shuffled and stored, facts filed. 'You've already forgotten Donald Finney', we said.

'Donald who?'

'Finney: the councillor in Smethwick in 1968 who Prem reports as saying: "I've had a wonderful holiday – didn't see a nigger for a fortnight." '

'What's that got to do with sex and sound systems?'

'It's yet another example of the white British phobia with invasion – with violation and contamination. England's green and pleasant land, and all that. Never been invaded since the Normans except by the blacks. Kept the Germans out twice but let the coloureds in without a fight. It's all about invasion and pollution, the disturbance of the daily routines and assumptions of what Stokely Carmichael calls anglo-conformity.'

'That's what Manning and Ohri have said. Let me quote: "It is unlikely that a group of white people in a neighbourhood will choose the issue of racism and its effects on the black community to organise . . . 'their' neighbourhood is one which excludes 'the blacks' who live next door or over the road. For this very reason most community work groups end up being white with a white worker!" '

'Yes, if you can't make laws as in South Africa to keep blacks out of white residential areas, and if you aren't successful as they are in America in using house prices and restrictive purchasing practices to keep out blacks, then how do you maintain the pleasant everyday landscape of white anglo-conformity?'

'By not "seeing" black people, as Manning and Ohri suggest. If you don't see people, then they're no longer a blot on the landscape, or part of your community', replied Chris.

'It's even worse than that. There's the rubbing out of black history as a way of undermining the position of blacks in the present and future British landscape. Without roots, you can't grow. Listen to Malcolm X':

It's impossible for you and me to have a balanced mind in this society without going into the past, because in this particular society, as we function and fit into it right now, we're such an underdog, we're trampled upon, we're looked upon as almost nothing. Now if we don't go into the past and find out how we got this way, we will think that we were always this way. And if you think that you were always in the condition that you're in right now, it's impossible for you to have too much confidence in yourself, you become worthless, almost nothing. But when you go back into the past and find out where you once were . . . that you once . . . had made great achievements, contributions to society, civilisation, science . . . you know that if you once did it, you can do it again. . . (*1969*)

'The point that Malcolm X was making', interrupted Paul, 'was that by keeping black people cut off from their past, whites are tying them up on the fringes of society. It's another device to control. And when these defences and devices cease to work then many white communities tacitly allow their more racist members to drive out blacks by murder and violence.'

'Isn't it a bit over the top to talk about blacks being tied up on the fringes of society?'

'Your question raises the problem of knowledge: how do whites ever get inside the skins of black people to know what their experience of this society actually is? It's not just a problem of opportunities for communication and empathy, or of the fact that the two worlds of black and white hardly intersect. So many whites will remain ignorant about the black experience because at heart they're contemptuous of Asians, afraid of Afro-Caribbeans, and have too many interests to protect to face the consequences of what is the everyday experience of black people in this country.'

'One way to solve this problem of knowledge is to get it second-hand through other people's accounts. For example, you question the point about 'fringes of society'. Well, listen to Stephen Small's interviews with young black people':

In their statements and comments on Britain, individuals reveal an underlying tension between a desire to enjoy the rights and privileges of British society and the feeling of rejection as black people in a white society. They do not fundamentally reject the values and institutions of British society (as will be seen, many of them have desires and aspirations of a conventional kind), but they do reject a 'white society' which denies them the same chance of success and accomplishment that is offered to their white peers. And their sense of identity is strongly tied up with the ethnic group to which they belong, a group with whom they share similar experiences. Through their personal experiences they have found themselves rejected by British society and through their knowledge and perception of history they have come to conclude that, in general, black people have always been rejected or dominated by white people and by the British in particular, not only within Britain but through-out the world. This had led them to feel that they are not regarded or accepted as belonging to British mainstream society, that blackness is not an integral part of the society in which they live and that as black people they have little chance of full participation or opportunity to succeed here. For many this results in the conclusion that there is no place for them here. Most individuals feel much bitterness and a strong sense of rejection. Having reached these points of view individuals have reacted in a number of ways and to varying degrees; reactions which have a considerable influence on their assessment of what future lies before them. Several people expressed a desire to leave England at all costs, others seemed undecided, and some seemed inclined to stay regardless. These attitudes are tied in not only with their ethnic identity but also with their distinctive personalities, individual aspirations and the rights which they demand as citizens of the United Kingdom. (*1983*)

There was a pause in the conversation. 'It's not just a matter of trying to understand some of these matters – whether they be the structural or the interpersonal – but you've also got to find out how they operate within the neighbourhood. The neighbourhood is not just an empty vessel in which individuals rattle about driven by their own internal needs or by larger external forces. On the contrary, the neighbourhood contains a variety of mechanisms through which the internal world and the external are mediated, translated, and interpreted. Thus confronting white prejudice and racism is not just a matter of understanding the white psyche or racism as an ideology used to justify the slave trade or colonialism; you've also got to know how these factors are given expression or extinguished within the local neighbourhood.'

Another pause, another moment for re-grouping, the move to a conclusion. 'Anyway Chris, we've talked enough for you to see what we might be letting ourselves in for – especially you.'

'What's that supposed to mean?'

'It's going to be very painful; I don't mean just what you learn about yourself but when you start working on race then you'll get overwhelmed by the sheer crudity of what many white people feel about blacks, or what they can do to them. Look what they did to Mr and Mrs A in North London':

It was a three bedroom house. An English family had moved out and the GLC offered it to us. It was a good house and had a big garden at the back. The electricity was switched off when we moved in but my husband arranged for us to be reconnected. The same night our window-panes were broken by white people. There are also some Jamaicans in the neighbourhood, but they live rather far away. The next evening whites wrote on the front door: 'Get out and go back before it is too late.' My husband was a night-shift worker then. The next morning we washed the front door and he told us not to worry, they would calm down eventually. I was nevertheless worried, because they had given us a warning. On Sunday we had guests at our house. Five to six white people knocked at our front door. They had sticks in their hands and started shouting and calling us names. My husband told them that he didn't want a fight, that they should go home, that all we wanted was to live in peace. He told them that if they broke the window-panes again he would go to the police. Then those white people broke the glass of the front door. My husband stood in the door. They started to throw bottles inside and hitting my husband with iron rods. I started crying, I was pregnant at the time. We reported it to the police but nothing happened. Now we were really scared. The windows were unsafe, each room had a window and then they repeated their warning. I went upstairs with the children and locked us in, then I broke down in tears. The next day at about 9 p.m. they broke all the window-panes again. In the morning we went to the GLC and asked them to keep our deposit of £1,200 plus the £400 we had spent on decorating the house, altogether £1,600, and to put us back into our old flat as living in that house had become a constant stress and we were very much afraid of getting killed. We told tham that our children were very small and we didn't want to take any risks. We lived in fear that anybody might put a brick through our window at any time. The GLC told us that the house was ours now and that we could do with it what we wanted and that they couldn't help us.

'You see, you'll be entering a kind of frontier war, but the frontiers are as much in the mind as on the streets. You'll be forced to take sides. Listen to Mrs X from Brixton: "The problem is they're walking down the street and they're not safe." She's talking about her two children. She's not talking about being safe from sexual molestation or attacks by white gangs – she's talking about the threat to her small children that she feels comes from the police, from being picked on, hassled, roughed-up, lied against, kept in the police station. She's worried about the heavy policing of young blacks in some inner-city areas. If you want an elegant discussion of policing and the black community read the Scarman report or the Policy Studies Institute books on police and people in London (Smith *et al.*, 1983) which show, incidentally, that Mrs X's fears are not groundless – young West Indian males are more likely than any other group to be stopped by the police. Indeed, the shock of the Handsworth riots led one journalist to realize that "the only human contact many young blacks have with white Britain takes place when white men come to police them".

'On the other hand, listen again to Mrs X, talking about policing':

> I really feel violent about what's going on with black people, it's not nice. They [the police] only start more violence in people's minds, the way they're behaving, it's not nice . . . if you have a dog outside and you keep teasing him, he's going to bloody bite you . . . these are the things they want to sit down and look at, and get into it and work it out, and stop interrogating people. I mean if a child go out, or a man go out, and break the law, lock him up, that's the law. But not when he's walking down the street, you hustle him around, lock him up, tell lies on him, lock him behind bars, beating him till you kill him or knock him out of his senses till he's no use to himself . . . why treat human beings like that? (*Television History Workshop, 1981*)

'There's an interesting division of labour on the streets, though I wouldn't push the point too far: the Asian communities are being patrolled and harassed by gangs of young white children and by thugs from neo-fascist groups. The Afro-Caribbeans, on the other hand, are catching it from the police. The Asians are forming vigilante groups to protect themselves; many young

Afro's used the 1981 and 1985 riots to say "enough, we're not going to be kicked around any more". Being harassed by the police is not just unpleasant or painful or a blow to your pride and dignity: it has a critical effect on your livelihood if you are a young black. This is a point made by Mr C':

> You got to come to Brixton and live at Brixton to know what's going on in Brixton, right. 'Cos these police, they're going on the street, they're just picking on youngsters. If you could interview a hundred youngsters in Brixton today that don't have a previous conviction you'd be lucky, right. And if a bloke of eighteen and nineteen have three previous convictions, there's nobody going to give him a job, right. How long is he going to live? Maybe sixty, seventy, is he going to live that sixty or seventy years without work? He can't! He's got kids and if he isn't working and he had previous conviction and when he goes to the employer to ask for a job and he doesn't get that job, what is he going to do? Is he going to come back inside and look at his kids and say there is no money? There's nothing to buy sugar, he has nothing to buy property, or even buy a sweet. He's got to do something, right. And if he go on the street and he sees somebody with something that he wants, he'll steal it because the police has put him into a situation that he has to steal to survive, and that's what it's all about, see. Because if a bloke can't get a job, can't get no money, can't get no social security . . . he's got to live, somewhere there he's got to live, whether me, you or somebody else got to suffer for it, you see. And that's the kind of thing that's going on in Brixton. (*Television History Workshop, 1981*)

'You may think it's an exaggeration to talk of a "war" between young Afro-Caribbeans and the police. but the relationship *is* very difficult; for example, a report that the Metropolitan Police themselves commissioned found that "the level of racial prejudice in the Force is a cause for serious concern". It indicated that':

> Young West Indians are far more critical of police conduct than young white people, particularly in relation to false records of interviews, fabrication of evidence and the use of

force and violence. *The lack of confidence in the police among young West Indians can only be described as disastrous.* (*Smith* et al., *1983*; emphasis added)

'But the police are only one part of it; there's also the teachers, the employers, the housing officers, the estate caretakers, the doctors and so on. How long d'you think it'll be before the day comes when a crowd of blacks will assemble to stop a social worker taking a black youngster into care? It's not just the prisons, it's also the children's homes, the ESN schools, the mental homes and so forth that have a disproportionate number of black people in them.'

Enough is enough: it was time for Chris to go. At least, an agenda had been roughed out and some issues pinpointed. But Chris added one more thing to the agenda: just *how* was it possible to bring about institutional change? Was it through anti-racist training, exploding the myths of white cultural supremacy, pulling the rug from beneath the white norm? Is it possible to tackle racism without trying to do something about the worst effects of hierarchic practices, professional elitism and bureaucratic rigidities that seem to characterize so many local authority departments? And if racism was prejudice plus power, then didn't dealing with racism in an institution like a housing office or a social work department mean confronting the power exercised, on the whole, by white men?'

Chris had always been puzzled by the differences and similarities between racism and sexism. Both are based on fantasies about 'the other's' inferiority as a justification for exploitation. Chris found racism the harder of the two to explain – being founded on something as superficial as pigmentation. But women and men *are* physically different, thought Chris. Women bear children or have that potential (of which they are reminded every month for 30 years). Women are smaller, have less muscle and a less efficient metabolism. (There was, of course, the additional fact that having assumed, or being indoctrinated, with a posture of superiority the racist or sexist person realizes he cannot maintain it if he gives blacks or women access to the opportunities and privileges that he enjoys.)

There was another difference between racism and sexism,

mused Chris: it is possible for whites to go all their lives without ever meeting a black, let along being intimately involved with one. But the sexes are almost wholly involved with each other, and usually in a way that generates the deepest feelings and/or affects the definition of their own identity. But part of the perceived 'alienness' of blacks is to do with ignorance and lack of contact.

Chris's view was that the cultures of the two sexes in a given society are really complementary sides of one culture – each set of roles is intimately known to the other and is seen in practice all the time. Differences are therefore perceived as familiar, 'natural' and entrenched – and consequently their removal is a threat to the familiar world. Chris doubted whether white people considered the differences they perceived between themselves and blacks as part of the familiar and natural world, as complementary aspects of a single culture – and that was part of the problem.

Of course, women, like blacks, may react to oppression by creating a new culture all their own, which deliberately sets out to be *mysterious* to the oppressor. In short, lots of phenomena are probably common to all systems of exploitation and rebellion but, in Chris' view, it was the basis of the original oppression that made sexism and racism unlike.

Where Next?

We arranged another time to meet to continue the discussion. We took stock of the growing number of white community workers, of whom Chris was one, who wanted to be more effective in helping black people in neighbourhood activities. But we didn't know how to assist because we didn't know much about the issues – not least because the community work literature yielded little and the material from the American experience seemed, on the whole, less than suitable for the quite different conditions in this country.

There seemed every reason to do something to help. The issues around race and racism, participation and exclusion, were unlikely to evaporate; we accepted the argument that, leaving aside what we did in our own time outside work, we ought to do something in our professional roles, even though what we could do (some research, some training, a publication) might seem rather trivial compared to the experiences of black people on the streets. We saw, too, that if community work was to make a contribution in the emancipatory struggle of the black British, then part of this contribution would be through white community workers who make up the majority of British community workers.

We also felt that there were a number of challenges to community work implicit in the issues to be explored. First, the failure of moral crusades on racism to produce a practice theory useful to practitioners in their daily work brought community work itself into disrepute. And we could not ignore that there was a general expectation, as noted earlier by Cheetham, that community work did have something to offer. Secondly, the issue of black participation in neighbourhood activities is one of the crossroads of social policy and the theory of direct fieldwork practice. Barr has made the point that community workers are faced 'with the interaction of two major sets of problems: those arising from the structural, social and political forces which constrain attempts to relieve poverty and inequality, and those arising from the internal competitiveness, prejudices and misunderstandings between the component elements of the community' (1980).

But there is a sharper focus than that suggested by Barr. In the past, the saliency of structural factors has induced a culture of radical pessimism in community work that has led either to dismissing the neighbourhood as a base for intervention, or to being frank about the large gap between what community groups do in the neighbourhood and the structural causes of many of its problems. But in the issue of black participation, the community worker has both to deal with the broad issues of racial prejudice, disadvantage and institutional racism, and to devise his interventions in such a way as to support the membership of black people in community groups. In other words, the issues of white racism and black participation give community workers a structurally determined problem that is amenable to intervention and some change at local level. While workers might be excused from coping with, for example, the investment decisions of multi-national companies, there can be no excuse for not attempting to be more effective in both confronting local forms of racism and, in so doing, supporting black people in roles and responsibilities in local communities that augment their status, power and resources.

Thirdly, the issue of how black and white people deal with each other in local communities seems capable of exposing a number of lacunae in community work theory and practice. Of these, the most significant is the 'vertical fetish' most vividly demonstrated in that cartoon of a lonely community worker chipping away at the base of the local authority monolith. Community work has been far more concerned with the vertical relationship of community groups to power/resource holders ('action by the community') than to the horizontal relationships of people and groups to each other ('action within the community'). How community action relates to community interaction has hardly been discussed at all, although one useful pointer from the American experience is that community work with ethnic minority groups demands careful attention to the social, commercial and cultural networks of those groups.

After much discussion, we worked up a proposal to raise funding to explore some of the issues raised by Chris and other workers, and this year-long process and the content of the proposal are discussed in Appendix 1. The summer of 1984 came and went as quickly as most British summers do; we were now September's children, clearing the desk after the long break and sharpening pencils and resolve for the start of the project on 1 October. It was about half-way through September that Pushpinder and Hugh began probing:

'So we're supposed to be worried about the non-participation of blacks in community groups?'

'Yes, but we're not saying it's their fault', we said, sensing the drift of their question. 'For heaven's sake, nobody's suggesting they're suffering from "civic underachievement" or that they're too lazy, or indifferent or hedonistic . . .'

'Or too selfish, building up their business interests, being seen at the Temple, pushing the children through school . . .?'

'No.'

'But what!'

So they made us write it down and it looked like this:

We start from two assumptions:

(1) That there is a level of participation of black people in a range of social, cultural, religious, economic and political networks/groups within the black community that is largely unknown to or inaccessible to white community workers (and white researchers, like ourselves). The fact that this participation is inaccessible to us obviously means that white workers can fail to appreciate its significance and undervalue it; but this same inaccessibility also makes it difficult for us to evaluate critically the extent and quality of this participation in black groups and neighbourhoods.

(2) That, on the whole, black people are excluded, and will often exclude themselves, from participation in general-purpose neighbourhood groups (such as tenants' and residents' associations, action groups etc.) – groups which on the whole are dominated by white working-class members whose attitudes, ways of working and priorities often are indifferent or hostile to the interest of black people, white groups which on the whole do nothing to counter racism and intimidation that is rife in so many working-class areas. In other words, a major constraint on blacks today in civic and neighbourhood roles will be their experiences of racism and harassment in their daily lives.

Our study is then interested in a number of questions about participation including but not confined to, the following:

What is to be done, if anything, to support black and white people working together in general-purpose neighbourhood groups, and how do black people themselves assess those groups?

What role is there for white community workers in helping black people represent their interests both through black organizations and, where appropriate, through multi-ethnic community groups?

Now all this is rather long, and repetitive; it is also vague, cautious, cribbed and cabined with generalities. So why have we reproduced it? Partly, because we have learnt in this area of work that you do well to repeat and to re-state in different words (particularly in face-to-face discussions), for communication is poor between black and white, about black and white. We will return to that later. Another reason for reproducing the passage is that we have discovered how quickly whites lose confidence in their concepts and language; even in groups of black and white peers (let alone on the streets) the reliability of language diminishes, meanings are unclear or ambiguous, people listen but don't hear, stereotypes and prejudices filter, code and distort, intentions, assumptions, trust and good faith are clouded. In short, whites will not speak because they have learnt that their innocently conceived words may not be so innocent after all, and that these can be used to demonstrate their racism or prejudices. Whites fall into silence, or speak vaguely or in generalities; no risks are taken, no firm positions put forward, no challenge given or desired.

We want to talk about this later in the book but here are two examples. We asked in the quoted passage how white community workers help black people to represent their interests. Hugh and Pushpinder seized on this one afternoon in late September. Why did black people need 'help'? There was nothing wrong with them, they were not children or disabled in some way. Weren't we 'pathologizing' them? Anyway, why do we concentrate on 'representation' of interest? Blacks are perfectly capable of expressing their interest; the major problem is that white people and institutions are not capable of *receiving* and hearing those representations.

The second example comes from a letter to the *Radio Times* (24 October 1985) after the shooting of Cherry Groce by a policeman:

May I, through your columns, ask the Editor of BBC Television News why he chooses to use the word 'accidental' to describe the Brixton shooting? Though this may be the preliminary view of the police, and may be the truth of the matter, the word is firstly inconsistent with the BBC's own construction of the shooting (*Six O'Clock News*, 30 September BBC1), which suggests the shot was discharged after a verbal warning; and secondly, is a judgemental word that preempts the inquiry into the incident.

The word was not used, so far as I can remember, to describe the shooting of WPC Fletcher, though she was hit by a bullet apparently aimed at Libyan demonstrators . . . Such prejudgement by the BBC is a sign of what black demonstrators have referred to as a partiality in British society in favour of white authority and which they claim to be the root cause of their frustrations.

B. Garner

So you see how the common-or-garden taken-for-granted language of social welfare becomes a potential minefield. Why enter, why lose an arm and a leg? Why did two white teachers claim that the issue of black participation was as much their issue as a black person's?

The participation of black people is also about the viability of neighbourhoods as social, political and economic systems; and of democratic processes at local government and parliamentary levels, and within the trade-union movement. We believe that community groups are an important part of the political process and to be concerned with the participation of any section of the community in these groups is to be concerned with the inclusion or exclusion of that section from democratic processes. On both these counts, the issue of participation in local activities is one that embraces more than the experiences of individual blacks and groups; it is an issue about society and national life, its quality and values, and thus goes much further than the basic struggle about the resources, power, justice and opportunities available to black people.

In much the same way we would identify racism as a contamination of national life and purposes. We do not want our children to grow up in a society where black people continue to be subordinate and exploited citizens. Thus the struggle is not just for a 'better deal' for black people, but for a better society.

Our part in this struggle in our professional roles entails helping white community workers in their work with white groups and black people, because we think that community workers have a role in modifying those groups that are at present dominated by white people and white interests.

So, for these things, and more, we inched out of our ivory stockade to risk an arm and a leg, always mindful of the sanguinary words of Obi Egbuna:

> We do not want to put our hands in anybody's pocket but our own. And we do not want anybody's hand in our pocket either. If we find any stray hand in our pocket, we will saw it off, be it white, black, green, or striped.
>
> But since the hand in our pocket right now happens to be white, we are in the process of sawing it off. If anybody doesn't want his hand sawed off, he should keep it where it belongs: in his pocket.

Notes

1   Paul Hoch has written an interesting book on the themes of 'white hero, black beast'. He writes of how the 'alleged rapes of white women by black "guerillas" in Southern Africa is still used to whip up worldwide white hatreds . . .'. He notes the 'relish with which the Western media tars African and Asian rebels with the label guerillas . . . the term is identical in sound to gorillas, and this brings to mind all the frightening assertions of beasts breaking through the defences of civilization to attack 'our women'. Hoch also traces the theme of black beast in literature and popular entertainment discussing characters such as Caliban, Othello, King Kong and Darth Vader (*1979*).

2

Understanding Participation

> It would be dishonest for me to sit here and tell you that I
> have no caste attitudes. It would be dishonest for me to say
> to you, as a man, that I have liberated myself from my sexism.
> What I would say is that I am aware that my antennae are out
> and that gives me a code of practice. The code by which I live
> life.
> *Tuku Mukherjee*

Chris was looking for an acceptable code of practice as a person
and a community worker, on the assumption that a precondition
of change in others was a change in oneself. While it was
important to acknowledge the views of some colleagues that
racism was embedded in exploitative economic relations (between
people, and between classes and countries), it did not follow from
that particular analysis that the individual does not matter because
she or he has no power to change anything. My power *to* change,
Chris thought, is part of the power *for* change.

We had a telephone call in early November to say that Chris
had formed a small group of three white community workers.
Their primary concern was the participation of black people in
neighbourhood groups but they had soon decided that working
on this issue implied working on themselves. As a start, they had
signed up for some racism awareness training, and two of them
were also going to workshops at a local adult education institute
on working with ethnic minority groups. Colin, one of the group,
had been embarrassed in one of these sessions by how little he
knew about the history of black people in Britain. So they had
been reading *Staying Power* by Peter Fryer and were taking to
heart Salman Rushdie's warning:

> If you want to understand British racism – and without
> understanding no improvement is possible – it is impossible

even to begin to grasp the nature of the beast unless you accept its historical roots; unless you see that 400 years of conquest and looting, centuries of being told that you are superior to the fuzzy-wuzzies and the wogs, leave their stain on you all; that such a stain seeps into every part of your culture, your language and your daily life; and that nothing much has been done to wash it out. (*1982*)

The group were also looking around for classes in black British history and Chris was thinking of learning an Asian language and even of going to India or Bangladesh for a long summer holiday. It was not without apprehension that they mooted these activities for they were aware that, from the outside, they might look like a type of white 'student' liberal who black groups will look upon with utter suspicion. Being seen as over-sympathetic in addressing themselves to the well-being of ethnic minority groups could be interpreted by those groups as patronizing – a point at which their efforts to be effective workers would be without value.

They had come across a pamphlet by Jim Cowan called *Many Cultures, One Community?* (1982). They shared his assumptions about his community work in south London:

- that, whether white people like it or not, Britain now is, in terms of people living here, multi-racial and multi-cultural.
- that the institutions of society (including most voluntary and statutory agencies) have not really begun to take this evident fact into account.
- that multi-cultural and multi-racial services/groups will only emerge as a significant force for social change when *individuals* in those institutions are aware of the need for and significance of their actions in creating a multi-cultural and multi-racial society.
- that training is a key to generating this awareness of individual responsibility, change and effort.

What Chris's group of workers took from this was that their attempts to find a code of practice for themselves were not just about their own relations with black residents and colleagues but were also part of a strategy for changing attitudes and services in both community groups and their own agencies. Change in an agency (especially one with political and financial leverage in a borough) can become a way of inducing or compelling change in other organizations which come within the influence of its power and status, and which, at the same time, are being confronted by the needs and demands of black people themselves. 'We musn't give seed money unless we're prepared to seed ideas and values as well. In this way, we disperse the elements of our own code of practice,' Chris said.

They had borrowed a number of ideas from Cowan and had thus been able to use them to formulate the stages they should go through as individuals and as a group. Briefly, they were:

- locating themselves and their agencies within a multi-racial and multi-cultural community;
- assessing their racial identity and experience as white people;
- understanding the pervasiveness and effects of cultural racism, the dominance of the white norm, the devaluation of anything black;
- exploring the existence and functioning of racial prejudice and understanding racism as an ideology used to explain and justify the historical and present-day subordination of black people;
- assessing the extent and effects of racism with local institutions, and primarily within the assumptions, routines and practices of their own agencies;
- working out a programme of intervention, action and change.

They had a lot of questions about this process of change. While they accepted for the time being that 'racism was a white problem' (or a sickness, as some awareness training described it), did this mean that only whites could eradicate it? Could a group of white professionals working on their own be an adequate mechanism for raising awareness about their racism, and the racist routines of their agencies? What was the responsibility of black colleagues to work with them in training? They inclined to the view of a writer in a paper to Councils of Voluntary Service:

> Viewing racism exclusively as a white problem implies that black people are justified to shun responsibility for its solution: it seems to imply that simply because white people created racism (and perpetuate it) black people have no part to play in the genuine attempts by some whites to remedy the

situation. This kind of reasoning is obviously based upon a faulty premise firstly because, in the final analysis, racism is not a white problem but rather a human problem. Racism is like cancer (a problem facing all humankind) so that holding its sufferers exclusively responsible for its eradication is tantamount to holding cancer victims exclusively responsible for its cure or elimination. In the case of cancer, for instance, most of us would agree that abdication of help and responsibility by the medical profession, relatives and friends from its victims would be grossly immoral. It would be equally immoral for black people to shun responsibility for the elimination of racism. Thus, in order to cure white people of racism at both personal and institutional levels, black people have a moral duty to assist in the role of physicians, nurses, therapists, relatives and friends. (*J Owusu-Bempah*, *1985*)

But what was happening to the project workers? Hugh and Pushpinder were preparing for their field interviews but they were also beginning to collect flak from black community workers. Why were they collecting data on black people to be handed over to and interpreted by two white researchers? Wasn't the National Institute a rather lily-white organization? Why were they taking part in a study that was funded by the Home Office? Surely a handful of interviews in the black community couldn't be 'proper research'? And why were they bothering anyway – we all knew that the answer to the question of participation was racism. What else could it be?

Interestingly enough, Paul and David were running into other kinds of issues. They touched the proprietorial nerve of the race relations industry: why were they doing this research? They may know something about community work but what did they know of race relations, and particularly its sociology and research? Weren't there a good number of other academics who had been building up a reputation and credibility in race relations research – surely they should be doing the study? Of course, it makes good sense to have a group of experienced and expert people who 'know' about race and racism but to leave everything to them could perpetuate certain racist strategies. Hiving the race issue off (to CRC's, blacks, experts and so on) is a way for individuals and institutions to avoid change in their own worlds, in their own time.

The benefit that came from touching this proprietorial nerve was in its reminder that in looking at black participation there were other variables to be considered, not least class and economic position. How did the participation of blacks compare with that of whites in similar socio-economic groups? What was the extent and quality of voluntary participation amongst the general population? How did the poor participate? It is to these and related questions that we now turn.

Who Participates in What?

Two substantial sets of data on the nature and extent of voluntary participation in the United Kingdom are found in the General Household Survey (GHS) of 1981 and the National Survey of Volunteering (NSV) carried out by Field and Hedges in 1984. The GHS of 1981 was the first major survey of voluntary work, and the problems of methodology (including the definition of voluntary work) are clearly presented in Chapter 8 of the Survey. Its data are limited for our purposes: there are no earlier or later data with which to compare the 1981 figures; there is no breakdown of the data by ethnicity; and the range of activities counted as voluntary work is heterogeneous. It includes such diverse and different activities as raising money, giving advice to individuals, teaching and coaching, practical help to individuals, improving the environment, and working for a community or political group. In addition the data does not distinguish between voluntary work done in the respondent's own neighbourhood from that done outside it. The GHS data therefore gives us only a very rough indication of people's involvement in community groups and committees operating at the neighbourhood level.

Some of the main findings from the Survey on participation in voluntary work was that 'almost a quarter – 23 per cent – of persons aged 16 and over who were interviewed in the GHS in 1981 said that in the twelve months before the interview they had done some voluntary work – that is, work for which they were not paid, which was of service to others apart from their immediate family and friends'.[1] Women were more likely than men to be doing voluntary work, and the proportion doing voluntary work also varied with age – the peak was for those aged 35–44.

For both men and women, and for most age groups, those in the professional occupation groups were more than three times as likely to be participants in voluntary work as those in the unskilled manual group. In the professional group 43 per cent of informants and 33 per cent from the employing and managerial group had participated in voluntary work in the year before interview, compared to 15 per cent and 13 per cent in semi-skilled and unskilled manual groups respectively.

One of the conclusions of the Survey is that:

> The analysis presented in this section, while showing that those who do voluntary work are more middle aged and middle class than the population as a whole, does not support the hypothesis that voluntary workers would be drawn predominantly from those who would apparently have the most time to spare. On the contrary, groups which might be expected to have more time available, such as people without children, the unemployed, and perhaps the recently retired, show lower than average participation rates in voluntary work. Although it cannot be inferred directly from the survey results, it is possible that those who do voluntary work may tend to have a relatively stable and secure lifestyle, so that some of the spare time they do have can be given to voluntary activity rather than to sorting out their own problems or adjusting to a new lifestyle such as that imposed by, for example, unemployment or retirement.

To this must be added the finding that 37 per cent of the informants in the Survey had no regular commitment to any voluntary activity; only 9 per cent of all adults interviewed said they participated in at least one voluntary **activity** regularly each week.

The Survey presents an analysis of the types of voluntary activity undertaken. This is important because we need to make a careful (though rough and ready) assessment of how many of those doing voluntary work were involved in groups and committees through which they were able to develop civic skills and responsibilities. The most commonly undertaken forms of voluntary help were fund raising and giving practical help to individuals (41 per cent and 30 per cent respectively) and most of this fund raising was in raffles, fêtes, jumble sales and so on. Of the 23 per cent of the Survey informants who had participated in voluntary work, just over a quarter (26 per cent) 'had served on committees, or done the kind of work which is often associated with being on a committee, such as keeping records, writing minutes or looking after money'.[2] There was little difference between manual and non-manual volunteers from these groups in participation in fund raising; but volunteers in the non-manual groups were more likely than those in manual groups to have done committee work. The bulk of work done by volunteers in the manual groups was practical help to individuals and other kinds of practical work. This was also the case for the unemployed; in this group only 13 per cent of those doing voluntary work did committee work, compared to 30 per cent of volunteers who were in full-time work.

We can now look at who benefited from this voluntary work: those most likely to benefit were children and teenagers, the sick and the disabled, and the elderly. But the most significant finding for us was that:

> In general, those in the non-manual socio-economic groups were more likely to do voluntary work which was of benefit to children and teenagers, the local community and church or club members, whereas those in the manual groups were more likely to do voluntary work which benefited the elderly. From the analysis of types of activity presented earlier it seems possible that for voluntary workers in the manual groups, the elderly whom they help are neighbours, whereas for those in the non-manual groups the voluntary work may be of a less direct kind.

For example, volunteers in the professional and managerial groups were, on the whole, more than twice as likely as volunteers in the manual groups to be doing voluntary work that benefited the local community, church and club members and other groups.

There have been a number of studies, mainly American, which indicate that middle-class people are more likely than the working class (especially the poor) to participate in community activities and voluntary associations. This is confirmed by the GHS data, but the Survey also indicates that not only the extent but also the type and beneficiary of the voluntary work varies with the class of the volunteer.

It is difficult in the absence of comparative data from other years or countries to make judgements about 'high' and 'low' levels of participation; but it may be safe to deduce from these data that not only are the working class and the unemployed less involved but that their comparative lack of involvement in matters such as committees and groups implies their exclusion from the informal sphere of local politics and associations where some basic skills and confidence may be acquired. This is important not just because this sphere is, or ought to be, the base of the structure of local government and parliamentary politics (just consider how many councillors started their careers as activists in local community groups), but because there are studies (reviewed and confirmed, for example, by Tamney 1975) showing that voluntary association membership as well as the development of local relationships are related to participation and interest in national politics and issues.

The NSV data on the areas of interest of voluntary activity are illuminating, and are reproduced in Table 2.1. The data indicate the comparatively low levels of participation in community groups and local political activities.

The data from the GHS and NSV raise the issue we shall continually return to in this book: the balance between private lives and public roles that is appropriate for the viability of local government and parliamentary politics. This is such an important matter that even if nothing else comes from a six-month exploratory study, we can be satisfied if we have drawn attention to how little empirical or qualitative data there is about people's public roles and responsibilities in their communities; dredging for clues and making rough and ready deductions from limited surveys such as the GHS is not the way in which politicians and policy-makers are likely to come to a clearer understanding of the relationship between voluntary participation and democratic commitment.

The National Survey of Volunteering (Field and Hedges, 1984)

Table 2.1. Areas of Interest and of Volunteer Activity

	Areas of interest (past year) %	Areas of volunteer activity	
		Past year %	Longer ago %
Children's education/school	18	11	7
Religion	28	10	7
Sports/exercise	36	9	6
Youth/children (outside school)	11	8	10
Hobby/recreation/special interest	44	6	3
Health/safety	12	6	6
Social welfare	7	5	4
Local/community	9	5	3
Elderly	8	4	4
Citizenship	6	4	3
Education/general	12	2	4
Politics	5	2	4
Environmental conservation	5	2	2
Justice/human rights	2	1	1
Union/staff association	4	3	0
Other job-related	6	4	0
Disability-related	1	1	0
Base – all respondents	1,808	1,808	1,808

Note: For a full description of these categories, see the NSV shuffle cards reproduced in Appendix 4. The last three listed were not on the shuffle cards, but arose from separate questions in the survey.

confirms the major findings of the 1981 General Household Survey; it suggests that there is no such thing as a 'typical volunteer'. But the tendencies revealed in its data point towards volunteering being particularly associated with:

being educated to further or higher education level;
having a job;
being a white-collar worker (particularly professional and managerial);
being an owner-occupier;
having (and driving) a car;

having a telephone;
being white;
having children;
being aged 35–44 or, at any rate, somewhere below 44.

The NSV does provide an analysis by ethnic group but, sadly, it concludes: 'the number of ethnic minority members in the sample (60) was too small to allow much separate analysis, but the incidence of volunteering among them appears to be appreciably lower than among whites'.

We have noted already that the GHS data is not analysed by ethnicity. But is it possible to deduce (in the absence of analysis by ethnicity) from these other factors something about the extent and nature of the participation of black people in voluntary activity? On the one hand, from the fact that black people are found (disproportionately) amongst the manual groups and amongst the unemployed, then one would expect them to have a comparatively *lower* level of involvement in voluntary activities, and that they would be more likely to be involved in activities such as practical work or fund raising than in committees or other groups. This is only a guess, and goodness knows what differences there would be between Asians and Afro-Caribbeans and also within the Asian group. One might expect, for instance, that some Asian groups (and particularly the African Asians) would have a more pronounced middle-class profile and thus they might differ in the nature and extent of their voluntary participation from, say, Bangladeshis. On the other hand, the GHS shows that men and women with dependent children are more likely to be involved in voluntary activities, as would those under 40 years of age. These data would lead you to guess that some ethnic groups (because they have a younger age profile and their households contain more children than white households) would have a *higher* level of involvement in voluntary activities.

If this kind of reasoning and guesswork makes you unhappy (as it does us), then you would look in vain for alternative data that was more revealing. For example, one of the most recent surveys on black and white British was published by the Policy Studies Institute (see Brown, 1984). But it contains nothing on black and white voluntary participation, except for data that black people are generally more likely to join unions than white people, attend meetings with about the same frequency, but are much less likely than white members to hold an elected post. *Social Trends* (Central Statistical Office, 1983, 1985) tells us that membership and attendance at black churches have increased dramatically since 1970. For much else we have to turn to American studies but feel equally frustrated with them; Tamney's study of a neighbourhood in Milwaukee with respect to membership of voluntary associations and its effect on voting found little difference between the membership levels of black and white residents (1975). But we cannot easily rely on data from Milwaukee, or any other American neighbourhood, in a study on black participation in Britain.

So we are forced back to sifting through the circumstantial evidence. From a range of American and British studies (e.g. Schoenberg and Rosenbaum, 1977 and Wallman, 1982) we find three variables that seem to have a significant bearing on local involvement and participation. These are length of residence, home ownership and employment. There are, of course, other factors such as class and education but we have already dealt with these in the discussion of the GHS and NSV data.

Length of Residence

The NSV data on the effect of residence on volunteering is difficult to interpret, because of the effect of other intervening variables such as age, the 'sociable-ness' of an area, family formation and class. It concludes that length of residence in an area 'does not appear to have a very direct relationship to volunteering . . . [but] there appears to be some tendency for regular volunteering, at least, to increase with length of residence for the first few years . . .'

Brown's 1984 study on *Black and White Britain* indicates that there are higher rates of geographical movement amongst ethnic minority households, particularly amongst Bangladeshis. It is also worth noting 'that a quarter of all black council tenants have applied for and are still waiting for a transfer to another property. The proportion among white tenants is less than half this.'

Home Ownership

The findings of the NSV study are that 'owner-occupiers are appreciably more likely than council tenants to be volunteers. Other private renters lie in between these extremes.'

The tenure patterns of different ethnic groups are reproduced in Table 2.2. What is of interest is not only the differences in tenure between each ethnic group, but the balance within each ethnic group between different forms of tenure, especially the balance between owner-occupation and council tenancy. In both the 'white' and 'Asian' columns, home-owners outnumber council tenants, whereas amongst West Indians[3] there are more council tenants (46 per cent) than home-owners). It is also important to note the low level of owner-occupation amongst Bangladeshis, and the higher level of council tenancy. Brown's data (1984) also show that tenure patterns are tending over time to become even more ethnically polarized than they are already; in particular, there are fewer white council tenants, and more white households in private rented accommodation. This is marked in the inner-city areas where nearly a quarter of white households are private tenants. The concentration of Afro-Caribbean households in the inner-city areas in council tenancies and housing associations reminds us of how far American public housing is now occupied by such households.

Table 2.3 is reproduced to show regional differences in tenure patterns. Note in particular that in the inner areas of London, Birmingham and Manchester, the proportion of Asians in council tenures is about the same as for whites, although again even in these inner areas the level of Asian owner-occupation is higher than that of whites and West Indians.

What can we make of this data? If geographical mobility and owner-occupation are related to participation in community groups and voluntary associations, then we can say that the data predict a low level of such participation for Afro-Caribbean and Bangladeshis, and that the participation of other Asian groups would be expected to be higher (other things being equal, which, as we shall see, they are not). The data do not tell us anything about the different levels of voluntary participation to be expected from white, Afro-Caribbean and Asian council tenants.

Table 2.2. Tenure Patterns (percentages)

	White	West Indian	Asian	Indian	Pakistani	Bangladeshi	African Asian	Muslim	Hindu	Sikh
Owner-occupied	59	41	72	77	80	30	73	67	73	91
Rented from council	30	46	19	16	13	53	19	24	16	6
Privately rented	9	6	6	5	5	11	5	6	8	3
furnished	2	3	4	4	4	8	4	5	6	1
unfurnished	7	3	1	1	1	2	1	1	1	1
Housing association	2	8	2	2	1	4	2	2	3	*
Other	*	—	*	*	—	*	1	*	1	*
Base: households										
Weighted	2,694	1,834	2,851	1,150	751	277	604	1,339	748	520
Unweighted	2,305	1,189	1,893	726	518	197	411	937	481	349

* Percentage greater than zero but smaller than 0.5.
Source: PSI study, Brown, 1984.

Table 2.3. Tenure in Inner Cities by Ethnic Group (percentages)

	Inner London, Inner Birmingham, Inner Manchester	Outer London, Rest of West Midlands and Greater Manchester	Rest of England and Wales
White households			
Owner-occupied	29	62	61
Rented from council	42	28	30
Privately rented	23	7	8
Housing association	6	2	1
West Indian households			
Owner-occupied	28	48	52
Rented from council	59	44	30
Privately rented	3	3	11
Housing association	10	6	7
Asian households			
Owner-occupied	44	79	82
Rented from council	42	15	10
Privately rented	7	4	6
Housing association	5	1	1

Source: PSI study, Brown, 1984.

Employment

Both the General Household Survey and the National Survey of Volunteering indicate that the unemployed have lower and different levels of participation from those in full or part-time work. Schoenberg and Rosenbaum (1977) have also indicated that employment 'appears to be the most important single factor related to levels of neighbouring, organisational membership, and sense of personal control which residents express'. They go further and state that 'contrary to the literature on the subject, neither home-ownership nor length of residence affect the level of participation'. Their conclusion is that while home-ownership and length of residence may be important contextual factors for participation, 'programmes which provide jobs may be more important to mobilising residents on their own behalf than programs which promote neighbourhood population stability and mortgage guarantees'.

Brown's PSI study shows that the unemployment rate amongst West Indians is twice as high, and that amongst Asians one-and-a-half times as high, as amongst whites. Unemployment rates amongst some Asian groups are much higher, for example amongst Pakistanis and Bangladeshis. In no age group, either for men or women, do the levels of unemployment amongst West Indians and Asians fall below the white group. In addition, the duration of unemployment for black men and women is longer than that for whites.

The job levels of whites are much higher than those of Asians or West Indians, but there are variations within the black population and between men and women. As far as men are concerned, the proportion who are manual workers is 83 per cent for West Indian men, compared with 73 per cent for Asian and 58 per cent for white men. For women there is much less contrast between black and white; for example, the number of Asian women working in professional and managerial jobs is almost as high as that of whites, but both are much higher than that of West Indians. White people more often have supervisory responsibilities than black people, and, on average, white men earn substantially more than black men.

As we have already seen, the GHS and the NSV data show that voluntary participation varies with unemployment and job level, and Schoenberg and Rosenbaum (1977) provide supportive data on the relation between being in a job and being involved in the local community. From the PSI data on black unemployment and the proportions of black people in manual jobs, we would expect that black people would not be involved to any significant extent in voluntary organizations and community groups. This would be particularly true for Afro-Caribbeans, Pakistanis and Bangladeshis.

The Participation of the Poor

There was an interesting division of labour occurring in the project. We were looking at some of the *structural* factors affecting participation; although we had not yet considered the *direct* effects of racism and racial harassment on local involvement, we had seen how racism and discrimination operated through the employment and housing markets to affect participation. Chris and the group of community workers, however, were beginning to explore some of the *personal* and interactional aspects of the relations between black and white people.

We fed back our conclusions to Chris.

'Let's take the GHS definition of voluntary participation (un-paid service to others apart from their immediate family and personal friends): if we apply this to the black population, and take into account the data about employment, job level, stability (as indicated by geographical movement and transfer applications) and owner-occupation then we might safely predict single-figure levels of participation for the black population – especially for Afro-Caribbeans, Pakistanis and Bangladeshis.'

'Why single-figure?'

'Only 13 per cent of unskilled manual workers in the GHS have participated in voluntary work in the year before interview; let's assume that is the most optimistic figure for the black population. Take into account the direct effects of racism and harassment as well as lots of other factors (which we look at in a later chapter), then we might expect the numbers of black participants in voluntary action to be below 10 per cent.'

'But we already know from our personal experience that black participation isn't great. That's how we all started on this project.'

'But these data do two things; they tell the individual community worker that the non-involvement of blacks in their particular neighbourhood isn't just a phenomenon of that neighbourhood, or of the way in which that worker is operating. And they tell us that no matter how salient are the direct effects of local and societal racism, black participation will not improve very much until their position in the housing and employment markets improves. Inter-racial co-operation presupposes racial justice.'

'Or until white people start listening. Blacks won't get involved if they feel in advance that white groups and white institutions will discount what they are saying.'

We each silently recalled the interviews in progress with black residents; a newsreel of comments from community workers plays on the inside of our minds. Someone remembers Margaret Page's comments in an ACW newsletter: 'black committee members have pointed out to me that their contributions are not properly listened to in meetings, and were not taken up, whereas white committee members who had said the same thing got a hearing'. John Rex has made a somewhat similar point in relation to trade unions which despite the loyalty of blacks to their unions 'at best ignore their grievances and at worst positively support more privileged native workers in preventing the immigrants from breaking out of replacement employment into the main parts of the labour market' (1979). Pushpinder makes this point more forcefully by quoting from one of her interviews with a man who was talking about a local group:

> I have attended a couple of their meetings, but the English people do not like to mix . . ., they do not want anybody to join them, and also our people do not have the time. Furthermore, when you tell them about our problems, they waste a lot of time in discussions and nothing practical is done. They have got a welfare officer on this estate as well, but *they* can't be bothered about our problems either, so why go and see them and waste time?

This gave Chris the opportunity to explore the value of the idea of 'positive action' in relation to black people's participation in voluntary activities and community groups.

'I can see the inevitability and strength of black groups but aren't they tantamount to positive discrimination in providing services – you know, providing separate facilities for black people with black staff and all that? Isn't that kind of positive discrimination in services seen as part of racism, now?'

'And positive action as opposed to positive discrimination?'

'Reorganizing attitudes and practices in an agency so that what black people want from it is given as part of the agency's mainstream responsibilities and services.'

'And positive action in community involvement?'

'Not sure yet; but it must imply blacks and whites working together in community groups. Look, you can't be complacent about the low level of black people's participation just because it is comparable to that of their white counterparts, according to employment and owner-occupation and so forth.'

'Why not?'

'Because positive action in community development means pulling black participation above the norm, because in that way you achieve two things. First, it is another way black people in the presence of whites begin to assert their worth and capacities; and second, if blacks and whites don't start communicating with each other then this society will fall apart in the inner cities.'

Communication: that gave us the opportunity to talk about Chris's racism awareness training, but our question was deflected with another.

'What do your employment and housing data tell us about black participation in black groups and networks?'

'We don't know yet; but we would need some pretty convincing arguments to persuade us that black participation in black groups was likely to be any higher than their voluntary participation as a whole.'

This last comment left an uncomfortable silence in the room; the discussion tacked to a slightly different course: 'One of the dangers for white community workers is to be sucked into working with people from the least disadvantaged black groups – Sikhs or Hindus, for example, or people who came from East Africa. The challenge in *all* community work is not to neglect the most marginal.'

Back to positive action and communication again. 'Have you analysed the groups you work with to see how many unemployed or unskilled manual workers are in them? You see, you've got this thing about "communication" between black and white, but we can't even get whites from different classes working together.'

'I do not have a thing about communication. I'm not talking about "better communication" as a kind of panacea. Communicating is a task, the first step. It doesn't make problems go away; it just opens them up, puts them on the table.'

This discussion took the project in a number of different directions, but the one to explore now is that of the participation of the poor in voluntary associations and community groups. The phrase 'the poor' is not an exact one but refers variously to low-income and low-class groups, the unemployed, those on welfare payments, the badly housed, and those that the education system has failed. It is an elastic phrase that stretches often to include the homeless, the single-parent household, and some of the elderly or the chronically sick and disabled.

There are two reasons for looking at the participation of the poor. First, many black people are amongst the poor as defined above, so that some of the factors that affect their participation in community activities will be those that affect the poor in general, factors that are not necessarily race or colour-specific. Secondly, because so many black people are poor in the above sense (and in the sense that they are grossly disadvantaged in housing, employment, education and other markets), their participation with white people in community groups is participation with economically and educationally disadvantaged white people. So the more we know about their participation, the more effective we are likely to be in supporting that of their black peer groups. And let us not mince words: you cannot expect people to bridge both the race and the class divide at the same time. As our interviews will show later, it might be rash to anticipate success in getting middle-class blacks to work with poor or working-class whites; or in encouraging working-class or poor blacks to feel comfortable in working with upper-working-class or lower-middle whites. It may be that the more a group of black and white people have in common (class, age, educational attainment, children, housing tenure) the more likely they can shuffle forward together to reach across the colour line.

There are some practical implications to this kind of reasoning: for example, to encourage the participation of poor or low-income blacks, the community worker may need to encourage that of poor or low-income whites in the neighbourhood. The community worker must also be able to disentangle those factors that affect the participation of poor people from those that are specific to ethnicity or colour, and which do not vary with income or class.

Those who have studied or written about the participation of the poor include sociologists, social psychologists, community workers and journalists. The insights of such a group are difficult to bring together, especially in a brief account. We want only to remind the reader of some of the salient points, and to ask him or her to use what is presented to assess their own work both with the poor and with members of ethnic minority groups. Anyone who wants a more comprehensive review of research on this issue will find it in O'Brien (1975).

We have chosen to present this overview in the form of a dialogue. This enables us to present each person's thoughts as fully but as concisely as possible but it also allowed the readers of the first drafts to enter the dialogue with their own comments. Some of the dialogue is reproduced from Paul Harrison's book, *Inside the Inner City* (1983) and from the article on interest-group processes written by David O'Brien (1981).

'Before we can ask questions about the participation of the poor, we need to ask why anyone bothers to participate in voluntary activities and community groups. If you take the "high" view, it's because people want to help others and themselves. There's a problem to be solved, a task to be completed. People are motivated by altruism, a sense of service, wanting to contribute to the public good.'

'And the "low" view?' asked Chris.

'People join groups because they're lonely or frustrated in some aspect of their lives. Or they want to get out of the flat, or away from the family. Or they've got a lot of time and energy on their hands, or intelligence or creativity not being used in their work. And some people have political ambitions, others are interested in personal power, status, publicity, their name in the newspaper and local radio.'

'But a lot of those intangible rewards only come to the leaders, to the chair or secretary. Why do people come as members or followers?'

'There's a moral dimension to this. People join in something because they identify with the collective ("the estate" or "Bermondsey people") and believe people should stick together to help each other out. The ability to identify with those around you, the idea of belonging to a community, is crucial here. People also join in when they feel strongly about an issue; perhaps they feel that when a council or some other authority wants to do something it is an injustice or an outrage. In other words, by becoming a member people are expressing a moral or political view, though they might not understand it in that way.'

'All three of these reasons', responded Hugh, 'have particular difficulties as far as the participation of black people is concerned. As a black person, you have to have a convincing argument that the expected benefits of a group's work are worth having, and make a worthwhile contribution to your livelihood. As a black person, you may also be interested in other activities outside the neighbourhood. You have to believe that the expected benefits will go to everyone and that the community group is not just a partial interest group diverting benefits to white people. Barr has also suggested that even on issues which concern all groups (for example, housing redevelopment) some people may want to deal with them on an ethnic group basis. Moreover, it may be that the Bangladeshi on a housing estate thinks of the dampness in her flat as "something I and other Bangladeshis on this estate experience", rather than "something I and other tenants on this estate experience". Another problem is that there could be a discrepancy between what the individual sees as a problem in his environment and what his extended family or reference group defines as one, and the individual may choose, or be obliged, to give up his own definition.'

'Intangible individual benefits like status and the exercise of influence are equally problematic', added Pushpinder. 'You would have to believe that you have the possibilities of exercising such power as a black person, both in society, and in the white-dominated residents' group. Besides, you may seek these intangible benefits through your own ethnic organizations, churches, and the extended family.'

'And the moral or political thrust to join a community group depends on a sense of injustice and outrage. To be effective, this has to be seen as an injustice against a group with whom you identify, and it may be the case that for some black people they are unable to see (for example, a housing department decision) as an outrage against "all us tenants", or may see such events as injustices against themselves as particularly vulnerable individuals. To join something on the basis of outrage also assumes three things: you think you and others can do something about it; you have a certain level of political awareness; and you have had access to information about the issues and problems – the issue has come to your attention. All three of these are particularly problematic for some ethnic groups.'

'Let's look more directly at the participation of the poor. Why have community workers had so little success in organizing amongst the most marginal and disadvantaged?'

'Because they've failed to realize', answered Chris, 'that mobilization is a process. It takes time, staying-power: you can't mobilize the poor in a two-year project. Especially when the poor are often so mobile and transient – not just in and out of work or between areas but in and out of prison, or hospital. There are so many things that take them away either physically or emotionally from the work of a community group. There has also been too much pressure on community workers (often coming from employers and community groups themselves) to achieve tangible results and outcomes – whereas working with the poor demands time and skills in longer-term process goals.'

'Then there's that whole bit about the poor having to work on their day-to-day survival needs, being oriented to the present and unable to plan ahead. There's also the internalization of feelings of worthlessness, the objective and the felt feelings of powerlessness – and the sheer remoteness and inaccessibility of people making the decisions who have to be influenced. Not to mention the disenchantment amongst the poor with the will and the power of political leadership to do anything about their situation.'

'David O'Brien has a lot to say on those matters', interjected Paul. 'He argues that one of the most popular explanations for the empirical fact that the poor do not get politically involved is the "culture of poverty" thesis. The thesis is that the poor feel powerless to effect change in their lives, through political or other means, because they have internalized a subculture – the culture of poverty – that defines the world as removed and unamenable to change and the poor person himself as relatively powerless to effect changes in his life situation. This culture, it is argued, accounts for the apparent "vicious cycle" which keeps poor people in a dependent state from generation to generation.'

'But hasn't much of this work on the culture of poverty been called into question?'

'Yes, and we also have to be careful about social psychological explanations. These go like this: if we cannot ascribe the behaviour and attitudes of the poor to a unique culture, perhaps we can ascribe it to psychological states – such as anomie, alienation, or apathy – that are a result of the structural conditions of poverty. This explanation, then, focuses on the situation of living in poverty and its causal relationship to the attitudes of persons living in that state. Thus, a number of writers argue that the poor feel powerless, alienated, or anomic because the general social disorganization of slum life and its lack of supportive subsystems (for example, the lack of a stable family) affect the personal perceptions of individuals living under those conditions. In short, the argument is that the poor fail to use their resources for political purposes because they are relatively passive and apathetic members of our society. But again research on the poor indicates that they are not nearly as passive and apathetic as we were led to believe by earlier sociologists.'

The point of the preceding discussion is to emphasize, in O'Brien's words, the fact that the poor must be viewed as purposive actors who consciously try to make adaptations to their environment. However, the nature of the environment that they have to cope with forces them to spend most of their resources on non-political activities. On the one hand, the conditions of living in poverty force the poor person to see life in terms of immediate needs. The poor, unlike most of us, face a daily struggle to provide the bare minimum for sheer physical survival. Because of this fact of life, they are unable to afford the luxury of engaging in political activities that only promise to yield results in the future, even if those results might be more rewarding than results gained from short-run activities. Thus, if the poor person does not support a movement to change the basic structural conditions of his life (for example, to eliminate poverty through political action), it is not necessarily because he is alienated; rather, given his condition, he simply cannot afford the luxury of getting involved in such activities that only promise some relief to his plight in the future. On the other hand, if the poor feel powerless (and express it on alienation scales) it is because they really are powerless *vis-à-vis* the forces that control their lives.

From this analysis, O'Brien argued that situational constraints on the behaviour of the poor explain in large measure why poor black people in North America appeared to be so apathetic about the civil rights movement. They were primarily concerned with immediate, tangible things like jobs, decent housing, and the quality of public facilities. The civil leaders, however, were concerned with less tangible goals like ending *de facto* segregation of public facilities and neighbourhoods. One can make a cogent argument that if the goals of the civil rights groups were realized, there would be, in the future, a marked change in the condition of all blacks *vis-à-vis* whites.

But O'Brien's view is as follows:

> there was no incentive for the poor black man to invest his resources in action that only promised to bring about change in the future; given the immediacy of his needs, he was not particularly interested in long-range social change. In fact, the civil rights leaders often asked him to sacrifice his immediate needs for the pursuit of long-range goals . . . civil rights leaders often opposed construction of hospitals or schools on the grounds that they would reinforce 'de facto' segregation. Yet, many poor blacks were primarily concerned with receiving better hospitals and schools, whether they were segregated or not. Thus, when the poor blacks refused to support the civil rights leaders, they were acting in their own rational self-interest. (*1975*)

The fact that the civil rights movement was unable to offer any incentives to the poor undoubtedly was, according to O'Brien, an important reason for the emergence of black-power ideology and community organization activities in the 1960s. Both the ideology of black power and the activities of community organizers emphasized the need to organize the poor around the immediate problems of their lives like schools, the quality of housing, and public services. In short, attention shifted to 'grass-roots' organization, especially at the neighbourhood level.

Pushpinder came into the discussion at this point to ask if this shift led to better organization among the poor.

'No, O'Brien found that despite the growth of ideologies supporting neighbourhood organization (for example, black power) and the emergence of skilful political strategists (for example, Saul Alinsky), there was certainly not a grass-roots revolution in the slums.'

'But if, as O'Brien has argued, the poor do not have a unique psychology or culture that permanently immobilizes them politically, then why did they not support collective organizations (that is, neighbourhood organizations) directed towards their immediate concerns?'

'O'Brien's answer to that question is that community workers have failed to involve the poor because those workers have not resolved what he calls the Public Goods Dilemma. This is that people do not *have* to join community groups in order to enjoy the benefits to the whole collective that comes from a group's work. A public good is defined as a good that is non-divisible; that is, it is available to everyone whether or not they pay for its costs.'

'You mean a public good or benefit like improved maintenance on an estate or stopping a post office being closed? In such a case the poor will benefit from the work of a group whether they participate or not.'

'So that given the pressures in their lives, a poor person is behaving as a rational, sensible person when she refuses voluntarily to spend scarce energy and resources on community activities from which she will benefit anyway. And the other, divisible benefits of collective action – power, status, prestige, and so on are part of an incentive structure that attracts the more able, the better-off in a community.'

'Let's change direction for a moment, and look at the contextual or situational factors that constrain the participation of the poor. Jane Jacobs and Oscar Newman, for example, have shown how space and design affect social interaction and local involvement. And Paul Harrison has called the housing estate the most disastrous architectural invention of this century. He describes the model for the housing estate as the college or monastery, where intimacy is made tolerable by reinforcing a common purpose. But families, argues Harrison, require privacy as well as neighbourly contact. The estate thrusts them into a proximity that becomes increasingly intolerable as cultural diversity grows and social cohesion and control decay. Excessive intimacy, like an invasion of personal space, generates social isolation and hostility.'

'That reminds me of what residents said to Craig Robertson in his interviews on Craigmiller: "They hoped to make themselves safe by means of being separate; they were afraid or pessimistic. They found that collective action would lead them into more 'pain, shame and blame.' Their lives already were plagued by painful relationships, they said; so they were not going to 'volunteer' for still more pain. They 'knew', in advance, their collective action would result in their being mis-used for someone else's purposes – and they already suffered too much domination and manipulation." '

'In his 1983 book on the inner city, Harrison has written of how most people stake their hopes, not on changing their environment, but on getting out of it, not in collective action, but on individual escape. This attitude is one of the strongest obstacles to change . . . there is a belief in most people, again based on experience, that it is usually more profitable to devote energies to bettering one's personal situation than to get involved in collective actions which may not move in the direction you wish, or if they do, may not succeed, or if they succeed, may produce, at best, only modest improvements. There is a widespread escapist mentality, that it is easier to try to get out of bad housing or bad employment than to fight collectively for improvements that benefit everyone, and by the same token, that it is easier to get out of the inner city then to stay and fight to change it. And if that fails, it is easier to bury your head in the sand, to slump in front of the television, to obliterate your troubles with drink or drugs, than to press on in a relentless struggle for justice.'

'This attitude of individual escape seems particularly strong amongst many groups of black people; after all, they have made the most heroic of individual "escapes" in their epic journey to this country. Some blacks are learning quickly that to survive they must rely on their own efforts and on their family and kin.'

'And when local authorities don't have the resources any more, this must reinforce the emphasis on individual escape . . .'

'And release negative forces within poor communities, the brunt of which are borne by individuals from ethnic minority groups.'

'Yes, Harrison has suggested that those who were hurt by slump and government policies could, in theory, have channelled their aggression towards its real causes. Crisis could have mobilized them into protest, demonstration or conventional political action. In practice several influences worked against this. The poor and the disadvantaged, drained of morale and self-confidence, are the hardest of any group to mobilize. Television has anaesthetized the distress of this slump, much as coca-chewing stills the hunger pains of Andean Indians. More significant perhaps is the widespread lack of class-consciousness and of awareness of the root causes of exploitation and inequality and their intensification, partly due to the absence of radical critiques and documentation in the dominant mass media. Against this chorus, the efforts of the Left at political education were practically inaudible.

'Thus it was that, instead of becoming a creative force for change, aggression remained bottled up inside poor families and poor districts. The slump led, not to organized protests, let alone revolution, but to an increase in chaotic conflict within poor areas, dividing the disadvantaged against themselves, weakening them further, and adding to their deprivations.'

'Harrison pointed out three kinds of obstacles to change from within the inner-city neighbourhood: there are *physical* barriers, to involvement, such as lack of cars and bad public transport, more people working unsocial hours, one-parent families unable to leave children and the sheer exhaustion brought about by much manual work; all of which hold people back from evening meetings. There are *psychological* factors: the fear of crime, a lack of confidence in one's articulateness, a dislike of public arguments, cynicism about the responsiveness of established powers and disbelief in one's own power (both derived from long experience in every sphere of life). There are *social* blocks, such as the constant shifting of population, especially of those elements best suited to provide leadership. There is the mass of cleavages based on race, language, behaviour . . . all of which atomize communities into their constituent households.'

'There's a concern in Harrison's book with "problem" or "dump" estates.'

'Yes, once an estate acquires more than a certain proportion of disadvantaged tenants – perhaps, say, one-fifth or one-quarter – it can find itself trapped in a descending spiral which may continue

until it is demolished or massively rehabilitated. The prepon-
derance of single-parent families and families with conflicts
caused by low income or unemployment weakens parental discipline, so vandalism and crime are more prevalent. The atmosphere of demoralization and the culture of silence make it harder
to form effective tenants' organizations to press for maintenance,
or for individual tenants to get their own repairs done. The
"better" tenants, with higher incomes, savings or skills, or more
persistence over getting a transfer, move out and are replaced by
more disadvantaged people. The estate acquires a reputation,
usually worse than the reality, which discourages those with any
hope for their own future from even viewing a flat there . . .'

'He makes the consequences sound almost inevitable.'

'They are. The very ecology of the place divides tenants up and
creates a mass of conflicts and cleavages: young versus old;
delinquents against the law-abiding; victims against the parents
of perpetrators; top-level maisonettes against middle-level
maisonettes; those on upper floors against those on the ground
floor; those who are concerned about cleanliness and those who
are not; the quiet against the noisy; pigeon-feeders against
pigeon-haters; dog-owners against non-owners. To these we can
add more generalized divisions that arouse deep emotions: rent-
payers against squatters; tax-payers against claimants; black
against white; not to mention political, moral, religious, sexual or
class cleavages.

'There are a score or more possible divisions, and most of them
cut criss-cross through each other, creating a multi-dimensional
matrix with more than a million possible compartments, whose
inhabitants will be set against the rest on at least one divisive issue.
The community is atomized, ground into fragments like sand on
the beach. The stress of poverty and uncomfortable proximity
intensify the conflicts. The architect of Dante's hell economizes
in places by using the souls of the damned to torment each other.
The inner city achieves the same effect, setting the victims of our
society against each other so they cannot effectively organize to
change the causes of their predicament.'

'Perhaps this is a good point at which to end the dialogue.
We've shifted a little from the black British to the poor British as
a whole, but at the moment that is no bad thing. Phenomena such

as the extent of the animosity between young blacks and the police, the physical harassment of blacks and the general hostility between blacks and whites – they're all suggestive of the "complete breakdown in communication between white and black society" that Chris Mullard (1973) predicted over ten years ago. Both racism and the disgust of black people with white society are finely exposed and magnified in the inner-city council estates. But the breakdown is also evident in the ordinary, everyday encounters between white and black, both amongst working people and amongst professionals such as ourselves. We shall look at this issue in the next chapter.'

Notes

1   The NSV picked up higher levels of volunteering than the GHS (23 per cent) or the Wolfenden Committee (1970 – 15 per cent). The NSV figure is 44 per cent. The differences are attributed by NSV almost wholly to differences in survey approach.
2   The NSV figure is 36 per cent, but because of difficulties of definition the two surveys are not really comparable on this point.
3   Brown's report uses the terms 'Asians' and 'West Indians', and we will do the same when using or referring to his data.

3
Learning About Each Other

. . . granted that racism is a white problem, it is incorrect to assume that only whites can or should solve it . . . Racism is a human problem; as a disease, it is whites who are afflicted by it, but it is black people who suffer most its effects . . . the dehumanising problems of racism cannot be resolved at any level . . . without the co-operation of black people.

J. Owusu-Bempah

As Brown's study from the Policy Studies Institute shows, the issue to be addressed by motivated politicians and policy-makers is the removal of those barriers put in the way of the black British in their access to comparable levels of employment, housing, education, health and so forth. But the issues to be faced by the white practitioner are different but no less complex. They are, first, is it possible for me to, and how do I, change in my self-awareness and dealings with others? And secondly, if I am employed in an agency that gives services to the community, how do I define obstacles which impede equality of access to, and experience of, those services by black people? How do I remove those obstacles?

Many black and white workers in community work have suggested that racism awareness training is a potent medium for both individual and agency change, though as yet there is little evidence for this based on British experience. Cowan and others have argued that the two go hand-in-hand:

if public services wish to respond positively to the needs and issues which arise because of the black community, then changes in the services should be preceded by, or at the very

least paralleled by, training in staff awareness about racism
. . . There is a widespread tendency to want to remain silent
on the issues of race. This 'culture of silence' is, in fact, the
first and greatest obstacle for the staff of any agency to
overcome. (*Cowan, 1982*)

We shall look at the issues of silence later, but we note here that
Cowan refers to the silence of both black and white people:

Inside statutory services, racism is not visible to most white
staff. Black staff are either silent about racism, confused
about how they should challenge, or located as a threat and
pushed to the margin and rendered powerless. This context
of institutional racism fosters silence, collusion and isolates
and confuses people in the structure.

Cowan goes on to describe, as part of efforts to change
institutions, a process of 'owning' one's colour, and this passage
is important to the themes of the rest of this chapter:

whether one's skin colour is yellow, brown or black, there is
a lot of evidence to say that in terms of location and
experience of British society, there is a basic 'black experience'. Within white society, very few people see themselves
as white. Many white people consequently find the above
hard to accept. Because white people see themselves first and
foremost as individuals, it is very hard to accept, that in
relation to black people, white people also have a distinctive
location and experience of British society. Furthermore, it is
very hard to see how the black experience of a basically white
run society will change significantly until white people, as
individuals, start seeing the white experience so that they can
change it. One of the goals of racism awareness training is,
therefore, to begin the difficult process of 'owning' one's
whiteness and recognising that by doing this an individual
greatly benefits.

The importance of owning whiteness and the white experience[1]
cannot be over-stressed, but in so doing we must not obscure two
points about blackness and the black experience that are rarely
articulated. The first is that black people are also involved in a

process of owning their colour and experience and that the process did not begin or end in the 1970s with the black pride movement. Secondly, if whites are to own the white experience and to evaluate its impact on their personal and work relations, then so, too, must black people become aware of the impact of their blackness (colour and experience) in their personal dealings with whites. Without such a *mutual* acknowledgement of self, there can be no grounds for honest dialogue and working together.

We want to look at the issue of owning colour and experience by quoting from a letter to the ACW newsletter, from a worker with twelve years' experience of working with Asian groups in a project run by a local CRC and later by a social services department. She writes:

> The 'facilitator' chose to adopt an aggressive style and responded to any questioning by bombarding us with our white 'imperialist past' and accused us of seeing Asian people as a problem . . . this approach . . . had the effect of alienating or intimidating many people . . . to spend a day in the name of training and being harangued and misinterpreted was not a particularly beneficial experience for any of us. (*Mary Foley, March 1985*)

We start with this quotation because the primary vehicle for exploring colour and experience is some form of training. The point raised by Foley's letter is *how* that training is carried out, and the sophistication or otherwise of black and white trainers in their theories about how people learn about themselves, and begin to change perceptions, attitudes and behaviours. The tone, and hence implicitly the androgogic theories of much racism awareness training, have been discussed by Gurnah, who describes them as 'accusatory . . . moralistic . . . highminded . . . accusative . . . incriminating . . . guilt-trip . . . pentecostal . . . confessing . . . recantation . . . shame and lecture into action'. But Gurnah suggests that this approach is mistaken 'because individual guilt rarely leads to positive action; and then, it is unclear that even if it *did* that it would constitute the right kind of action.' (1984). In addition to the paper by Gurnah, there is also an

s kind of discussion, the distinction between role and
pers. important; let us risk the generalization that most racism
awareness training reaches the person and not the role, though
this may be less the case for those doing jobs (for example,
community and social workers) where the boundaries between
role and person are considerably blurred. Owning up to racism
and whiteness is not simply a good in itself but ought to be a step
for professionals towards redefining their role and responsibilities
in their relations with, and services to, black people. Gurnah has
rightly criticized racism awareness training for both its theoretical
poverty about and its practical guidelines for the links between
personal, role, organizational and structural change.

Part of the anguish in Foley's letter (and we find it time and time
again amongst white community workers) is that the training she
experienced focused on person and not on role and all that the
white workers could get from the course tutor was that they
should resign! There is a need for more understanding in
community work, amongst both black and white, about the
possibilities for personal development within the organizational
and group constraints with which most people work and live. In
other words, changes in person and role have to be paralleled by
efforts to bring about supportive changes in organizational and
group characteristics.

The movement from person to role to organization is the process of establishing an anti-racist strategy of positive action in
both service agencies and community groups. No matter what
the changes in person that are brought about through anti-
racism training, they are of little value if the individual is
constrained in his role by more embracing agency traditions,
routines and procedures, or by the attitudes and roles of other
people in the organization. The constraints on person and role
that are inherent in a white- and male-dominated organization
are often felt acutely by middle-level managers, such as the area
officer in a social services team, or the secretary of a Council for
Voluntary Service. Annamanthodo has clearly made these
points in relation to CVS involvement in forms of racism awareness training (RAT).

it seems most unlikely that (white) individuals taken out of their everyday environment can sustain change back in their organisation, without a real understanding of how it operates and how structures need to change. The nature and extent of institutional racism mean that individual ideas may not be the best focus. Organisational structures and practice are so deep rooted and persistent that they have to be dealt with on that level rather than 'deracising' the individual. . .

Sometimes organisations have sent one or two representatives on a RAT course. The assumption is that these two trained people can come back and now train their own colleagues. At least, it is hoped that what they have learnt will somehow rub off. This is an impossible idea and may, in some cases, even be counterproductive. Individuals who have been energised by the course may come back full of hope and good ideas, only to be discouraged by other staff. They themselves are disappointed without support and interest, and the whole anti-racist initiative dies before it has really started. (*1985*)

Annamanthodo points to the need to see personal training and agency change as a *process* rather than rooted in one-off events. She writes that racism awareness training:

should concentrate on a clear review of the structure, policies and practice of the organisation . . . RAT should take individual attitudes into account but the plan of action towards race equality is more important in the long-term for real change. What we are talking about here is 'training in organisational development for race equality' rather than race related training' . . . unless the training is followed up by changes, and supported by structures to implement and monitor these changes, the training may relieve a few guilty consciences, but have little real long term impact.

When seen as a process within an institution, anti-racism training has the potential to pay equal attention to person, role, organization and services. These four provide the means to look at differentials of power and status in an agency between black and white staff, and between white staff and black users of the agency.

Recognizing 'White Speak' and 'Black Speak'

We encountered the problem of role and person in our two workshops, but in our notes we used different phrases to describe it; both black and white community workers came on the workshops to discuss issues of practice (role) and to learn from each other. But the discussions in the workshops never left the realm of testing out people's basic assumptions (person). Not only did the tension between practice and basic assumptions persist throughout the workshops, but the exploration of assumptions/person was confined to external manifestations of what was presumed to exist inside. For example, some of the black participants in the workshop sometimes seized upon single words and phrases, and they were treated as if they were a full and adequate representation of another person's assumptive world. This pattern of communication set up a vicious decline: as complex ideas and feeling were reduced to a critical examination of a single word used to express them, so participants began to give out only the most crude and unambiguous of statements leading to a narrowing and hardening of the categories in the discussion.

Suttles has noted the same issue in the American neighbourhoods that he has studied: differences between black and white people that became serious in local relations were not so much differences in norms or goals or basic assumptions but in the *notational devices* that each person from an ethnic group relied upon to express his or her views about these values and goals:

> the participants are like schoolboys using different number systems while trying to explain to one another the same arithmetic problem. Behind their misunderstanding is the same mathematical system and possibly the same answer. However, unless they can make the necessary transformations, they cannot possibly agree . . . so long as each group does not know how to translate . . . they go on misunderstanding one another and incorrectly interpreting each other's behaviour (*1968*)

Suttles's comments enable us to ask about the *extent* and *quality* of communication between white and black people. We have been able to observe this communication among white and black fieldworkers; we have had some opportunity to assess whether this communication between white and black professionals is likely to be successful in helping each other, and those with whom they are in contact at work (for example, residents' associations) to learn. One cannot yet be optimistic on either of these two matters, and we want to indicate our reasons for this conclusion by looking at further aspects of communication.

Most people who have contact with members of other ethnic groups have two qualities of discourse; this is almost a truism. White people communicate with white people in a way that is different from their communication with blacks, and one can make the same statement about black discourse. This truism is not simply a statement about vocabulary, dialect, pronunciation, measure and pace of speech, but is also one about the decisions people make about what they can take for granted in the assumptive world of those with whom they are talking. Most of this chapter will be concerned with communication, but our first observation is about the existence of a 'moral language'; it is easy to spot this language in, for example, the slogans and banner goals of organizations such as ACW, or in the public proclamations of agencies about their equal opportunity employment principles, or in the personal declarations of white individuals about their racism awareness training or their intimate relations with blacks. The moral language to which participation in racism awareness training has given rise has been briefly commented on by Gurnah. He writes that racism awareness training

> has a tendency to render discourse *precious* where both trainers and trained talk in hushed sincere voices about their search for the inner meaning of their feelings . . .
> . . . it provides white officials with the acceptable language of anti-racism, with which to disarm black criticisms . . . It is reminiscent of men's groups, where men learn the correct language with which to cope with feminists they know. Thus, instead of achieving the required transformation of racist thought and behaviour, RAT may very well unintentionally encourage tokenism. (*1984*)

This moral language or 'white speak' includes saying the right things in the right way about black politics or art or music, or the right things about the police and so forth. The purpose of this form of 'white speak' is to reduce uncertainty, risk and the difficulties that come with interpersonal explorations; sometimes its purpose is to define the white person or organization as 'sympatico' and to prescribe the parameters for an encounter with black people.

But the language of 'white speak' is, particularly in public, also a language of circumlocutions, euphemisms, reserve and diffidence, and is often marked by a disproportionate reverence for the views of black people in a group. One example of 'white speak' is the letter sent to the ACW newsletter in April 1985 in reply to Mary Foley's earlier letter. In this case the imperatives of 'white speak' drive the letter writer ('a white radical feminist') to defend a black male teacher even though she was not a participant of the event he organized. The letter illustrates a destructive aspect of 'white speak' – that no matter how indifferent, poor or outrageous is the method and content of what a black person does, it can be legitimized as 'good' or 'right' because he is black and those who criticize are white:

> It *is* painful to be identified as an oppressor, particularly if you believe you are working for a new just world. But some of the most basic awareness must include the understanding that oppressed people have a right to be angry, a right to name and confront the oppressor, and a right to adopt whatever 'style' they consider to be appropriate.

Two further points can be made at this stage about the 'moral language'. First, we shall see later that when even 'white speak' seems risky, the alternative for white professionals is silence. Secondly, 'black speak' amongst black professionals is no less harmful to the validity of group discussion.

We assume that one of the goals of training is to show how much part of a racist strategy such a moral language is, and how inimical it is to communication that is grounded in genuine attempts to negotiate what the other person is feeling, thinking, believing and so on. But one of the most adverse consequences of this 'moral language' is that it seems often to lead to the suspension of the critical faculties of both white and black people in dialogue with each other.

This last point was commented on by a reader of an early draft of the book:

> there is no substitute for getting to know a wide variety of black people. In my experience the Jewish saying about two Jews and three opinions is just as true of black people. Direct experience of this helps to give confidence in discussion with individual people of whatever colour who claim that everyone of their colour (or class, occupation etc.) agrees with them. A problem in the race training area is that the single black trainer (or two people who work together because they support each other's view) can imply that their views and interpretations are right, unchallengeable (unless you are a racist) and reflect what every right thinking black person (i.e. politically educated, non-uncle Tom) thinks.

White workers seem to get enormous relief (as well as other benefits) from racism awareness training; it gives them an experience that can be injected into the 'moral language' and helps them, it is often believed, to establish their credentials. Yet one assumption of racism awareness training is that knowledge of others is no substitute for knowledge of oneself. Such self-knowledge may lead to seeing how fallacious is the 'theory of proper motivation'; this is the theory that in order to be effective in work with black people, the white person need only develop the right political and sociological attitudes to black people and racism – in short, to be a 'good guy', demonstrating all the appropriate stances about racism, ethnic development and so forth.

Manning and Ohri dispose of the 'good guy' position by calling it the 'anti-racist-racist position'. They write as follows, making reference in their last sentence to the unhelpful consequences of 'white speak':

> It takes the form of community workers being very active in campaigning organisations against the National Front, whilst being involved in little or no activity to challenge institutional racism. Obviously such workers need to be

commended for recognising that racism is a cancer which should be reckoned with, but they fall into the trap of becoming Sunday-anti-racists. Such workers either fail or refuse to recognise racism as a reality in situations where they hold either power or responsibility. It blocks the possibility of such a worker being able to evaluate how her/his current community work at a neighbourhood level either colludes with or challenges racism. The worker begins to assume that being anti-racist at a campaigning anti-N.F. level will automatically translate itself into anti-racist work at the neighbourhood level without monitoring his/her actions or the strategy of the group. It also becomes unsafe for anyone to raise the issue of racism in an honest, self-critical and constructive way, because of the defensive stance which such workers take, believing themselves to be committed anti-racists, but fearing to put that to the test. (*1982*)

Unhappily for them, people working the 'good guy/girl' position are invariably seen through; no degree of proficiency in the vocabulary and slogans of 'white speak' can disguise the hollowness of communication. Astute blacks have learnt to put the words of whites into the context of body language, eye contact and a range of other factors, such as a sense of rapport, a *feeling* about whether or not the white person's communication is authentic. Both blacks and whites find it hard to describe adequately how they recognize this authenticity of communication; one reader of the first draft of the book commented:

I was fascinated by the description of 'white speak' . . . It certainly rings true and does not lead to real communication or trust. I believe that one of the ways of breaking down this communication barrier is by helping people to speak more honestly, openly, and directly and receiving the same in return to be used as helpful feedback with which to modify behaviour where appropriate, not criticism which results in defensiveness and avoidance.

You may ask if this is possible and realistic or just naively optimistic. Well, I have often been accused of naivety, but perhaps it is just this quality which has enabled me to go into situations where a more careful person would keep out . . .

My approach was always to be direct and open and talk to people even if they didn't want to talk to me. Just as important I tried to prove that I had something to offer (actions not words), that I could be relied upon, was not sectarian, and not on an ego trip. I think it works.

Knowing oneself is part of the process of owning one's colour. There are many beneficial consequences for white people in doing this; for example, it is through the process of owning colour and its advantages and liabilities that the white person can understand how he protects, maintains and repairs the structure of self and group interest that is connected with being white. Being able to acknowledge what you protect and defend is not just a useful first step towards personal change; it also begins to alter the nature of black responses, and hence can lead to a shift in the quality and content of communication between white and black professionals.

Much of 'white speak' is designed to help white professionals survive intact in their discussions with blacks, and thus to protect their interests as white individuals and as a white group. 'White speak' is part of a purposive strategy used by many whites to adapt to, and develop within, a changing and more challenging group environment; as such, it is reminiscent of the survival technique used by poor blacks that was known as 'tomming'. Besides white speak, there are two other devices used by white professionals to control their communication with blacks, and to maintain intact the advantages of the white experience. The first of these is what Ley (1970) has called the minimax criterion that governs relations between black and white people: this is the most pessimistic rule that can influence decision-making and interpersonal relations because it assumes *maximum* hostility in the environment, leading to the *minimization* of all risk-taking by the individual. The minimax criterion influences blacks and whites alike, and is quite clearly a potent factor, as we shall see in a later chapter, in determining the participation of white and black working-class people in community groups.

The third device alongside the minimax criterion and 'white

speak' is the strategic use of silence. What is common to the development of all three is the learning by whites that in both personal and public discussions language is no longer something that can be relied upon and whose effect on the listeners can reasonably be predicted. Indeed, whites soon learn that trying to talk openly about black and white relations, and about racism, is one of the riskiest of undertakings in a group with black people; keeping silent, however, is not just a way of minimizing personal risk but is also a potent tool for maintaining power and control, as Tuku Mukherjee has observed: 'Your racism has been your silence. It has been the inability of people to debate this issue.' The silence and deference of whites is often felt as controlling because black colleagues never know what white people are thinking about them and their work. One participant on one of our workshops described how he was 'numbed and deskilled' by white deference – though he also pointed out that the silence and deference were quickly replaced by scrutiny and questioning once black workers started to ask for resources or change.

Behind Ghetto and Stockade

We have thus observed that the minimax criterion, 'white speak' and silence are adaptive/survival devices, as well as exploitative ones. But their combined effort is to place white professionals into safe intellectual and emotional enclosures; whites have learnt the survival value of self-stockading. The white stockade is not only a haven in the group for those who are timid and apprehensive about blacks, but also a necessary defence against black participants who are, or are felt to be, intimidating. The white stockade is, of course, reinforced by a range of emotional and psychological factors, whose exploration is outside the remit of this study. The psycho-sexual fear of the black man and the myths, stereotypes and fantasies that have brewed in the white psyche for generations help to construct and strengthen the white stockade. Not only is there a timidity and sense of superiority behind the white stockade, but guilt about the advantages of the white experience becomes transformed into anxiety about how the black victim is going to deal with you. The white person knows that in a group discussion she can become the receptacle for a sizeable deposit of legitimate anger and outrage. The existence of the white stockade prevents the development of adult relationships between black and white people, and there are no better indications of this than the use of 'white speak' or the emergence of patronizing and degrading parent–child relationships.

From behind the white stockade, blacks become a menacing homogeneous group (most especially Afro-Caribbeans), having a hostility and separateness that, for whites, is confirmed by the emergence of articulate and rejecting black separatist organizations. This perception from behind the white stockade of united and uniting homogeneity amongst the blacks in a group makes it impossible for whites to appreciate the individuality of the black people in the room with them, prevents recognition of real differences (based on class, age, sex or political position) between blacks, and thus inhibits blacks and whites from making alliances with each other over points at issue in a discussion. The perception of black homogeneity leads easily into insecurity and lowered self-confidence, a point made in an article in *Spare Rib* by three black feminists: 'you know that white people are afraid when black people get together in groups. They seem to think that we'll be scheming some trouble or something' (*Dolores, Gerry and Sunita, 1983*).

A consequence of the white stockade is that

> a white image . . . contracts around a limited number of dimensions. A conspicuous minority crystallizes into a monolithic majority, a threatening and unpredictable community. Causes are rejected, and consequences alone are observed. Only the visual enters the image. The white perspective congeals into a static tableau – a tableau of limited variety, emotionally and evaluatively laden, and resistant to change. (*Ley, 1970*)

The congealed image of a monolithic, hostile black experience is perpetuated in group encounters by public displays of loyalty between blacks that conceal real differences of view, and by the 'noise' in the system of what Ley has called exotic data about blacks: coded language, ethnic gestures, dress, and so forth. The feelings of the white practitioner when confronted with such group encounters is honestly described by Parkes in his account of working in a youth club:

> In contrast to his or her black counterpart who encounters white majorities daily, the white person rarely, if ever, finds himself in a wholly black situation. The experience is not a comfortable one, at least not at first. One feels isolated and self-conscious and acutely aware of looks or glances which are cast in one's direction. One becomes extremely sensitive to half-heard comments or any suggestion that one is being mocked. Language which is unfamiliar to the white ear becomes a barrier whilst the profusion of black style – locks, tams, Rastafarian memorabilia – and the constant pounding of the reggae beat are bewildering. The sensation is made more acute by the fact that because of their unfamiliarity black faces are not easily distinguishable one from the other. This may sound like a racist cliché but is nonetheless true – though the fault is clearly in the eye of the beholder. (*1984*)

The congealed image we have described is also perpetuated in the group discussions we observed by the inability of whites and blacks to create a culture in which they could openly disagree and dispute with each other, to make and learn from mistakes, and by the vitality of the first principle of 'white speak' that informs the conduct of many white professionals in public: the assumption that the legitimacy of what a black person says derives not from logic, fact and reason but from his being black. Likewise, it is not uncommon to encounter black professionals and activists who choose to operate on a cardinal principle of 'black speak': the assumption that those whites who err or disagree in discussion do so from blindness or malevolence that is the fruit of their racism. All these factors make communication ineffective: blacks and whites deal with images of each other, and these images act as gatekeepers to filter and code any information that manages to survive 'white speak', silence and the minimax criterion. The possibility for mutual influence in such a situation becomes remote. This is a serious situation in which white and black professionals find themselves, not least because racism is a relationship, as Gurnah has astutely observed: 'What is profoundly mistaken about the slogan *"racism is a white problem"* is that it fails to recognise that racism is a *relationship*. In a relationship one cannot fruitfully focus on the *nature* of the individual in the hope of solving structural inequalities' (*1984*).

One might add that precisely because racism is a relationship, one cannot expect much of a change in the nature of the white individual – in her attitudes, behaviour, and dealing with others – unless and until whites and blacks work together in understanding the dynamics of that relationship. To do this effectively presupposes a quality of communication that is rare in black–white discussions. It presupposes, too, a change in the reasons why blacks participate in anti-racism training, enabling them to shift from the role most frequently assigned to, or taken by, them in training – that of putting pressure on whites, inducing guilt and extracting confession and recantation. But even prior to this, the analysis of racism as a relationship implies, too, that whites and blacks must accept the need to work with each other, rather than stay separated as in the kinds of training described by Satow (1982). This point has been forcefully made by Owusu-Bempah:

> It is undoubtedly true . . . that racist attitudes are very often developed in the absence of any personal experience with black people; nonetheless, it is equally incorrect to assume that white people can unlearn their racist attitudes in isolation from black people. Learning and unlearning are two different processes and therefore require different approaches. Under the right conditions unlearning of racist attitudes can be greatly facilitated by exposure to black people. This means that black people have an invaluable part to play in anti-racist activities, including racism awareness training, and hence need to be actively involved in the process. (*1985*)

The paper by Satow is typical of many from racism awareness training, and contains yet another superficiality about black–white relations that has gained as much currency as the slogan 'racism is a white problem'. This is the belief that all whites are racists, though there may be different views about how whites arrive at, and are maintained in, this condition. Anti-racism training does not pretend to remove the stain of racism, only to allow whites to understand it, confront and control it in themselves and, through so doing, hopefully to make changes in the white structures of which they are a part.

The statement that racism is an endemic characteristic of being white is at one level true; but it is superficial. It is about as profound as the statement 'all people are sinners'. It is superficial because it presupposes an aggregate 'white experience'; but many whites, for example, claim they did not have an imperialist past. Indeed, many (the Irish, Jews and perhaps the Welsh and Scots) experienced English colonialism, often at its worst, and suffered the subordination of their language and culture, as well as the exploitation of their labour and natural resources. A contentious point, perhaps, but it tells us to be aware of other, perhaps more potent, cleavages in the white experience: those of sex or age, and certainly those of class and region. The saliency to many people of their sex and age may also lead us to question the general applicability of Cowan's view (but one that is common in awareness training) that 'white people see themselves first and foremost as individuals' (1982).

The conception of racism as a structural blemish in the make-up of anyone white is also superficial because it is not verifiable empirically and, indeed, if it were, then only one case of a white person not being racist would be enough to undermine it. A major problem with the slogan is that it has become such a part of the 'moral language' of black–white relations that it has obscured and prevented the quest for greater differentiation in our thinking. For example, if all whites are indelibly stained with racism, how is the racism of the young different from the old, that of the working class from the middle class and that of men from women? What are the differences between the racism of those who are in contact with blacks at work or at home and that of those who are not? Are there no differences in the manifestation of racism towards Asians from that towards Afro-Caribbeans? How does the nature and quality of racism vary with political insight and allegiance? How is the racism of the intellectual different from that of the labourer, the powerful from the powerless, the employed from the unemployed? If white racism is maintained and repaired by vested interests and by white institutions and structures, how do the powerless, the victims, the marginal, the isolates and so forth absorb their racism? How does racism vary according to the *type* of white institutions and structures that are said to maintain it, and vary with the position, role and status of those in these institutions? How does racism manifest itself differently through different aspects of a white person's life – through, for example, the different roles they take on (mother, tenant, worker, darts player and so forth)?

These are important questions. I am not optimistic, however, that there will ever be sufficient time or resources to find answers to them. The immediate significance of drawing attention to them is, first, to ask for more awareness about the complexity of both white racism in particular and, in general, the whole gamut of feelings and emotions that define a white person's interactions with blacks; and, secondly, to try to put an end to forms of training and discussion between blacks and whites that are based on crude and dubious generalizations about racism.

The effect of pursuing a more differentiated approach to the personal racism of whites is that beliefs about whites will cease to be blanket appraisals. And blanket appraisals that 'racism is a white problem' and 'all whites are incurably racist' are just that – as blankets they keep myths and stereotypes warm, and smother contact, inquiry and exploration. They protect whites and blacks from encountering with each other. How can our ideas and actions against personal and institutional racism have any cutting edge if they are based on superficial propositions that homogenize whites and ignore the complexity of their personal dispositions towards blacks?

It is important to note that the existence of the white stockade itself contributes to the lack of differentiation in understanding white attitudes and behaviour; it makes it difficult for blacks to discover (and for whites to reveal) that the disposition of whites to blacks cannot be explained wholly as 'racism' or by reference to self-interest and race/class superiority. But the most obnoxious feature of the white stockade is not just that it is part of a racist, controlling strategy but that it forces blacks into unwittingly perpetuating that strategy. In group discussion, there is much pressure on blacks to take the white stockade by storm; aggression and anger, fuelled by the failure of whites to eschew communication through image, makes the black participants even more intimidating to the beleaguered white participants. The expressive and often threatening gestures and body language of the black members in attempting to get through the stockade is interpreted by many whites as the boundary markers of an exclusive, homogeneous group, and is perceived as exotic, thus reinforcing white stereotypes within the stockade. Thus the white stockade forces blacks into saying and doing things that perpetuate the fears and myths from which the stockade is constructed. Communication deteriorates even further when blacks threaten to leave the group or to set up their own black enclosures ('the black caucus').[2]

One of the interesting moments of Chris's racism awareness workshop was when the group was discussing cultural racism and was asked to find examples in literature of how the words 'black' and 'blackness' were associated with evil, wrong-doing, worthlessness and so forth. Two examples were discussed in the group – an extract from a book by Jerzy Kosinski, and a poem that Chris had written some ten years ago. Kosinski's book is about a 6-year-old Jewish boy wandering in Eastern Europe in the opening weeks of the Second World War:

> She called me the Black One. From her I learned for the first time that I was possessed by an evil spirit which crouched in me like a mole in a deep burrow, and of whose presence I was unaware. Such a person as I, possessed of this evil spirit, would be recognised by his bewitched black eyes which did not blink when they gazed at bright clear eyes. Hence, Olga declared, I could stare at other people and unknowingly cast a spell over them. (*1972*)

This passage linked with Chris's poem because each made reference to the eyes, and the sessions in the training workshops had made the participants realize the importance of eye contact in communication, as well as its negative value in maintaining the white stockade. Chris was invited to read the poem to the group:

> Dim light
> Furry cat
> Wistful in the dark
> Dimly dreaming
> Dear cat
> Let me stroke your dark fur
> Flash those eyes
> Not shining, dark
> But glaring
> A straight
> Glower of hate
> Not moving
> Not trying anything
> We cats, helpless
> Our time is not yet
> But one day – or one night . . .

The group discussed two aspects of this poem. It was about the inevitability of black emancipation, whether in Britain or America or Azania. Indeed, one of the seeds for the poem had been planted by the book *Black Rage* by Grier and Cobbs, and particularly by the following passage:

> consider the intensity of the black man's grief . . . It is the transformation of this quantum of grief into aggression of which we now speak. As a sapling bent low stores energy for a violent backswing, blacks bent double by oppression have stored energy which will be replaced in the form of rage – black rage, apocalyptic and final . . . a welling tide risen out of all those terrible years of grief, now a tidal wave of fury and rage, and all black, black as night. (*1969*)

The second aspect was the predatory atmosphere of the poem, because the poem had been stimulated by a dream about a black cat springing on to Chris's back. But the group was taken aback when the trainer observed that the predatory aspects could not be divorced from the erotic. The trainer confronted them with their own fantasies about blacks and sexual predation, with what Angela Davis has referred to as the myth of the black rapist (1982). The group members were asked about the ethnicity of the people featured in their dreams and in their mental reconstructions of newspaper accounts of sexual attack. It came as no surprise to the trainer that they were often black; indeed, many of Chris's imaginings about any form of physical assault on people or property featured black men, and the trainer used this to show that Chris and the others in the group had caught an important truth about black and white relationships – that blacks were forced to storm the white stockade (and in so doing put themselves even further beyond the pale) in order to win not only resources and power, justice and fraternity, status and recognition but also the ingredients of real communication. The white stockade had to be negotiated every time a black person had to deal with an official or department, or when she came through Passport Control after a holiday abroad. As one reader of the first draft commented:

> You talk of whites behind their stockade; but to black people, that stockade is experienced as being around *them.* Black people in this country are in a stockade – we are surrounded by white natives with spears, patrolled by white policemen with truncheons, guarding a land of opportunity and resources beyond. We want to burst out of the stockade – and that's what you see beginning to happen in Brixton, and in Tottenham and other places.

But as Chris found, the white stockade also existed in each individual's mind and in the way whites handled themselves in groups in which they participated with black people. Yet if the white stockade existed both as an objective, physical reality (not least in American suburbs with their electric fences, handguns and Dobermans) and as something in the minds of white people, was this also true of the black ghetto? What was the ghetto in the mind of black people? Could we think of it in the ways one had thought about the white stockade? Again, this was far outside the scope of the six-month project upon which we had embarked. But we did have some tentative ideas on the ghetto-in-the-mind that seemed relevant to a study about participation in community groups.

We first of all drew Chris's attention to the way in which the time and the energy of black people were taken up in anticipating, dealing with and defending against racism and prejudice. The black ghetto both as a residential area and as an attribute in the mind was partly about protection and regulating encounters with others presumed to be hostile:

> a black norm has developed – a suspiciousness of one's environment that is necessary to survival. The black man must be on guard to protect himself against physical hurt. He must cushion himself against cheating, slander, humiliation and outright mistreatment by official representatives. If he does not protect himself, he will have a life of such pain and shock as to be unbearable. (*1973*)

Saunders's conclusion is that if the community worker is to work with black people, 'your primary function is not to change the man but to help him effectively change his environment. The appropriate changes in his behaviour will come when he recognises the need to acquire new adaptive techniques because those he previously used are no longer needed or effective.'

The importance of risk-management is as obvious from our interviews as from the group discussions we observed. One of the black people interviewed in Birmingham said:

> As I say I've taken steps to avoid confrontation. As I said I don't have any social contact so we're not going to be in a social situation where there's going to be a breakdown of the relationship. I work away from the estate, quite a distance away from the estate, so when I do get home it's usually the evenings and I sit, watch television and read and talk to my daughter or something. So there isn't really much scope for us to have the type of contact that they have with other people on the estate that has led to some of the breakdowns that I've seen.

As for the possibilities of working together with white people on the estate, the respondent was even more careful.

We as a group must take steps to get closer to each other in order to be able to do something about our condition. The question is of course who is going to make the first step. I wouldn't want to go and say to white people on the estate, well listen, I think we all have the same problems – and they say, well Jesus we don't have the same problems as you do, you know, you're poor black people, we're white and we're all right; this kind of response might happen, maybe not in those same very clear terms but the implication would be there. You know they probably feel that they can go to the housing authorities and communicate to them as white people to white people and anything to do with black people will be diluting their cause and just creating more problems for themselves rather than actually strengthening their position and therefore helping them to cause a change that will benefit everyone.

The gap between the white stockade and the black ghetto on one estate is vividly captured by the same respondent as he talks about the fragility of communication that is based on stereotype and myth:

I suppose you could get into situations where there are misunderstandings because we have no knowledge of each other, very little knowledge of each other, maybe white people decide to stereotype black people's behaviour and consider certain types of behaviour to be antisocial and directed at white people. There have been incidents that I've seen where the police have been called in over fairly trivial matters that I think could have been sorted out amongst the two groups of people if they had been prepared to discuss it. Usually the whites in my experience have adopted an intransigent position based on what they consider to be their position of strength because it's *their* country and they've called in *their* police force who come in and take *their* side and brutalize black people maybe who were being 'insolent' by a stereo being played too loud or somebody parking *their* car where you normally park *your* car. The bankruptcy is such among these two groups of people that they are unable to say, OK, you know we both drive cars, we both pay road tax, we don't own any part of the road, you know if I park here it doesn't really matter, you can still park behind me or in front of me; but you know I've seen incidents of that really petty nature because of ignorance of each other or suspicion of each other or hatred of each other, blacks and whites have not been able to work it out, the police have been called and it has ended all rather badly. So there are types of disputes and problems that can arise from different racial groups not being much aware of each other on an intellectual level because people don't read books or bother to read newspapers that have any content at all and go on to cause each other endless aggravation as a consequence of this mistrust and mutual hate.

Living Together but Differently

Chris had become concerned with what a colleague had referred to as 'the almost super-human effort needed to develop a sophisticated understanding of white racism. Without it, we haven't got a hope in hell of changing anyone.' Trying to change white professionals means more than naming and confronting them as oppressors; it is not just a rational process of enlightenment but an emotional penetration in which whites are presented with information about themselves, their racial identities and experience, the norms they live out about white superiority and the position of race as an organizing ideology in their lives. At the very least, the presence of the black ghetto and the articulation of its interests represent a massive challenge to the cosy anglo-conformity of the white stockade.

Chris had been impressed by the dialogue with white and black community workers while on a visit to Holland. One of them had declared that 'you can't deal with racism by taking a leap'. The distance between the white stockade and the black ghetto was such that many people needed help to shuffle forward, and to learn to encounter with each other through a series of small steps, working in very small and local situations, 'improving relationships by more co-operation in action as well as cultural activities'. They also tried to deal at the same time with 'abrasive spots' in the locality such as noise, rubbish disposal and the harassment per-petrated by young children that had such a deleterious effect on black–white relations. And they had learnt about the importance of changing role as well as person. For themselves, these commun-ity workers worked on the assumption that improving the quality of black–white relations depended not only on securing racial justice but also on improving the general set of relations in a neighbourhood between people and groups. Thus they wanted to reconstruct their own roles and techniques to make them more effective community workers at the horizontal level.

Another aspect of this reconstruction involved the relation-ships between the black and white workers in the project. A key moment in this reconstruction had been Harry's 'donkey explo-sion', as they called it. Harry was one of the black field workers and in one staff meeting he stopped what he was saying in mid-sentence and turned to the white workers:

'You're like a lot of nodding donkeys', he shouted. 'Why d'you agree with everything I say?'

They were treating him in public as if he were infallible, but in private they voiced their doubts and disagreements. 'It was a hell of a strain for me and it meant that as a group we just weren't communicating.' But the white workers argued that the nodding donkey syndrome was not simply their problem: it was inter-actional, a product of the black–white relationship in the project. As such, the behaviour and attitudes of the black workers that helped to produce this ingratiating and timid response from the whites had to be understood and changed also. Constantly calling the whites to account for their imperialist past, for example, made the whites more defensive and intimidated, strengthened rather than breached the stockade, crippled communication, tripled frustration and zeroed the possibilities of learning and personal development.

One of the most controversial moments of Chris's visit to this Dutch project came when one white worker suggested: 'To do your job properly, you have to know what white working-class people think and feel. What pressures and stresses make them racist or prejudiced? What sort of burdens do they carry in their lives that having to cope with strange coloured people seems to be the last straw? You can't stop them being racist until you start empathizing with them. I don't expect black people who are being victimized and harassed to empathize but black and white professionals should be doing it.'

This comment reminded Chris of a review by Janice Fleming and Mark Harrison in *Youth and Policy*, in which they insisted on the necessity of a view of racism as an integral dynamic of British society: 'racism exists not only in the present, but comes from the past situations and is linked with the breaking up of the feudal system, the slave trade and the emergence of capitalism, imperialism and colonialism' (*1984/5*). They said that one had to be careful in evaluating this dynamic on groups such as the working class. Simply to blame the working class (especially its young people) for the existence of racism 'seems just to be changing the victim to blame'. They argued that one must not see racism as a pathological condition of any group but as the consequence of a range of exploitative economic relations, both present and past, that infect society as a whole. Moreover, thought Chris, it was possible to see how the history of conflict between British people of different colours and races was partly a history of the miseducation of the working class and, in recent times, the poisoning of their attitudes by some politicians, notably Enoch Powell. One small part of this miseducation has been the neglect of an important truth about ourselves: to be British is to be a member of a country of many races – that is the way it always has been, and ever will be.

It was obvious to Chris that racism was about the cultural and economic subordination of black people; as such, it could be seen as an ideology, a set of organizing principles and attitudes, that had developed to explain and justify the exploitation of countries in Asia, Africa and elsewhere. But the critical question for the community worker was this: was racism as an ideology amongst the working class merely a handed-down version of that elaborated within society as a whole? Or was it 'used' by the working class to explain and justify *their* control over resources and power (such as they had) at the local level? White people who had influence in community groups, or managed community centres, who had their name in the paper, or hob-nobbed with the local MP were enjoying responsibility and power in their local patch that was both a rewarding and a scarce experience in their lives.

They were bound to protect it fiercely against black residents and other white people, and the availability of racist data about black people in the area could be mobilized (even unconsciously) to explain and justify their exclusion from community groups.

This was the material explanation of racism at the local level; as an ideology used to explain and justify subordination it would have an autonomous, local character, though nurtured on society-wide myths and stereotypes about black people that were put about on television and in the press. But there was more to it than this: the oft-heard racist complaint, 'I didn't get the maisonette because it went to a black family', is an example of scapegoating that allows dispossessed whites to escape from recognition of their own exploited position, and thus to evade the responsibilities inherent in collective action to change conditions. In addition, must not the denial of solidarity with blacks lead inevitably to the denial of solidarity with anyone? Thus at the local level, racism as ideology may be used both to justify the exclusion of blacks from what meagre allowances of power and authority can be enjoyed in community activities, *and* to maintain a façade of superiority and well-being that allows many white people to avoid an evaluation of their own objective economic/social position. So it was a truism that excluding blacks from community groups was part of the functioning of the white stockade; but this had to be understood in terms not just of contamination theory ('England's green and pleasant land'), nor of the conservative suspicion of outsiders, nor the psycho-sexual fears surrounding blackness, but also of the protection of those few resources and rewards that white working-class people had achieved through community activities.

While Chris was reflecting on this, the Dutch worker who had made the comment about empathy was getting into hot water with two of his colleagues. Wasn't he just colluding with racism? How could you empathize with young kids on the estate who had recently tattooed a swastika on the belly of a Turkish woman?

He wasn't, he replied, thinking about extreme forms of racism of that kind; he was thinking of the white people in the community groups he worked with whose behaviours and attitudes were much more amenable to change. It was essential to put yourselves in their shoes in order to understand (but not necessarily agree with) how they saw the culturally diverse neighbourhood around them. 'You won't get anyone to change by calling them pre-judiced or racist; what effect do you think it has on a white person to be told (by an outsider, like ourselves) that she's racist? Would it help someone to read or write if we publicly confronted him as 'illiterate'? The people round her are already up to their necks in problems – most of them are out of work, for a start, and they live in rotten houses and flats – and you expect them easily to cope with what they see as yet another burden foisted on them. They resent their poverty, they resent their powerlessness, they resent having to cope with strange people with a different language and customs and most of all they resent the fact that the cosy white working-class community that they used to depend upon to cope with such stress has virtually disappeared.'

It is a bit like community care, thought Chris, which also asks under-resourced neighbourhoods and over-stretched people to cope with yet another responsibility.

This was an important point that the Dutch worker was making: the response of the white urban working class (particularly its racism) to the black residents around them should not be considered separately from the impact of unemployment, urban decay and the deterioration of services and facilities. Chris recalled that Bridges and Fekete had argued that any theories about racism and the disintegration of urban working-class culture should not be isolated from 'the overall economic restructuring of capitalism presently under way and its increased dependence on central state power and the use of the police for political and social control' (1985).

The discussion among the Dutch workers continued unabated: 'There are so many strata of emotion about the race issue that unless you begin to identify and name them you'll never be able to develop a theory of change, a theory of informal education with adults in this neighbourhood.'

'That's what this project lacks', said one of the black community workers. 'There's an interesting point here: there's an incredible contrast between how complex it is for white community workers to work on racism with the white working class, on the one hand, and, on the other, the simplistic level on which black and white community workers engage with one another. In other words, there's a lot of confrontational-type "education" going on between white and black workers which is no model at all for our involvement with people in the neighbourhood. It's not just enough', he said, turning to Chris, 'to have a correct analysis about racism or racialism; you've also got to have a theory about how best to get blacks and whites to encounter with each other in this neighbourhood, to talk, to work together, to conflict, to work out contracts for living together. People have got to develop the skills for living together.'

'Living together but living differently,' added Chris.

Notes

1   Presumably the process of owning one's colour is difficult partly because racism awareness trainers would not want white participants to own their whiteness in the way that National Front Members or South African whites do.

2   It is interesting to note that Cashmore has drawn attention to another kind of stockade that many academics in the field of race and ethnic relations have retreated behind. He describes much of their discussion as an impenetrable thicket, and he has produced a dictionary to let in some light (1984).

4

Coming Out: the End of Closet Neighbouring

> ... a significant number of people in the inner city and outer estates are friendless and desperately lonely ... large numbers of people in urban priority areas are deprived of 'community' by being excluded by *poverty or unemployment* from fulfilling relationships in their neighbourhood ... Poor people can be forced into isolated and lonely lives ... where sound networks have not developed to meet human needs for interaction ... The concern was rather with a 'privatization' which is inflicted upon people by circumstances ... The result is an acute form of urban deprivation: deprivation of relatedness, of esteem.
>
> (*Archbishop of Canterbury's Commission, 1985*)

Chris was not unaware of the criticisms made of the white English that, with few exceptions, they had seldom in recent times been obliged to develop skills in living differently, in living in a cosmopolitan culture in which they would have to tolerate differences in the values and life-style of those around them. But it seemed to Chris that this issue of living differently was secondary to that of whether people in urban areas had the capacity to live together.

The idea that people in urban areas had forgotten or neglected the skills to live together intrigued Chris as the study visit continued in Holland, and then in northern France, to Lille and Paris. It wasn't so much that they had forgotten; it was more that people had made a number of radical adaptations in their relations with others as the urban environment had changed and been changed; specifically, they had evolved a way of managing their relationships by withdrawal into the household, choosing to live more separately from one another. This adaptation to the insecure and unpredictable around them had been encouraged by the development of their roles as domestic consumers of an expanding range of goods and services. The home had become less important as part of a network of neighbourhood roles and responsibilities, and more important as a micro-consumer unit, providing reparation for those in work, and containment for those out of it. Perhaps it was to be expected, mused Chris, that as residential densities increased, and as more and more people spent more and more time in their neighbourhood, and as working class areas became more socially and ethnically heterogeneous, then people would seek to manage their relationships with each other by withdrawal rather than through engagement.

To say that people in urban areas had been 'adapting' to a changing environment concealed a complexity of social and market forces. Many people had chosen a private life behind their front door because of their fear of crime, and others because they had given priority to groups or communities of interest not based in their neighbourhood. Some people were constrained by factors beyond their control to lead private lives: much accommodation in the inner city was literally homes without neighbourhoods (for example, high-rise towers); both unemployment and the location of work outside the areas where people lived meant that work-based relations could no longer provide the basis for neighbourhood relationships. Similarly, the dispersion of people to commercial and recreational facilities outside the neighbourhood weakened the role of neighbourhood resources (for example, the corner shop) in putting people in touch with one another. Moreover, the different shopping patterns of people in a neighbourhood (for example, the elderly able to use only local shops, while the younger population had access to stores outside the locality) lessened even further the chances for social interaction.

The consolidation of private lives was made inevitable by the appropriation by the state of responsibility for a number of neighbourhood-based functions: people's declining involvement in social care, social control and socialization made social interaction less necessary. Seabrook comments:

It is one of the ironies that those values which the best of the working class forged in oppositon to the poverty and insecurity of capitalism – the mutuality and the sharing, the sense of a collective predicament, the imaginative understanding of other people's suffering – were precisely those which shaped the idea of the welfare state. It looked as if those very things which working people had created to mitigate some of the harshness of life were going to be vested in the structures of society itself. The welfare state looked to many working people as the public acknowledgement of things they had always known: that security, care and comfort must be given unstintingly to those in need. It seemed as though that unofficial and unsung ability to care for each other had come to a wider recognition at last: enshrined in the institutions and statutes of the land.

Forty years later, it doesn't look quite like that. We can see now how values have been expropriated, drained out of the communities and become frozen in cumbersome, bureaucratic and indifferent structures. (*1984*)

So all of these different factors lay behind withdrawal as an adaptive technique. But private domestic life had also been made possible by the steady improvement of housing standards, the extension of mortgages and credit facilities to the working class, and the miniaturization of commodities, such as washing machines, that were necessary to the efficient functioning of the self-contained household. A combination of advertising, easy-payment facilities and built-in obsolescence turned the home into a haven of personal enjoyment and provided the volume market for their commodities that British and international manufacturing companies so desperately needed. The international producer met the domestic consumer in the privacy of the home; for neither was the neighbourhood or the management of social relations with others a necessary ingredient in developing their market relationship. For the individual who was not poor, time invested in neighbourhood activities was time he or she could not give to acquiring more money; for the manufacturer, a person's time invested in social roles and responsibilities was time and energy not spent in enjoying the goods that he wanted to provide for 'in-home or in-car entertainment'. Geoffrey Moorhouse, writing about race relations in the Black Country in the *Birmingham Evening Mail* (28 August 1964), described the consequences, in a piece of prophetic analysis:

> There is certainly some fearful social sickness affecting the Midlands as a whole which seems to be compounded of a desire to make money fast while the going is good, a willingness to go to any lengths to achieve this . . . This is a full time job, leaving space and energy for no other consideration . . . Their wages are high because they work ridiculous extra stints in overtime. When they get home some of them say, they are fit for nothing but flopping down in front of the television set or in supine contemplation of their other riches.
>
> They are so worn out by their headlong pursuit of wealth that they cannot even enjoy normal family activity. How can a feeling for community expect to survive in such a climate?

Making a Living

Chris's concern with the management of neighbourhood relations came close to Sandra Wallman's concept of 'managing livelihood' (1982). In her research in South London, Wallman set out to define the resources necessary to a decent livelihood, and to identify some of the ways in which people from different groups managed these resources. Wallman rejects the conventional economic view that livelihood is dependent on access only to housing, people and services, and goods and money:

> Livelihood is never 'just' a matter of finding or making shelter, translating money and getting food to put on the family table or to exchange in the market place. It is equally a matter of the ownership and circulation of information, the management of skills and relationships, and the affirmation of personal significance and group identity . . . A realistic description of living in the city ought therefore to take notice of social as well as economic tasks.

Wallman asks a number of basic questions relevant to this study:

What makes for viability in contemporary urban life?

In how many ways do ordinary people manage a livelihood?

How do households of differing ethnic origins living in the same area together manage their separate livelihoods in relation to each other and to that area?

How far do people of different ethnic origins living in the same area have similar goals and expectations at similar life stages, and how far do they differ in the management of their livelihood?

In which aspects of managing livelihood is ethnicity a resource which individuals can, for some purposes and in some circumstances, mobilise to their own advantage; which will have no value or relevance to them in other situations; and which will, in still others, become a liability to be escaped or denied as far as possible?

Wallman and her colleagues chose to add three social resources to the economic ones: time, information and identity. What is important for this study is not those three particular social resources but, first, acceptance that livelihood depends on a range of social resources; secondly, that any evaluative questions about the functioning of city areas must assess the importance of social resources; and thirdly, the fundamental proposition that livelihood has to be managed. The necessity of management is a truism in relation to economic resources but social policy-makers have rarely grasped that social resources also have to be cared for and developed if they are not to be wasted, or to atrophy, or if they are to be used to secure the greatest benefit from economic resources, or if they are to offer opportunities to residents for creative and socially productive roles within the neighbourhood. The growth and development of a range of social resources (friendships, networks, personal significance, leadership, knowledge and information and so forth) lead us to consider the idea of sponsored community development which we will take up later in this chapter.

In the rest of this book we will often refer to the tasks of 'managing social relations and resources' or to 'how blacks and whites manage their relationships'. The word 'manage' is used as it is used in the phrase 'managing a livelihood', that is, 'making a living'. We will use the word 'manage' to refer to the process of tending to and developing relationships and social resources. The word is not without its difficulties, as one reader of the first draft noted:

> This theme of managing race relations is a bit unfortunate – isn't that what's been happening since the 1960s and long before? Empire equals management equals administration. Each neighbourhood is to have its own District Officer – a super manager . . . the idea of managing black–white relations in neighbourhoods verges on the callous or even obscene. It's not the right language. How did you manage Toxteth or any of the other places in 1981 which erupted? Agencies have managed to stay above the conflict. Does our new multi-cultural community worker appear as a re-run of the old colonial District Officer?

Point taken. But we are primarily interested in what support and resources are needed *for people themselves* to develop and look after (manage) relationships with those living around them.

For the moment, we want to consider some issues about how urban residents manage their livelihood, and, in general, how they manage their relations and encounters with each other. Of special interest, of course, is how white and black people work out their relationships with one another, but we believe that it may be helpful to look at the particular case of black and white relations within the context of the competence with which all social resources in a neighbourhood are managed. Where relationships in general are poorly managed, this presumably will affect relations between particular groups; thus strategies aimed to improve sectional relations may be most effective where efforts are made to help a neighbourhood maintain *all* its social resources more competently. In much the same way, looking after sectional relations (such as those between black and white) will be affected by the level of economic and material resources in a neighbourhood. This applies as much to the general quality and maintenance of the environment as it does to the access of black and white people to comparable levels of housing and employment. Community workers cannot expect success in putting black and white people in touch with each other, and to be touched by one another, if each group is being pinched by poverty and disadvantage. The effect of the material on the social has been described by the GLC report on racial harassment:

> In common with every other estate on which the Unit has worked, the poor service for repairs and maintenance was the greatest single cause for dissatisfaction. The anger and frustration which many tenants express towards the repairs service often spill over into their attitudes towards the estate in general and their feelings towards other tenants and neighbours. On Ocean Estate, this has serious implications for social harmony with some tenants choosing to blame the newer residents and especially the Asian families for the decline which has resulted, in fact, from deteriorating standards in maintenance. A responsive and efficient repairs service will make a very real contribution to good neighbour relations and greatly improve tenant satisfaction with the Council's service. (*Greater London Council, 1984*)

So Chris was finding that in order to work more effectively in the neighbourhood with black people and groups, attention had to be given to:

(1) The general quality of social relations there.
(2) The influence of the physical environment and the availability and quality of neighbourhood facilities on social relations. The work of Jane Jacobs, Oscar Newman and, more recently, of Alice Coleman (1985) has indicated the effect of design and layout on social behaviour and interaction.
(3) The availability of decent housing, employment, health care and so on.
(4) The extent to which the management of social and economic resources was supported by neighbourhood facilities such as play groups, and other services needed by households at varying stages in the life cycle.

This was somewhat perplexing for Chris: if social resources, including those needed for managing white–black relationships, were so connected to material resources, then perhaps the idea of learning an Asian language or going to Bangladesh in the summer

ought to be dropped; maybe it would be better to learn about
tenants' co-operatives or small-business development and the
working of community enterprises. At the very least, Chris was
aware that there were a number of *indirect* strategies for supporting the involvement of black people in community groups and
that a white person might be more effective at working on these.

But even more perplexing were the connections between different kinds of social resources; how, for example, were relationships between residents, or those between black and white
neighbours, affected by the presence or absence of one of the most
crucial of social resources – the possession of power over matters
that affect one's household and environment? The Louvaine
Action Plan quoted in Wallman (1982) describes the feeling of
powerlessness when dealing with authority as the worst of all
blights because it affects people's minds. The feeling of helplessness and potential risk in the face of both neighbours and
authorities comes through strongly in another part of the
Wallman book when she writes:

> neither colour and language, nor the presence of 'blacks' and
> 'Greeks' are actual or persistent issues. Those most often
> cited are: faceless bureaucrats, ambitious politicians, people
> who ignore the council's skips and leave their rubbish by the
> dustbins, council employees who will not take this large
> rubbish away, people who have noisy and frequent parties,
> and worse, are thought to charge a gate fee and to admit
> strangers to their parties . . .
>   . . . better use of the housing stock has created a surplus
> over the residents' requirements. This must, according to the
> rules, go into the council's hopper to be allocated to 'any-
> body' on the housing lists.
>   This possibility is a focus of anxiety . . . 'Anybody' will
> not be known to us . . . will only use the place to get a
> house . . . will not really want to live here . . will not have
> people here . . . will not care about the place . . . will run it
> down . . . will move on . . . Residents therefore encourage
> each other to find amongst their acquaintance 'somebody'
> who wants to live in the area; who would move in and would

stay; who would become 'us'. Even in this context, ethnic ratios and affiliations are beside the point . . .

Chris wondered if it was reasonable to hypothesize a relation between helplessness/powerlessness on the one hand, and poor social relationships and communication between people on the other. And there was, of course, community workers' own helplessness: most felt unable to develop a substantial *local* strategy to give residents more influence over factors affecting their well-being that emanated from outside the neighbourhood, for example in Brussels or Tokyo (though producer and consumer co-operatives and other forms of community enterprise could contribute to creating a small degree of defensible space around a neighbourhood).

On the other hand, there were local sources of helplessness – for example, if you were a council tenant, the inability to influence lettings policy, or repairs, and decisions made by council departments. So practitioners were going to have to re-think their ideas on tenant management and participation; Chris had already noted how Jeremy Seabrook had grasped the nettle of residents being involved in a vetting procedure for prospective tenants (1984). In addition, there was the matter of residents' feeling of powerlessness to influence the behaviour of those living around them who were being offensive, anti-social and criminal. Was part of the job of the community worker to help residents develop 'contracts' about the local social order, helping them to take up a collective interest in defining shared agreements about public behaviour and responsibilities? Chris hypothesized that the more local residents could become re-involved in functions such as socialization and social control the more they would begin to lose their sense of helplessness about events in their environment. Feeling helpless was, in other words, the price that people paid for retreat, for withdrawal, for self-interest and for disregarding social resources in the single-minded belief that it was access to, and consumption of, only the material that produced the good life.

From our reconnaissance interviews with black residents, there seemed to be six areas of major concern (many of which overlap with each other) that affected relationships between all residents, and which often had an effect on black–white relations on a housing estate.

(1) The security of one's person and property.
(2) Noise, from other people's televisions, sound-systems, love-making and quarrels.
(3) Rubbish and hygiene.
(4) Car repairs and maintenance in public areas of an estate.
(5) The abuse of lifts and other common facilities.
(6) The noise, disruption and aggression of children.

These six are the major abrasion points in community relationships. We can capture their effect on livelihood by reading a few extracts from our interviews with black residents. Each extract is taken from a different interview.

I'm forever keeping an eye out for an opportunity to move to something better, something where you can come home and not be surrounded by garbage and noise and lot of kids aimlessly rampaging up and down . . .

I don't know very much of the people on the estate. I know the former tenants that were living here when I moved in and we got along pretty well. But these that are moving in now is a kind of younger generation than I am . . . and they're a different type of people that you're even afraid to talk to them or approach them because there are so much muggings and break-ins going on around us that you don't know who is who, you're afraid to invite anybody in in case something happens. And I don't visit.

Some of the neighbours treat me right and I treat them all right, but we had one near by that's my nearest neighbour and they make a lot of noise and the front garden is full of filth and all that until they have a rat.

Some of the people in this tower block seem to use the lifts as a toilet. . . I've got black people downstairs and along the corridors. Sometimes I ask the guy downstairs to be reasonable when he's turning up his music at 11, 12, 1, 2 in the morning. I think it's totally unnecessary so therefore I tell him to turn it down. But we don't get on . . . a lot of the white people on this block have a tendency to want to look after it, they don't want to move out of it, they're happy, they're friendly, they look after my little boy. The little black girl next door, they take her downstairs with them, they're just like one family down there but some of these blacks, them young black kids and some of the parents, they seem to have a different mentality – well, I call it a chip on their shoulder. But to me some of it is just pig ignorance.

As far as I'm concerned the estate is all right. But the people who are in it, to me they're just out of order . . . you'll have blokes who lives in this estate who were robbing people's homes in broad daylight . . . you have white kids calling 'you black bastard'. And there's always arguments, fights. There's always something between families, right . . . now me personally, I play me music, right. But there are times, now they call it the prison block on that end, those people who live in there are not tenants as such, sometimes they're playing music till seven o'clock in the morning . . . and I'm telling you it's loud . . . there should be something done about it . . . a lot of black people make things bad for themselves, right. To me, the ones who were born in this country, they're the ones who cause most of the trouble . . . I think a lot of we people, right, our black people – that's all they want to do. The youngsters anyway, right. All they want to do is sit on their bum and do nothing and claim money . . . You know, it's wrong. It's wrong . . . I think people have got a big chip on their shoulder – black people, they've got a big chip . . . but to me you've got to forget about the past, right, and think about now . . . starting with black people they're too bloody noisy, number one right, they're too noisy, talk nasty talk . . . They throw their rubbish everywhere, right. I'm not saying white people don't do it, I've never seen them, but with the white people I mean everything fits – when I go into Brixton market they're indoors and they're just sort of like shut away. Now after that, after dark and after hours it's the black people who take over.

Q: Who shot Mr Dispal's son?
A: Two white boys shot him dead. That's why Mr Dispal

was transferred. I have no small children, that's why I don't have any problems, because most of the fights in flats start over kids.

Q: Are there any problems with white kids on this estate?

A: Not for the past year; before, these kids were a real problem. They used to tease Asian women and beat our children.

Q: Do they sit there all day long on the wall?

A: Yes, they do, during the holidays. They play until midnight. They sit in front of Asian houses just to upset and scare us. . .

Q: Who does the cleaning outside?

A: We Asians do most, the other tenants don't care too much about cleanliness.

Q: Do white people clean as well?

A: Yes, when one asks them. Otherwise they abuse us and moan all the time for nothing . . . they don't like us, we know that. We try to be nice to them, but they take our behaviour otherwise . . . the white people are mostly uneducated, because they do not take much interest in their education . . . sometimes when white people tell their children off, there are shouts and noises, impatiently replying in raised voices to each other and this is bad for our children when they hear it.

These extracts reveal a number of points about community relationships, not least the indications of scapegoating and cleavages within ethnic groups as between them. But for the moment, compare them with the following extract from an interview with another black resident describing the estate he used to live on:

Well the estate I lived on in Greenwich was a local council estate, it was a new estate – by that I mean it was built within the past ten years. It was multi-racial, I had Asian neighbours to the right of me and West Indian neighbours on the left. It was a large estate; to an extent it wasn't managed very well by the local council, a lot of rubbish and that in the streets, lot of dogs about the place littering the place and that, but it was friendly and you know there was a community feel to it, people did know one another, you did hear music being played you know, and people didn't complain about that type of stuff.

The contrast between this last extract and the others leads us to the question: what makes some neighbourhoods or estates 'work' and others not? Why is it possible on some estates for neighbours to develop informal agreements or understandings about behaviour and relationships? Why do some neighbourhoods but not others manage to evolve a satisfactory *modus vivendi* between residents in which people can comfortably live together but live differently? The above extracts point to the difficulties in constructing a local social order in the face of differences of age, class, education and life-style; we would have to take into account the stability of a population, as well as the size of an estate or neighbourhood, both of which considerations come through in another of our interviews:

There's not many black people on the estate. And the odd bits of racial tension have come as a result of something that's been perpetrated, i.e. they've thrown a stone at your window and you've told them off and then they come back with racial abuse and that's not necessarily victimization simply because you are black. We know most of the people on this estate, you know the faces, we know most of the people but that's gradually changing as new people come in. But I think we've been able to tackle anything that's really come up directly with the perpetrators simply because it's small and you know where they live . . . I mean there's no fear or anything like that, and as I've grown up on the estate as well, now that I'm sort of like a young woman on the estate; before I was a youngster so I mean I've grown up and I know – I'm fairly familiar with the surroundings, yeah.

There are two points to be considered about the evolution of a local social order that influences people's dealings with each other. First, people need to be able to recognize and know each other, and the households from which they come. Conversely, there is a need to recognize strangers and to understand what they might be doing. Often it is the size or the design of a neighbourhood that prevents this happening, or mobility within the population. Second, people must feel they have the capacity, or that it exists in the community, to act in relation both to neighbours and outsiders. But in many neighbourhoods and estates individuals are too frightened to take an initiative, the tenants' association is seen as ineffective, the housing department as next to useless and the police uninterested or, in the case of black people, likely to side with whites. White and black tenants alike feel they have nowhere to turn; witness the following interviewee who thinks his estate 'is not too bad except for the neighbours'.

They have been doing stupid things like putting paint in front of my door or taking the spy hole out and putting dogs' mess in front of the door.

Q: Really? Why do you think they are doing that? Are they white tenants?

A: I don't think it's the grown-ups, I think it's the teenagers, because they used to knock before for things and at first when I first moved in, I used to give it to them. Things like sugar, flour, tea bags, cups, anything, sausages, fish fingers, and when I stopped they started putting things outside the door.

Q: So what do you do when you have complaints?

A: I usually see the caretaker but he can't do much about it, so I see the tenants' association representative but he says he can't do much about it either, should report it to the police.

Q: Have you taken it to them?

A: No.

Q: Why?

A: I think it's too petty. I've spoken to them next door about it.

Q: And have they stopped?

A: Not really, it's still continuing.

Q: This happens every day?

A: No, not every day, every now and again or they throw dogs' mess over our garden.

Q: So you're never quite sure what will happen here?

A: No, not really, but it doesn't really bother me that much, only the dogs' mess.

This last extract sums up much of the anguish about neighbourhood life; matters which are of importance in a person's livelihood (and what could be more harrowing than to be in fear of abuse and victimization from one's neighbours?) are evaluated by that person as too petty to report; when they are reported, the attitude of 'officialdom' is crucial, as Seabrook has perceptively noticed:

> You can tell from the intensity with which she talks that the broken fence is a metaphor for other anxieties. It looks like a trivial matter – a broken fence, there are hundreds on the estate. But what seem like minor matters to officials often have a much greater significance in the lives of the people concerned with them; and they become invested with all sorts of displaced feelings and anxieties. To ignore them or brush them aside is to deny people in a very basic way. (*1984*)

Much of the preceding material made each of us working on this project think about our own homes and neighbours. Pushpinder and Paul who have small children had more contact with more neighbours than Hugh and David who had no young children; we could each account for neighbours it was difficult to get on with, and neighbours who had complained about something we had done or not done. But it appeared that in much public housing the way of life of individuals was organized around reducing or eliminating contact with neighbours, and certainly with unknown locals in the urban neighbourhood. People around one were seen, on the whole, as an undifferentiated, possibly hostile, group from which people were predisposed to expect trouble and aggravation rather than support and help. This was particularly the case in modern large-scale public housing with a population that had been brought together from different parts of a borough or city. People were living together, but, in the absence of interaction between them, a moral order about their shared lives had not emerged; the result was conflict and even more withdrawal and the giving up of the search for trust and commonality. In this kind of situation, Suttles has made a comment about the particular significance of ethnic group relations: 'a more basic problem . . . is the residents' search for trustworthy associates in a population where the grounds for trustworthiness are so scarce. In the absence of any other grounds for trust, they rely upon ethnic and residential unities' (1968).

The False Security of Self-Management

Chris was aware, then, that in urban areas self-management had become the norm in the pursuit of livelihood. Community workers knew this from their own experience, and from the welter of reports from social journalists such as Paul Harrison and from social researchers such as Barry Knight and Ruth Hayes. Sometimes they used the language of 'withdrawal to the household', 'privatization' and sometimes that of 'home-centredness'; often demographers would point to the growth in the population of single-person households in the inner city. The reality of the single individual or family coping on their own with little, if anything, in the way of neighbourhood support also emerges from the range of reports on neighbourhood care. There was even a high moral tone behind some middle-class observers' views that, above all, people valued *privacy*; they didn't want to be bothered by others, they wanted the peace to live their lives as they wanted, they were quite happy, thank you very much, with not having any public roles and responsibilities in their neighbourhood. All they wanted was that their neighbours should respect this privacy and be quiet, law-abiding and socially responsible. And what was wrong with that?

There was nothing wrong with it, thought Chris, but it was an illusion; most urban areas were no longer homogeneous enough for the individual to assume consent on the part of his or her neighbours to a common code of behaviour that regulated their living together. In these days, such a code of neighbourly practice has to be forged from the heterogeneity of people and their different values and life-styles. It was a paradox, but the only way to enjoy a private life for those who could not escape the inner cities was to be more active in getting to know, and working with, those around them. Anyway, Chris doubted that the value of privacy was dominant outside the middle class; some studies had shown how impoverished working-class people had felt they had become since 'the loss of community'. And what about all those people (parents at home with children, the unemployed, the retired and so on) who were often desperate to find other creative roles for their time and energies?

Chris began to conceive of the neighbourhood where people live as a place for developing a number of networks and groups concerned with different aspects of locality life. The primary task of community workers should be to promote *membership* of people in these networks and groups, to help them achieve their goals, to prevent them becoming closed and oligarchical and to help people learn and develop through their membership. This object of encouraging and supporting membership is what Plant (1974) has called the transforming element of community work – changing people's description of their social experience from that of isolate and subject to that of member, from that of being acted upon to that of actor. This is a process of putting people in touch with one another, of supporting groups, of promoting membership and, in general, fostering interaction in the community as well as action by the community. The existence of a social framework in which people feel they fit and in which they are able to meet some of their own needs and those of others, is such a necessity for people (particularly those denied the opportunity for group association and activities, because they are out of work, or unable to work) that Chris could not understand why it had never been a central goal of social policy.

The employment of community workers is a means at the disposal of policy-makers to encourage this process of locality development. They are especially needed in those areas of greatest need where existing skills and resources are at their weakest and where feelings of membership at their lowest. Community workers are needed, thought Chris, because without them large sections of the population would be excluded from, or feel marginal to, participation in local activities and civic affairs, and out of touch with one another.

Chris also recognized that the existence of neighbourhood networks may be crucial to the development of political significance and competence. Helping people to participate more knowledgeably in politics is more than a matter of organizing skills and cognitively understanding political issues. An authentic source of political motivation may be the strength of the relationships that hold people together, and the sense of common purpose that this can provide. Tamney, for example, has indicated that there is a link between national political participation and the degree of involvement in local relationships:

> This evidence suggests the interesting idea that the expression of involvement in any social unit might be related to the degree of involvement in the immediate environment. Action, in general, may be affected by the degree to which we experience life as real. When does life become like reading a novel? When does the distinction between reality and fantasy become unimportant? We suggest that to the extent we are not involved in the environment of our daily life, a newspaper becomes a novel, and we lose the sense of urgency necessary for action. Perhaps involvement 'in the environment of our daily life' is necessary to make life real. (*1975*)

Jeremy Seabrook has made a similar point in his observation of neighbourhoods in Walsall:

> In one sense, people don't live in the neighbourhood at all. There they simply exist. The living is done inside – not only inside the houses which, in spite of the shabbiness and poverty, are for the most part warm and not without comfort, but inside the head, where fantasies and the images from the media and the television penetrate poorest and well-to-do alike, with their invitations to escape, to dream and to forget. It is those images, those stereotypes of living which come to dominate even the most dispossessed – that constant stream of images of a better world that exists, tantalizingly, hauntingly, just out of reach, but in such close parallel to that worse one which most people here inhabit, that world of unemployment, mislaid giros, junk food, debt, anxiety, mental breakdown, fear of the future, hardship and sickness, the appearance in court and the geriatric ward. (*1984*)

Seabrook observes the disengagement of people from each other at a deeper level: the not getting involved, keeping your head down, staying out of trouble, closing your front door, walking by on the other side. Contact with staff and neighbours in the neighbourhood office provides informality and warmth:

> In some people's lives you can feel the social gap it fills – the

sort of conversations occur that might have been associated with the casual exchanges over the garden wall, on the front door-step; so much casual and informal contact that has been silenced by TV, drowned out by amplified music in public places, stifled by Walkman earpieces, submerged by the clamour of capitalist selling.

These consumer goods are, for Seabrook, signs that skills in a range of social roles (as well as the confidence and sense of legitimacy that go with them) have atrophied or have, as in the case of the younger generations, never at all been learnt or valued.

The relationship between daily experience and political ideas and participation is likewise noted by Seabrook within the work-ings of the neighbourhood office.

This means that even though the practical problems the staff deal with are real enough, they are often only a fraction of deeper wrongs and greater grievances; even though the people themselves are not quite sure how to express them, how to give them voice. What is visible here is the way in which so many of the issues raised – intensely political, many of them – are not seen as part of political debate at all. Why can't the young understand the experience of the old? How can the old people say the young are lucky when they have been brought to a life in which they have no function or purpose? Why do I feel so alone? Why do I need tranquil-lizers for a life that is so empty? Why do I feel I'm finished when I should be in the prime of life? *The political has been diminished, set apart, removed from the deep things of our lives*, as though it had nothing to do with private life, that very place where capitalist ideology creates its ravages unre-sisted.

The difficulty with Seabrook's observation is that he pays less attention to the other aspect of the relationship between neigh-bourhood and political interest. This is the effect of political activities and traditions in sustaining local identity and other social resources. Not only do healthy political practices need vibrant communities, but vibrant communities need healthy political traditions. The reorganization of local government has physically and psychologically removed the centre of political and administrative decision-making. Kosmin has drawn attention to this in his article in Wallman's book on South London:

> the new political boundaries of demographic change meant that suburban, bourgeois interests began to prevail, both in the new Borough of Wandsworth, and in the vast Greater London Council. Burn's solution of municipal socialism gave way to the state socialism which he had forecast will increase the powerlessness of poor people . . . The survey on 'Living in the City' which forms the contemporary core of this volume shows ordinary working-class people to be almost totally divorced from political work and the activities of community and leftist groups . . . Politics is now run by elites without roots in the periphery, and local governments are independent of their environments . . . The two big parties may have welcomed the new political quiescence it brought, but introspectively it has also contributed to social disintegration through a loss of identity at the grassroots. These losses are essential factors in the syndrome of inner city disadvantage because healthy communities need vibrant political traditions. People who care about the quality of life in inner city areas may learn from the Battersea case that local identity has been one of its most valuable social resources. (*1982*)

Chris began to appreciate how profound was the link between neighbourhood roles and the effectiveness of democratic values and practices. But there were some pit-falls to be avoided. The emphasis on social resources such as identity does not mean it is desirable or feasible to enwrap people in some warm spirit of 'community' feeling. The emphasis for Chris was not on fostering 'a sense of community' but on developing roles and responsibilities in the neighbourhood that are of satisfaction to the individual and of service to others. In other words, ordinary people could be helped to develop a more even balance than exists at the moment between private lives and public roles.

'But do people want this?' asked a social worker whom Chris met on the visit to France. 'Our own Voltaire and your Anthony Crosland have insisted that most people want only to tend their gardens and watch their televisions. Is this true? If it is, are people leading private lives because that is what "human nature" is like or because of a long process of social conditioning, or, as Marx argued, because of the division of labour that separates people in their productive and social relations?'

'Whatever the answer to *that* question', replied Chris, 'there is a *moral* issue of whether, in a society where more people are spending more time in their neighbourhoods, we ought to neglect so thoroughly social roles and responsibilities.'

'But if people want to use their freedom to choose privacy . . .'

'The time has long passed when we could afford to engage in philosophical titillation about privacy and about whether we ought to enable or induce people to take on more public roles; the decay of the social fabric of many urban localities is now so advanced that each day spent considering whether "we ought to" means that we shall be that much less successful when we are forced to.'

'But', persisted the French worker, 'I always thought it was part of the British working-class culture to keep oneself to oneself.'

'Maybe, but such individualism was part of, or complementary to, a rich social context in which people were members of wider networks within the locality or based on the work-place. Without that social context, keeping oneself to oneself is anachronistic and dysfunctional in the inner city. Look at it this way: there are some more or less deep-seated needs in most people. They need', Chris continued, intentionally quoting Marie Jahoda, 'to structure their day; they need wider social experiences; they need to take part in collective purposes (and they want the products that result from collective action); they need to have a sense of personal status and identity. Through what aspects of our social structure have these needs been habitually met? Through employment and, for the working class, through the existence of a particular kind of localized culture in which an individualized home life (keeping oneself to oneself) was a complement to, and was made possible and endurable by, other social contacts. In areas of unemployment and/or where relations and contacts between people have deteriorated over the years, these needs for participation, association and significance are not being satisfied, and it is important

that we begin to define how these needs can be met by recon-
stituting the neighbourhood as a more valuable part of our social
structure in urban neighbourhoods.'

The French colleague still had 'freedom' written all over his
face, so Chris continued: 'When you talk about privacy I think
you are defining freedom as an absence of external constraints.
My concern is with another definition of freedom: the capacity to
have a measure of control over the material and social circumstances of livelihood. And that means being able to develop a
level of interdependence with others through which people can
use their resources to exert influence – yes, on each other, and as
a means of managing the material conditions that affect their lives.
For this reason, it is impossible to think of freedom independently
of community. Let me quote you something I was reading on the
train from Holland':

> The conception of freedom as absence from social constraint
> is a pipe dream, whose basis is the 'isolated individual' of civil
> society. In reality, . . . this appearance of individual isolation
> arises only because within bourgeois society the real connec-
> tions between individuals, through division of labour and
> exchange, confront them as an alien objectivity. Human life
> is irreducibly social, and human emancipation can only
> occur *in community*, by developing forms of *social* relation-
> ship through which individuals can begin to control the
> circumstances of their lives. (*Sayer, 1985*)

Chris's understanding of the importance of the moral or
political issues in the study of the contemporary urban neighbourhood was based on an awareness that more and more people
are spending more and more time in their neighbourhood.
Unemployment, early retirement, shorter working hours, job-
sharing, other factors such as the cost and scarcity of energy
needed to be mobile, demographic changes such as the increase in
the proportion of older people, and social policy initiatives
towards community care mean there will be more people spending more time at the point of residence and neighbourhood. In
some areas, the significance of the neighbourhood will be
enhanced by regeneration of the economic base through local
employment initiatives, and other attempts to improve the

material base of livelihood. Such initiatives recognize that the neighbourhood is a unit which can command sufficient resources to establish alternative institutions such as co-operatives, community business, and alternative and complementary forms of education and health care; and it is large enough to be a political force though also small enough for most individuals to relate to it, being a point at which people feel comfortable enough to come together to organize themselves for changes to improve their well-being.

But if the neighbourhood was to be significant in expanding the material base of livelihood, where, asked Chris in some despair, was the recognition that livelihood depended as much on expanding social resources? There didn't seem to be any sign of creative social policy initiatives about the neighbourhood. On the contrary, Chris detected an acquiescence in the high consumption of drugs, alcohol and television, more sophisticated monitoring and surveillance of the population, and the re-consideration of conscription to the armed forces. In the absence of creative strategies for the neighbourhood, these and other forms of escape, sublimation and control may be relied upon to contain peoples' clammed up creative energies, and their pent-up resentment about their poverty and helplessness.

More control through the better surveillance and policing of urban areas is clearly a policy option, though the desirability, cost and effectiveness of such an option have always been in doubt. It is uncertain that a democratic society has the will or the means to enforce a degree of control in the inner cities that is capable of quelling the anger, helplessness and frustration that is a consequence of bad housing, unemployment and poor education. The riots of both 1981 and 1985 suggest that heavy-handed, insensitive, ill-informed and often discriminatory policing is sufficient to stimulate an angry reaction from those kept without hope and prospects on the fringes of an affluent society.

The point has been made in an editorial in the London *Evening Standard*, a paper without reputation for progressive views on black people and on inner-city deprivation:

there are the facts of inner-city life which local police have a special responsibility for understanding and coping with: the desolation of areas such as Handsworth, the hopelessness and lassitude created by high unemployment, the racial tensions especially between West Indians and Asians, the problem that the young black community is doubly disadvantaged by colour and by lack of job prospects.

What needs to be established is whether the Birmingham police are handling these problems as well as they could, or whether there is any truth in yesterday's allegations (some of them by rioters) of police harassment, particularly during drugs searches. (*10 September 1985*)

It would be insufficient to draw attention only to the criminality of those involved in street riots. This would be a superficial explanation because we need to describe those factors that are responsible for the criminalization of many urban working-class young people, and for their hard and indifferent behaviour, their increasing addiction to drugs and alcohol and their remoteness from values and standards of behaviour considered important by adults and other authorities.

Opening Bolts and Locks: the Key to Coming Out

One of the most interesting benefits of Chris's visit to Holland was an appreciation of the laissez-faire tradition to the neighbourhood in British social policy. It has usually been seen as the milieu or environment or background to the functioning of other systems such as the family or the small group. Few had grasped that the neighbourhood could be seen as a social system in its own right, about which it was legitimate to ask questions concerning its functioning and state of repair. The idea of social development – of managing social resources in the pursuit of livelihood – was on the whole absent from social policy (with the possible exception of its application in the growth of new towns). In short, British social policy had failed to accept locality as a real and proper element of social structure.

French social policy had included some recognition of the role of the *animateur* in social development and, interestingly enough, it was the chance remark of a community worker in an advice unit on an estate on the outskirts of Lille that helped Chris's thinking to move forward: 'The good community worker', he said, 'must know how to tread water for a long time.'

Chris looked quizzical so he elaborated. 'Because you have to start where the group is at, work at its pace, help it to find its directions. And you have to maintain your position, otherwise you'll be swept one way and then another by the currents in a neighbourhood . . .'

'. . . and be swept up as yet more flotsam and jetsam on the beach of failed social policy initiatives', interjected Chris, guessing his continental drift.

You also had to wait for the right wave to come along, thought Chris, and weren't there already enough signs to show that the 'community wave' was just about to break? After all, there had been the Willmot and Thomas review of the significance of community in social policy (1984), and the initiatives to decentralize local authority services and to develop patch social work both indicated a concern to bring some significance back to the local. And perhaps the publication of the Coleman report (1985) on public housing might lead eventually to the massive programme of design modification that was necessary if tenants were once again to venture with confidence into neighbourhood-based relations. But it would be overly deterministic to think that architectural and administrative reforms, however necessary, could on their own enhance the significance of the neighbourhood for ordinary people in urban areas. They *were* necessary, but they were not enough, and such reforms could only provide a congenial and supportive environment for other efforts to manage social relationships and resources.

Chris now had a rather pointed question to ask: if the development of private, home-centred lives had been partly an adaptation to the environment, how might we now change that environment in order to encourage or induce people into a different form of managing their relationships with each other? What were achievable goals that policy-makers might look for, and community workers might help to bring about? One of the French community workers gave the following reply, which struck Chris with its ingenuity:

'The work of community workers is to help people to come

out, to put an end to closet neighbouring and to re-establish community pride. All this high-faluting stuff about the significance of community is nothing more or less than giving people the confidence to start the process of coming out, of moving away from their private life in front of the video behind the closed front door. Coming out as neighbours is no different from coming out as gays; there are real and imagined fears to be overcome, self-confidence to be acquired and roles and relations with those around you to be re-defined. We must move from an audio-visual culture to a more tactile culture where people come out to be in touch with, and to be touched by, those who live around them. We must help people move from the role of consumer to that of actor, from private consumption to social interaction. Coming out as neighbours means a change, too, in people's political experience. At the level of local, informal politics, working-class people must learn to work together with people with whom there is little in common by virtue of work-place, ethnicity, roots or even common cultural experience. This is the politics and the community of limited liability – of people working together, not from the basis of traditional working-class solidarity, but in task-centred co-operation to achieve specific goals on specific issues.'

Although this reply was insightful, its quality was poetic rather than specific; it certainly did not address the question of which changes were necessary in the environment. But which environment? The kinds of administrative modifications that are presently occurring (for example, the decentralization of services) will be necessary whether one is talking about a housing estate or a terraced neighbourhood. But if we look at public housing, whether it be inner-city estates or high-rise or peripheral housing estates, then there seem to be four areas in which essential changes are needed to permit people better to manage their livelihood together, rather than apart from each other.

First, a programme of modification to those aspects of design and lay-out that encourage crime, vandalism and so forth, discourage social interaction and produce fear and isolation. The critical areas for modification are described in the Coleman report (1985).

Secondly, resources to provide a high standard of repair and maintenance (one can hardly expect tenants to care for each other if the local authority is unable to care for them) and to remove or ameliorate points of abrasion (for example, rubbish disposal) in community relations.

Thirdly, a coherent strategy to end tenants' feelings of dependence and helplessness in respect to their own accommodation, and those factors on the estate that determine their enjoyment of it. Tenant management schemes may be necessary to this, and might well include a major role in vetting and selecting prospective tenants. There are obvious dangers in such a role but the gains to be made in turning tenants into actors with the possibilities of influence over their environment and each other must be carefully evaluated. It must be stressed that people will participate in tenant management schemes only when the power and the resources that they command are genuine and substantial.

Fourthly, a strategy (to overlap with design modification) to deal with people's fear of crime, and that will, in particular, remove the threat of violence experienced by black people within and around areas of public housing. If people are to maintain neighbourhood relations, then they must enjoy a sense of security and feel able to venture outside their homes, without danger to themselves and to the property they leave behind. They must feel free to complain about anti-social or criminal behaviour without fear of threat to themselves or their children. People will not come out to participate in neighbourhood activities if they fear those who live around them, although Kohfeld and her colleagues (1981) have indicated a vicious circle here: the existence of neighbourhood organizations has an effect in reducing crime, but people will not join them if they fear crime.

Some of the issues about personal safety go wider than the specific effects of, for example, attacks on old people, women and ethnic minorities. These issues are captured in the following passage from Jeremy Seabrook:

She says that it was a nightmare when she first started trying to get things done, some of the nuisances removed, some of the mess cleared up, some of the unofficial junkyards regulated. There were threatening phone calls, promises that she would get her windows put in, that her house would be fire-bombed. It is difficult for people who have not lived on the poorest estates to realize to what extent they can be controlled by the strongest who live there; there are districts that are almost no-go areas, in which the police can do very little, because of the silence that surrounds everything that goes on. The ruling villains have imposed their will on the residents; and the fear of reprisals is the most effective form of control. After all, the people who live here have nowhere else to go; the police at best can maintain an intermittent presence. Sometimes there may be anonymous denunciations by neighbours. What many of the poorest communities lack are the leaders who will create an alternative atmosphere to the bullying and intimidation – so many of those who might have helped raise confidence have long departed. What happens is the reverse of solidarity – a resentful silence, where secret grassing to the Social seems the only intervention likely to provoke any response from the authorities. That has changed now. But it does show what pressures were brought to bear on Mrs Smith and those who did remain, out of loyalty, for a principle, because they had hope or wanted to stand by the people whose lives were shadowed by these things. (*1984*)

In other words, managing social relations, whether on a public housing estate or in a terraced neighbourhood, requires a set of norms and undertakings about behaviour without which people's lives become miserable, and their feelings of helplessness exacerbated. Suttles (1968) has described this as the development of a moral order that includes all those present, and without which people who routinely occupy the same place will fall into conflict, or withdraw from each other. The development of this moral order as a social resource in managing livelihood depends on opportunities for informal interaction, information-exchange and communication between residents. Its development may also require the existence of viable institutions (churches, PTAs, community groups, tenants' associations and so on) and networks not only to facilitate such interaction but as a means to arrive at and embody shared common values, and to negotiate differences and conflicts. Morris, drawing upon her own research and following the work of Bott and others, has indicated that:

when there are numerous linkages between the people who make up a social network then they are more likely to develop shared ideas about appropriate ways of behaving. It is also the case that this interconnectedness provides the means by which deviation from agreed patterns is detected and controlled. (*1985*)

The Nominal and Interacting Community

In order to continue this discussion, it is useful to introduce the notions of the *nominal* and the *interacting* community.[1] The nominal community is depicted in the following quotations from our interviews with black residents:

I think it's a place to lay your head.

People are so isolated here, I mean so compartmentalized on the estate that there may not even be enough contact for there to be conflict.

Everyone's just too fast going, nobody has got time for anybody . . . those days were better when we used to talk to neighbours and neighbours used to talk to you, but now that doesn't happen.

I live at home but it's – I do so many other things that my time really is nominal.

The nominal community is one in which people live in the presence of each other but have few, if any, interactions with one another. The interacting community means what it says: people have different kinds and intensities of relationships with each other, ranging from casual verbal encounters through to different kinds of neighbourly and co-operative work together, either informally or as members of neighbourhood groups. The nominal–interacting distinction is, of course, a continuum, and a locality's place on this continuum will be determined both by the quality of interaction and its extent. It does seem possible to describe some sections of one locality as having only a nominal membership, while other sections might be more of an interacting community. For example, those in a locality who are housebound through infirmity or old age may enjoy only nominal member-ship, and this might also be true of some ethnic minority house-holds in a community. For example, Pushpinder reviewed her interviews with Asian tenants in public housing as follows:

> The relationship between the ethnic minorities and white tenants living on a housing estate is that they live in areas together, but quite isolated from each other. Although there is some superficial mixing, relationships exist in a negative; black tenants are aware of racial hostility, and conscious of being watched, noticed and pointed at for being different. This leaves them feeling uneasy and exposed and very threatened. This makes them very uptight and tense, result-ing in sticking close to their own ideas, and customs. They feel their only solution from the present situation and having some 'freedom' is by getting out.
>
> They participate in their own religious groups and visit their friends and relatives. There is very little time left to socialize on their estate with other white tenants, or partici-pate in any other activities. They feel indifferent to changing the physical conditions on their estate, and avoid any direct confrontation in day-to-day living.

The factors that conspire to create the nominal community are as varied as those social and economic factors that have produced home-centredness; we have noted that these include not only fear and distrust, but the effects of public housing design, the absence of on-site facilities for social mixing (for example, shops and launderettes), and the struggle for day-to-day survival that involves overtime, moonlighting and unsocial work hours that produces tired people. A nominal community is often created when success or failure in earning a living, together with *necessary* participation in schools, churches and so on, leaves no time or energy for *voluntary* participation. The tragedy for many people is that the struggle of day-to-day survival drains them of motiva-tion and energy for necessary participation in, for example, the activities of their children at school. We might also take into account the break-down of traditional bases of working-class solidarity, and the dispersion of people outside their locality in the search for friends, recreation and religious worship. There may be few institutions or organizations in a locality to promote and embody feelings of membership, and those that do exist such as tenants' associations are often held in contempt or indifference. The effects of insensitive housing allocation policies must be considered in the creation of nomimal communities, as must the lack of involvement of council tenants in the management of their estates and the selection of prospective tenants (see Richardson, 1983).

One of the characteristics of the nominal community is that it is dichotomized by concentration/dispersion. There is a concentration of energy, time and priorities in the household, and the dispersion of social and economic life beyond the neighbourhood; such a dichotomy makes the emergence of a common neighbourhood social order impossible to negotiate and sustain. Interactions with neighbours will be necessary rather than voluntary. The nominal community is also paralysed by outside forces and, following Suttles, may be described as 'defeated':

there are areas in most cities which are left undefended and open to invasion by almost any sort of resident. The entrepots of our large cities are a prime example. Properly speaking, however, it is not that the residents of such areas lack the impulse to defend their areas but that they lack the wherewithal to do so. They might better be called defeated neighbourhoods than undefended ones. The defeated neighbourhood is in some ways the reverse of that which is defended by a combine of political, administrative, and business interests. It is subject to insufficient or quixotic enforcement of building standards, zoning rules, police protection, and wide disparities in the delivery of all the available community services. Above all it is a community which citywide, regional, and federal agencies treat as an object without much fear of retaliation from a local constituency. Typically, then, the defeated community . . . is unable to participate fully in its own governance. Sometimes this is because it is so heavily populated by new residents, ex-felons, aliens, and transients that even the ballot box is not a significant avenue of influence. At other times it is a community so heavily stigmatized and outcast that its residents retreat from most forms of public participation out of shame, mutual fear, and an absence of faith in each other's collective concern. Skid rows illustrate the former weakness of the residents, and some of our worst public housing projects illustrate the latter. (*1972*)

In other words, in the nominal community residents may not have the motivation, the organizational skills and confidence, and the feelings of potential influence to manage the range of individual and institutional violations of their neighbourhood space. No one manages and defends the physical and psychological boundaries of the nominal community. Not only do individuals feel helpless as *persons*, but they do not believe that there are any *roles* or *organizations* available to them that will provide opportunities for influence over each other and outside institutions.

It is to be expected that an important guiding principle in the nominal community is the minimax criterion; this moves people to interact with others only in situations which are safe, predictable and controllable, and in which there is some assurance that other people will not be so bad as they are said or expected to be. In this situation, people are dependent on public signs of trust and predictability, and are heavily influenced by rumour, stereotype and fears about social and ethnic difference. Suttles has suggested that in this kind of situation people establish relations only with their own kind and then evolve a hierarchy of safe enclosures for meeting others. He suggests that residents may take refuge in those ethnic orbits of trust they brought with them from another country. Residents may also retreat from all social contacts beyond those of the nuclear family, which, in any case, cannot be avoided. Children are kept off the street, watched every minute, sent to a safe local school, and warned against strangers. Adults view their neighbours with suspicion and remain circumspect in their admissions. Local events are derided or avoided and, at most, non-relatives are faced in the confines of a church or other 'safe place'.

A nominal community is perpetuated partly though not wholly by fear of ethnic differences; but the fear surrounding differences, whether ethnic or other kinds, cannot be removed precisely because people are not able to encounter with each other. The nominal community is one in which people are living together but separately, where differences are exaggerated and not negotiable, and where agreements and understandings about how to live together are unable to emerge. Not only are differences exaggerated and fear about them aggravated, but there is a great difficulty in being different; the pressure on people is to avoid anything that makes them stand out. This is, of course, something that black people find difficult to do; there is an immense strain when people are confronted with pressures to play down differences in culture and so forth that they value. As an interviewee put it, 'If you try to start out as being a black person not fitting in with what's going on around, you can actually cause a problem.' Clearly this respondent, from one of three black households on an estate, was feeling the restrictive covenants of anglo-conformity. But in general the points of contact between white and black in a nominal community are so limited and of such a formal nature that attitudes and behaviours are invariably determined by stereotypes. There is between white and black what Ley has called an 'informal segregation' which 'has created two worlds which scarcely intersect, with a vast uncertainty between'. He describes a constant misperception of reality between blacks and whites in America as 'a dysfunctional social system of communication failure' leading to a social gap of such magnitude that it threatens not just the viability of particular communities but the existence of the nation as a whole (1970). The same point about this country has been made by Rushdie:

> Britain is now two entirely different worlds, and the one you inherit is determined by the colour of your skin. In my experience, very few white people, except those active in fighting racism, are willing to believe the descriptions of contemporary reality offered by blacks. And black people faced with what Professor Michael Dummett has called the 'will not to know – a chosen ignorance, not the ignorance of the innocent', grow increasingly suspicious and angry.
>
> What has been created is a gulf in reality. White and black perceptions of everyday life have moved so far apart as to be incompatible. And the rift is not narrowing; it is getting wider. We stand on opposite sides of an abyss, yelling at each other and sometimes hurling stones, while the ground crumbles beneath our feet.
>
> I make no apology for taking an uncompromising view of

the reasons for the existence of this chasm. The will to ignorance arises out of a desire not to face the consequences of what is going on; because if the white British allowed themselves to know, they would have to alter their picture of the world too radically for their liking. People don't want to do that; it is uncomfortable and difficult; and so they close their ears. Those who adopt the position of the ostrich invite a swift kick in the pants. (*1982*)

There is a range of other features of the nominal community that is worth exploring but to do so in any detail would take us outside the scope of this six-month project. But we will mention some in passing; for example, we would find a nominal community to be one in which people do not take on responsibilities for social care and control, and where acts of deviancy are left unchecked and unchallenged. It is the community in which the law of the strong prevails and the good samaritan has long since received a good kicking. In the nominal community, household priorities are almost wholly to do with the material terms of livelihood. But community business initiatives would not thrive in a nominal community because it does not contain sufficient of the social resources necessary for livelihood: trust, group identity, commitment and so forth. Membership in voluntary activities would be low, as would, perhaps, interest and involvement in both local and national politics. Listen, for example, to a voice from the nominal community.

> *Q*: What use does the tenants' association on the estate have for you as a black person?
> *A*: I think – just personally – I don't think they – I don't find them that easy to approach. They listen to you but they don't really seem that concerned or interested.
> *Q*: Can you tell me what kind of things might stop you taking a great interest in these?
> *A*: I think it's – because when you approach them they're not very welcoming or friendly so they're not – really wanting you to get too involved with them.
> *Q*: How would they have to change that you might join in?
> *A*: I think they'd have to be friendlier and show that they're willing to accept you or whatever.

Q: Are they a very close-knit group?

A: Yes, they are very much friends. You usually see them walking together and talking. I mean, if you see them and you smile at them they don't usually smile back or anything like that.

Q: Do you have any friends on the estate?

A: Not really, no.

Q: Would you say you get on well with people on the estate?

A: I say 'hi' and 'bye' and that's it. They hardly see me.

Q: Is that because of work?

A: Yeah, basically.

Q: Do you have any social contacts with your white neighbours, do you meet them quite a lot, go to bingo or something?

A: No. Nothing like that.

Q: But what do you like about people around here, or is there nothing special?

A: I don't really get too close.

Q: Is there anything you dislike about them?

A: No, not really.

Q: Do you feel as if you belong around here, do you feel settled now?

A: I don't feel settled.

Q: You don't? Why is that?

A: Because I don't feel that here is for me, no.

Q: Where would you prefer to be?

A: I can't really say off-hand where I would prefer to be.

Q: Are there any community groups that exist around here?

A: I've never looked for them really.

Q: Do you take part in any groups?

A: Not at the moment, no.

Q: So why don't you take a greater interest in any groups?

A: There's too much squabbling. Internally, you don't really get what you want in the end.

Q: How do you spend your free time or leisure time?

A: I don't find myself having very much free time.

Q: Do you take much of an interest in politics?

A: I listen to it.

Q: You're up to date with the news?

A: Yeah.

Q: What about local politics, do you take interest in that?

A: No, hardly.

Q: Is there anything else you'd like to tell me about living round here that I haven't asked you? How do you find living round here?

A: I think it's a place to lay your head.

It is self-evident that the *interacting community* is defined by the extent and quality of different kinds of relationships, networks, obligations and responsibilities between individuals and groups. It is characterized by a degree of voluntary as well as necessary participation in neighbourhood life. It contains a number of organizations (churches, schools, community groups and so on) that express and promote neighbourhood relationships and which can work, either singly or in co-operation, to manage the relationships of the neighbourhood with individuals and authorities outside it. Thus people who live in an interacting community may feel less vulnerable and powerless in relationships with outside forces. People manage the social as well as the material bases for livelihood. While the interacting community is also dichotomized between concentration and dispersion, the dichotomy is blurred and we find that people are able to identify and cluster around informal leaders or organizations in the neighbourhood. This feature of clustering, around each other and around leaders of different kinds, makes it possible in the interacting community for individuals, organizations and social groups (e.g. black and white) to exert a mutual influence over each other in the development of agreements about how to live together. The basis for viability and the capacity to manage the tasks of living together is linked to patterns of communication and interaction that allow for mutual influence rather than enforced segregation of residents. Thus the process of moving along the continuum from a nominal to an interacting community is indeed the process of coming out to be in touch with, and to be touched by, those around you, because it is only through coming out that mutual influence is attained. It may be labouring the point to emphasize that coming out means both emerging in public and giving expression to feelings of *membership* that had been repressed or too dangerous or threatening to own in the past. Coming out means trying to acknowledge one's status and potential as a social being, and to own the rights and responsibilities that go with that status. Part of our learning in this project is that nominal communities do not provide the social resources for black and white to manage their livelihood together; black and white people cannot begin to own their colour until they begin to respond to their status and potential as social beings in their localities where they presently live. It would not be wholly light-hearted to suggest that what is needed is 'neighbour awareness training' in which people are helped to acknowledge their isolation and to define their social roles and potential in them.

Building Community Capability

So far we have described interacting communities as having the social resources (though not necessarily always enough material ones) for people to manage their livelihood together. It may be said that interacting communities have what both Wallman (1982) and Schoenberg (1979, 1980) describe as 'viability' and what we refer to as 'community capability'. The phrase 'community capability' is suggestive of people's capacity to solve problems that affect their living together, and to solve problems for themselves or for sub-groups that are caused by outside agencies – the quality of their interaction gives them the capacity for action. The phrase indicates a level of responsibility for, and coping with, tasks such as social care and social control. In this project, we are particularly interested in how communities develop the capacity for black and white people to live together but differently.

There lies behind these particular meanings of community capacity a more general notion, defined by Schoenberg in the following way: a capable or viable community is one in which its residents work together to influence various aspects of the local social order, in which residents set goals for collective life, and in which they have the ability to carry out work to accomplish these goals. Following, but building upon, Schoenberg's work, we would say that a locality achieves this kind of capacity if it can:

- establish mechanisms to define and enforce shared agreements about public roles and responsibilities. These would vary from neighbourhood to neighbourhood, but would certainly include agreements about personal safety, the identification of strangers, the maintenance of common property, the disposal of rubbish and the behaviour of children. (How can black and white people begin to live together when the livelihood of each is based on the expectation that each will be assaulted by the children of the other?)
- set up both formal and informal organizations in the locality which provide for communication, the identification of leadership, and the learning of skills, and the ability to define the various interests of the neighbourhood to those outside it.
- make inputs to policy and political decision-making that affect the neighbourhood.
- maintain linkages to public and private resource holders.
- establish mechanisms, formal and informal, through which exchanges are created between conflicting interests, needs and groups in the neighbourhood.

There are a number of points to be made about community capability, including the obvious one that in most working-class or low-income neighbourhoods these kinds of mechanisms and organization will not be created or sustained without the intervention of skilled community workers. We will return to this point when we consider the idea of sponsored community development later in the chapter. For the moment, we want to make the following two points.

First, if policy initiatives to establish community care, or crime prevention schemes, or community-based health and education facilities, are to be successful, then policy-makers must understand the concept of community capability which such initiatives assume and direct to it appropriate theoretical attention and practical resources.

Secondly, a major outcome of this limited inquiry would be recognition of the further work to be done on the notion of 'community capability', particularly to establish those factors that help communities of black and white people to develop a viable means of living together.

There are a number of objective or structural factors that help to determine whether a community will be nominal or interacting with the capability to carry out the tasks of living together, for example, modifying architectural and design factors. But what else can be done by professional workers to create conditions that support the development of an interacting community with a degree of capability? The challenge faced by professionals in fields such as housing, health, welfare and education is to deliver services to meet individual needs in a way that enhances people's autonomy and self-respect and their ability to work together to solve common problems. At the heart of the development of capable communities is this understanding that the *way* in which professionals carry out their role (the neighbourhood-sensitive way in which they carry it out) is as important as the meeting of needs that individuals bring to them.

As far as community workers are concerned, they cannot do very much until they begin to see themselves, and to be so recognized by politicians and policy-makers, as instruments of the development of communities into capable social systems, rather than as agents of particular groups in the community with a specific but limited task. Clearly the creation and support of such action groups is essential to collective problem-solving, but they need to be seen as only a part of the development of the interacting community. Both community workers and policy-makers need to eschew their fetish with the vertical, and begin to develop their understanding, and skills in promoting, horizontal linkages at the locality level. Their job is not only to help local people establish the kinds of mechanisms identified by Schoenberg (1979) as necessary for community capability, but also to help people to participate in them, to make them work, to take up membership in groups, to make efforts to sustain networks and communication patterns and, in general, to acknowledge their significance for the pursuit of livelihood.

There are three kinds of contributions to be made by the community worker in developing the interacting community. The first is helping people to know about each other, and developing the interest they take in those in the community around them, being responsible for what goes on about them, and seeing the ways in which it is possible for residents to be in touch with the fortunes and tribulations of their neighbours. Secondly, they must identify the different possibilities for role development in a locality, that is the opportunities for residents to take up roles (neighbour, volunteer, party activist, association secretary, PTA member and so forth) that are satisfying to themselves and of service to others, and which, in turn, strengthen networks and contribute to people's knowledge of, and interest in, each other. Thirdly, they should work to ensure that both local people and other professionals and politicians recognize the significance of social resources in the pursuit of livelihood.

Chris saw that the culture of the nominal community was one way in which people could choose to manage their relationships with one another. It was not necessarily a bad way and indeed may be highly functional in some circumstances. Such circumstances might include a certain level of homogeneity in the population, or where the individual members of households have sufficient personal resources (both material and social) to feel in control of the many factors that intrude upon their living space and neighbourhood.

But is the nominal community a functional way of managing relationships in a community where there are differences of, for example, age, class or ethnicity, or especially where individuals feel helpless and weak in shaping their lives and the character of their environment? In these situations, does the nominal community create the conditions in which differences are exaggerated and feared, rather than defined and respected, and in which stereotypes and myths govern peoples' perceptions of each other? If so, the existence of nominal communities (and their perpetuation through the persistence of the laissez-faire attitudes in British social policy to locality as a proper part of social structure) is inimical to productive black–white relations, to blacks and whites encountering with one another, learning to work with one another in civic affairs, and recognizing each other's need to do other things separately and differently.

It was as the cross-channel ferry approached the white cliffs of Dover that Chris saw the connection between black pride and community pride, and how the notion of community pride is useful in understanding the emergence of the interacting community. It has a complex order of meanings: to begin with, there is the pride in environment (and the consequent feelings of responsibility for it) that comes from the positive resourcing of inner-city neighbourhoods, from schemes of design modification, and from housing authorities providing a level of repair and maintenance that indicates the value they put on a neighbourhood or estate. Community pride, if you will, is another valuable social resource in the management of livelihood which policy-makers may decide to promote or to neglect. But community pride is also something that is associated, as the Department of the Environment priority estates programme indicates, with a broader-based strategy of community development in which the growth of local organizations is encouraged, and tenants are involved in substantial areas of the management of the housing stock and environment. One of the desirable consequences of the existence of community pride is growth in the capabilities of a community as defined by Schoenberg, that is, the emergence of leaders and organizations to manage the dealings of the community with those outside, and the creation of a number of internal linkages for defining common goals, objectives and ways of expressing conflict and disagreement within the community.

The emergence of community capability provides an element of defensible space for its residents, in so far as a variegated system of management appears that can monitor and control the boundaries of the community. Such defensible space in relation to outside influences may create the physical and mental energies, as well as a feeling of legitimacy and confidence, for community leaders and organizations to think creatively about managing the internal relations of their community, particularly relations between groups such as young and old, black and white and so forth. And here Chris came to a further meaning of community pride: behind this rather ill-defined notion is that of the self-pride of individuals and groups in a community, feelings of self-respect, of personal worth and esteem, of significance, of counting, of mattering. One of the key elements in the development of black–white relations is the process of how *groups*, for example, an ethnic minority group, develop a level of self-confidence and pride about themselves, and how this transforms their dealings with other groups and authorities in the community. But as important is the process of how *individuals* measure their self-esteem and status; for example, we shall see later how members of some Asian groups believe that low status comes simply from being a tenant in council housing. We can take this further and ask how far the design and facilities of much public housing are supportive of the emergence of ethnic self-confidence and capability. Suttles, for instance, has argued that public housing does not lend itself to the kinds of minor entrepreneurial ventures that have been important in the past in the upward mobility of various ethnic groups. It does not allow for friends and family to settle near one another, and creates, too, a culture of impermanence where contacts with neighbours are short-lived, or expected to be so.

But the self-esteem and status of individuals have other aspects which relate to our previous discussion about experiences that help people to own up to their racialism and to own their colour. It must be very difficult for someone to own their colour if he or she feels that there is nothing at all about themselves or their group that is worth owning. In other words, low self-esteem and confidence, as well as feelings of helplessness, amongst white working-class people may not provide the best basis for working with them in the process of owning their white colour and experience.

Community pride, self-respect, confidence and esteem are yet more examples of the kinds of social resources that are necessary in the pursuit of livelihood, in managing relationships with one another, and in the development of community capability. We have stressed that such social resources need to be managed, just as the material bases of livelihood have to be managed if individuals and groups are to prosper and flourish. The management of social resources implies, at the very least, a commitment to give up a laissez-faire attitude towards locality as part of our social structure, and to bring to an end a long period in British social policy in which such social resources have been neglected and wasted. More particularly, the management of social resources implies a commitment to providing environments that are conducive to the strengthening of these resources, and to constituting at a local level the kinds of facilities, support and expertise that are necessary to produce interacting communities and the development of social resources and relationships.

The management of social resources thus suggests the importance of local strategies of sponsored community development. The term 'sponsored' is important as a counter to traditional laissez-faire attitudes, and to the myth of the 'natural' community. Indeed, the laissez-faire attitude within British social policy derives from the potency of this myth that, by one means or another, communities would develop by themselves, perhaps with their own bootstraps, based on class or kinship solidarities, and assisted by some 'invisible hand'. This myth of the 'natural' community and the efficacy of the 'invisible hand' has been buttressed by what Suttles has called an assumption 'that government could not contrive communities any more than it could regulate love affairs' (1972). Chris guessed that the reluctance amongst policy-makers to sponsor the development of communities was further reinforced by the debunking of neighbourhood in the 1970s both by some British sociologists and by the bulk of the Community Development Projects.

'Have I anything to declare?' asked Chris, walking off the boat towards the customs area. Only this: that what I have learnt so far about black and white participation in community groups points to a realignment of attitudes and values, without which the social organization of urban areas will continue to deteriorate, and relationships between black and white will forever be based on minimal contact and poor communication, and be mediated by stereotypes, myths, and fears. This realignment would mean acceptance that:

- the neighbourhood is a proper element of social structure;
- social resources are important in livelihood and need to be managed and developed;
- the nominal community is a self-destructive adaptation to urban stress and environmental change;
- the development of community capability is about the management of a neighbourhood's external and internal relationships;
- social resources and community capability are not only influenced by objective, structural factors such as poor housing, low incomes, bad design and so forth, but their development also requires local strategies of sponsored community development. In most low-income urban areas, the state of disrepair of the

social fabric is such that it would be folly to believe that the development and management of livelihood will occur 'naturally', by chance or accident or through the efficacy of the invisible hand;
- that the phrase 'sponsored community development' implies a programme more fundamental than the activities hitherto associated with community workers, although their part in such a programme would not be insignificant.

Notes

1   I have adopted 'nominal' and 'interacting' from their use by Van de Ven and Delbecq (1981) to describe group decision-making arrangements.

5
Taking Part in Community Life

Better a near neighbour than a far brother.
(Caribbean Proverb)

This chapter is about how black and white people manage a number of social tasks and roles, and we try to identify some of the factors that constrain the participation of black and white residents in community activities. We want to look at how black and white people combine with each other both to improve the material aspects of livelihood, and to carry out what Warren (1963) has called locality-relevant functions such as social care, social control and mutual support. Much of the chapter will look at the various ways in which different forms and expressions of the cultural norm of white anglo-conformity and racism affect black participation in community groups, including black organizations.

In the preceding chapter, the issue of black–white relations was set in the context of the nominal community, which we described partly as an adaptation to perceived stress and uncertainty in the urban environment; people were managing livelihood by withdrawal, by an emphasis on individual consumption or, in the case of the poor, simple survival, with a corresponding disinterest in managing social tasks and resources. The poor levels of contact, communication and trust that characterize the nominal community provide, we suggested, no basis for the improvement of relationships between black and white people. We indicated that the capacity of people to combine to manage some aspects of livelihood was to be seen not only as a casualty of the nominal community, but also as a means to put people back in touch with one another; thus we argued the case for sponsored community

139

development, particularly as a way to restore contact and communication at the local level between black and white residents.

Managing the material and social sides of livelihood is not something that is done only by the individual; it is a responsibility that concerns a number of collectivities such as the small group, or a small business. It is something to which large organizations such as a school or a hospital have to attend. All these collectives carry out a number of material and social tasks, and manage a range of material and social resources. There are also other kinds of group (for example, trade unions) where people combine to influence matters that affect their livelihood; and in the place of residence individuals often have to combine with those around them in order to gain some advantage in their livelihood. Thus residents' associations and action groups, for example, are mechanisms that people use to influence the distribution of what O'Brien (1981) has called non-divisible public goods (for example, the provision of central heating in a damp block of flats). The existence of other types of groups to do with self-help, support and the provision of advice and services also indicates that combining at the locality level is potentially a significant factor in managing both the material and the social bases of livelihood.

Community groups are part of informal local politics and are thus a basic element of the democratic process that provides a source of influence, as well as opportunities for developing skills and confidence in public roles. As such, these groups are not to be seen just as a way of better managing livelihood, but as part of what Mary Follet has called the inner workshop of democracy, where civic skills and responsibilities are developed and political understanding enhanced. Where such groups exist, they provide one of the few opportunities for black and white people to leave their respective stockades and to deal with each other on the basis of real contact and information. All-white and all-black groups do not provide these opportunities, although they are nevertheless still an important part of the democratic process. Many people will want to opt for an ethnic group in order to carry out a number of social functions such as social care or recreation, or to contribute to political discussion and decision-making.

Sponsored community development is about the support of a

range of networks, groups and relationships, including ethnically exclusive ones; but should it not also provide for black and white people to work together to improve their livelihood, particularly those aspects that can be enhanced by attempts to solve problems collectively?

O'Brien's concept of the non-divisible public resource (which we discussed in Chapter 2) is essential to a discussion about the role of black and ethnic groups. Such groups are part of the political process, important to counter racism, to seek positive action in services and resources and to meet a range of social, recreational and some economic needs; but in the case of non-divisible public goods that affect the livelihood of black and white residents in an area (such as controlling pollution from a neighbourhood factory, or getting a better caretaking service) then it is appropriate to question the value of black or ethnic groups in influencing decisions about such public goods; a community worker may find the involvement of black people in a neighbourhood group a more effective way to bring about the desired change. In respect of non-divisible public goods black people who are excluded, or exclude themselves, from neighbourhood groups will still enjoy the goods in the short term; but in the long term their exclusion imperils the vitality and credibility of such groups and thus undermines their capacity to deliver benefits and services.

Thus the support of black people's participation in neighbourhood groups in multi-ethnic areas is important because:

- the long-term effectiveness of these groups depends on recruiting both white and black residents.
- they provide an opportunity (though not the only one) for blacks to take part in local political life and acquire/develop skills and confidence in public roles;
- they are a means for black and white to engage with one another as part of the process of learning what it takes to live together;
- black groups in a white–black neighbourhood may not be as relevant to the distribution of non-divisible public goods as they are in the influence of policy, positive action, special services and other forms of organization to do with self-help, religion and recreation. We want to look further at black

groups later in this chapter; but joining a black group is only one option for people to help them manage their livelihood. It must be considered alongside the other option of black people joining with white in different kinds of neighbourhood activities and organizations.

What Affects Participation?

The participation of black people in community groups is determined by three major objective or structural factors. The first is the extent of racism and the particular experience or fear of harassment. Participation will be low because black people recognize the general level of hostility towards them in society, and the particular expressions of that hostility through working-class racism and violence. The case has been put by Ranjit Sondhi:

> the involvement of Asian people in multi-racial community projects has been limited even where the projects have been sensitive to their special needs. This is partly due to the problems of communication and inability to understand different cultural and social frames of reference. But it is mostly due to the fact that such projects have made black people feel uneasy, if not unwelcome, since the most well-intentioned attempts to bring people together were invariably set against the background of sustained hostility towards minority groups that make them cautious of any contact with white society and its institutions. (*1982*)

The extent of violence against the person and property of Asians and Afro-Caribbeans has been documented in a number of studies, perhaps most authoritatively in that of the Home Office (1981).

The second set are those economic and demographic factors (most of which are themselves related to racism and discrimination) such as home-ownership, employment, residential stability and so forth that affect participation in voluntary activities. We saw in Chapter 2 that from data presented in the General Household Survey (1981) and the PSI study we could predict low levels of voluntary participation amongst many minority ethnic groups. Finally, the wider political climate in the country about immigration and nationality (as well as the absence of political will to tackle harassment, discrimination and disadvantage) will have an adverse effect on black people's motivation and confidence to participate with whites in community affairs. The effect of the political framework on the civic participation of the black British has been noted in another context by Booth (1985).

Within these three sets of factors there are a number of other important matters that determine how, if at all, black and white people will, at a local level, manage together certain aspects of livelihood. Black people have come to experience and expect prejudice and racism in most aspects of their lives, particularly in the quests for work and housing. This experience in work and housing is indicated in Brown's 1984 study, for example. Thus black people may expect community groups to be no different, and perhaps to be a lot worse. How do the community worker and these groups signal that they offer a different experience? The community group has to 'welcome' black members, and also be responsive to their interests and needs, and to the ways in which they wish to think and act in formulating group plans. It has to translate its literature into different languages and ensure that meetings are not held at inappropriate times or non-welcoming places. Quite apart from the threat of racism or harassment, black people will not be motivated to pursue their livelihood through community groups if those groups do nothing to counter negative messages in a neighbourhood such as racialist graffiti and propaganda, and the verbal abuse of black people by young white children. In other words, black people will not join community groups if the environment for participation is not supportive; not the least of these environmental problems on housing estates is the physical siting of black tenants. The PSI study shows that black families tend to get the flats furthest away from the ground floor (Brown, 1984); thus they are both physically and psychologically removed from the centre of community activities.

There are, for some ethnic groups, particular issues about participation to do with language, culture and religious prohibitions about the mixing of sexes in public. There are factors about education (32 per cent of Asian women in Brown's study, for example, left school before they were 12), and there are different expectations about the roles of the sexes between ethnic groups, and Barr has indicated the relevance of rural/urban background:

> The degree of attachment to traditional values and experience of, and exposure to, alternatives are key variables in determining the ease with which people may participate in institutions based on different values and culture. The urban dweller is likely to have been more exposed to changing ideas than a man from a rural background even in the same area. (*1980*)

The rural/peasant dimension is also apposite to a discussion about class as a basis of action, and the extent to which people had acquired in their mother countries experience in trade unions and local politics.

Attachment to traditional values and the anticipation of hostile or indifferent community groups are two factors which predispose some black people to pursue livelihood through black or ethnic groups. If people feel threatened in society, and if they feel that important cultural values are at risk, then the amount of personal risk they are prepared to take will be minimal. Involvement in community groups with white people assumes a confidence about one's self, values and culture, as well as an openness to change and to challenge. In a hostile society, such confidence and openness are at a premium, not least because one way of surviving such an environment is to hold on to traditional values and ways of doing things. One of the threats of working together with other ethnic groups is the threat of reducing racial identity and coherence; but in a hostile society it is precisely this coherence around tradition and custom that sustains the individual and his or her family. From the point of view of the community worker, neighbourhood organizations offer opportunities to develop new roles and responsibilities; but in some Asian groups traditionally conceived roles and responsibilities (especially those between young and old, parents and children) are weakening and felt to be under threat. These are not circumstances which help people 'take risks' in joining community groups but rather impel them to a protected zone, a safe haven, within the extended family and in the religious and recreational activities of their ethnic group.

There are other kinds of risks and difficulties that will face many Afro-Caribbeans in 'coming out' to join with whites in community groups. The PSI study, for example, indicates that some 40 per cent of West Indian households contain a single adult or a lone parent with children under 16; this proportion is higher within the inner cities (Brown, 1984). It requires little imagination to see how much courage and practical help (baby-sitting) would be needed for the single black person to venture out to a community group composed largely of white working-class neighbours.

The search for a refuge or protected zone is a natural consequence for black people who feel vulnerable in a dominant and domineering white society; it is, of course, another example of the minimax criterion in operation, as people define safe encounters as those largely within their own ethnic groups, and trust encounters with others only where there are clear 'guarantees' about the standards of behaviour of those others from outside the ethnic group.

Ethnic participation supports and is itself supported by another factor which accounts for the reluctance of black people to see membership of community groups as necessary to their livelihood. This other factor has been called 'the immigrant ideology' (Lawrence, 1975) as a shorthand phrase to explain why so few first-generation immigrants were involved in political activity. A core part of the immigrant ideology was the belief amongst black people that they would be returning home; they had no stake in the country, in their local community; they were only temporary residents in the United Kingdom, here only to pursue a livelihood in the most narrow sense of the term. Naturally, the immigrant ideology is fuelled by the refusal of many white people to accept that Britain is a multi-racial society, and their deep-seated fantasies that somehow black people will soon 'go home' either voluntarily or through induced or compulsory repatriation.

The immigrant ideology is another set of interactions between white and black British that helps to explain the disproportionately low number of black people in community groups in the neighbourhoods in which they live. Some of the dilemmas of the immigrant ideology are illustrated in one of our interviews:

We both want to get back to our homeland, when our

circumstances allow it. My husband has not yet completed his education, because, in order to get a good job, one needs education and experience. But back home, one only needs a certificate to get a good job. When we go back home, we must have savings to start a business, because the job conditions are different back home. My husband has no idea of job or living conditions back home, since he has been living in this country for the last 17 or 18 years. The sooner we go home the better, because when the children grow up, they might want to settle in this country, and then we would be in trouble because the family might split.

Even when black people come to accept their long-term residence in this country, many will remain heavily invested emotionally in their home country and closely follow its political affairs rather than those in the UK. Many second-generation black people are still caught up with their parents' countries either through religion, music or culture, or the prominence given to such events as the Golden Temple siege in Amritsar. People like Lawrence expected that the born-here generation would not be held back from participation in political life by the 'immigrant ideology'. This was too simple a prediction and underestimated the strong emotional ties that connect people to their parents' countries. It also ignored the growth of black and ethnic consciousness. Separatism has been seen as a desirable path of development, as a protective device against harassment, and as a safeguard of vital elements of language and culture. This new consciousness does as much as the 'immigrant ideology' to keep people out of the mainstream of British political life, including community groups and local politics.

There are two further aspects of the immigrant ideology that may affect involvement in community activities. The first are people's memories of, and conditioning by, the 'imperial past' which leads them to expect no better treatment at the hands of authorities (like the housing department) than they would have expected 'at home'. People refuse to claim welfare benefits 'because it is more than we would get back home'. Another expression of the colonial legacy is 'take what you are given', an attitude towards livelihood that goes hand in hand with a dependency on letting white people do things and decide things for you. (On the other hand, there is a good deal of ambivalence about this which again works against participation: Little's study of adult education noted that the bitterest complaint amongst Asians 'is that someone else decides what is good for them' (1982).) This misplaced gratitude that eschews making demands is, of course, reinforced by comments in the media about scroungers, and by the existence of beliefs in the importance of self-sufficiency.

The second aspect of the immigrant ideology is the reluctance of people to get involved because 'We don't want to make trouble.' O'Brien has captured this in writing about the poor and community action:

> if the poor feel powerless . . . it is because they really are powerless vis-à-vis the forces that control their lives. These forces, especially public welfare agencies and the police, keep the poor dependent and constantly in fear of sanctions. In short, the poor are more vulnerable to sanctions for participating in political activities than are other groups in our society. (*1981*)

The fear of 'trouble' is a particular issue for ethnic minorities because of the reaction not only of public institutions but also of working-class bigots and racists. (We all know what happens to 'uppity' blacks in American films on the deep South.) There is also a link here to people's worries about citizenship and rights to take up residence, and to other matters such as tax, so that people may not feel able to come forward to take on a public role as a member of a community group that gives them or their family publicity and local attention.

Besides that of legality, there are other aspects of the political economy of ethnic communities that affect their involvement in community groups. Like the poor in general, many blacks will be struggling to make ends meet, and will not have the time and/or the physical and emotional energy for community activity. According to a survey referenced by Cheetham (1985), three-quarters of West Indian and nearly one-third of Asian mothers are employed outside the home at some period during their children's pre-school years, many for substantial periods, compared with 45 per cent of the general population. Many black people will be working overtime and moonlighting in order to meet obligations to kin in the home country, or to save up towards the day when they will return home, or to pay off loans raised for business purposes. The pressure to earn money is explained by other factors: according to Brown's PSI study, three-quarters of black mortgagors relied on savings for the deposit for house purchase, and there is a relatively large proportion of Asians who have found it easier to borrow money for house purchase through banks but at rates of interest that are often higher than those of building societies (see also CRE, 1985). The PSI study shows that finding the money for house purchase is more of a problem for black people than white. Finally, it appears from this study that many black home owners may rely on savings and bank loans for home improvements rather than improvement grants: the grant scheme 'is not being used by some of those who need it most, and the explanation could be that the information on the terms, eligibility, the application procedures, and the types of work covered is inadequately targeted towards ethnic minorities' (Brown, 1984).

The PSI study also indicates that both Asian and Afro-Caribbean employees work shifts more commonly than whites, and these differences are even greater when night shifts are considered. This factor, when taken together with the working of long and unsocial hours (in, for example, the retail and catering trades), indicates again how little time and energy many black people may have for voluntary participation in affairs outside the household. What time and energy is available will be given to meeting the emotional and physical demands of the extended family, and of religious and cultural groups.

Families also make financial demands: amongst both the Afro-Caribbean and Asian groups (but particularly the latter) there are more dependants per earner than amongst whites (PSI survey). This is a result partly of differences in household structures, and partly of higher unemployment amongst blacks.

Participation in ethnic groups and networks is necessary not only because of traditional values and obligations, but because people rely on such networks for information about basic essentials in their livelihood, not least the opportunities for work and earning extra income. Many black people will conserve their energy outside work and family obligations to do only those things that enhance their skills for employment, survival and progress. Little has commented on this in respect to adult education facilities for ethnic minorities (1982). The priority of these instrumental goals (which, of course, reinforce individual escape rather than collective action) may mean that there will be little interest in general community groups based on leisure, recreation or even on issues that affect livelihood. We might note, too, that as the National Survey of Volunteering (1984) suggests, many people join community groups for social and affective purposes (such as meeting people and making friends), and this may be less important to some ethnic groups whose members receive these social benefits through religious and cultural activities based in their own group. Some of these social needs may also be met within the larger households to be found in some ethnic groups: Asian and West Indian households frequently contain large numbers of adults when compared with white households (Brown, 1984). One further point about relationships needs to be made here. The NSV data show that amongst those involved in community groups, being introduced through someone they knew was a particularly significant feature in joining such groups. This suggests that participation in general community groups by black residents living in predominantly white areas presupposes the existence of a network of relationships and contact with white neighbours involved in, or knowing about, those community groups.

We have already considered the connection between religious and cultural activities and the economic aspects of livelihood; but such activities are also bound up with political interests and affiliations, although these may as often be about political issues in the home country. We shall see in the next chapter how in the black and hispanic communities in America community politics and other forms of organizing are inseparable from the functioning of social networks. These networks are not locality-bound, and this is inevitable in neighbourhoods where members of ethnic minority groups form only a small part of the population. Yancey and his colleagues have also indicated that the development of neighbourhood networks in ethnic communities is connected to the existence of 'ethnic institutions' such as shops, bars, schools, churches, mutual aid clubs and voluntary associations. Where such local institutions exist, local relations will develop and be maintained. They quote Raymond Breton: 'The institutions of an ethnic community are the origin of much social life in which the people of that community get involved and as a consequence become tied together in a cohesive interpersonal network' (Yancey *et al.*, 1976).

The existence of such institutions is related to the growth of ghettos or ethnic residential concentrations. There are, nevertheless, two factors that the community worker needs to remember even when working in neighbourhoods which have not become ghettoized. First, the dispersion of people to ethnic institutions such as churches or shops outside the neighbourhood clearly constrains identification with locality, and the time available for local forms of organizing. Secondly, the absence of facilities in a neighbourhood (for example, a black hairdresser, a shop selling saris, black shop assistants) may have an important effect on how far people feel they belong or fit in. The development of small businesses and co-operatives in a neighbourhood amongst ethnic groups, and the campaign in local firms to take positive action in the provision of goods and services (as well as equal employment opportunities), are not to be seen solely in terms of small-scale economic development but also as an essential element in the sponsored development of the community as a whole.

White Groups, Black Issues

One of the arguments put forward by black radicals to explain the non-involvement of black people in neighbourhood organizations is that black problems, just like black people's social networks, transcend the framework of the local community. Mike Phillips, for example, has argued that black people have specific needs and problems which are not recognized by authorities and would not be catered for in a white working-class organization such as a tenants' association (1982). It is argued that even in the case of a problem such as damp housing that affects everyone in an area, black people will want to deal with it on an ethnic group basis, not least because general community groups will be seen as expressions of white interests and racism. Donnelly and Ohri make some similar points:

> To obtain the agreement of groups to work together on aims and ends is never easy. This co-operation is even more difficult in the arena of British race relations. For it is not self-evident to any black group that any white group sincerely shares a common objective with it, nor indeed is it always clear when scarce resources are being distributed among black projects themselves whether their particular cause is served by joining with another group. The scars of imperialism run deep; not only did they divide the colonizer from the colonized, they also divided the colonized themselves. Not only is there a lack of trust on the side of minorities, there is so often that naive belief of the British community worker that the interests of the black community are identical with those of the white working class and that a special negotiation and discussion with the black group itself is not necessary. (*1982*)

One of the most articulate exponents of the separatist view has been Stokely Carmichael. In his book with Hamilton (1967), he identifies three myths or fallacies about blacks and whites working together. They are, first, that the interests of black people are identical with those of community groups such as tenants' associations; secondly, that it is possible to secure co-operation between the politically and economically secure and those who are politically and economically insecure; and thirdly that joint work can be sustained on a moral, friendly, sentimental basis, by appeals to conscience, fraternity, good faith and so forth.

He suggests that a particular problem for blacks getting involved in community groups is the superiority of white working-class people towards their values and ways of living. A consequence of 'anglo-conformity' is that newcomers are not made to feel welcome and/or they must adjust to fit the style and mores of the group. Anglo-conformity assumes that it is desirable to maintain 'English' institutions, the language and English-oriented cultural patterns as standard in the life of the country.

The development of black community organizations is not simply a reaction to the domination of white interests in general community groups; it is seen also as a way of expanding self-determination and encouraging self-confidence and skills through independent development, much in the same way that many women are choosing not to join male-dominated groups.

The quest for identity and strength through separate development is not to be dismissed as the concern only of a small number of black radicals, or of inward-looking Asian communities locked into traditional patterns of religion, language and culture that they wish to protect from contamination in white Western society. On the contrary, the experiences of slavery and colonialism have left a legacy about origin and identity that is being augmented by nationality and immigration laws that cut people off from their homeland and their kith and kin who live there:

Q: How hopeful do you feel about the future for black people in this country?
A: If you want my honest opinion, I think there will always be a core of black people who do survive, but generally speaking it's going to be even more serious than it is now, because there's going to be more black people in the prisons, there's going to be many more in mental institutions, there's gonna be greater unemployment. So with all those types of pressures and plus the things that underpin the community – yeah, such things as unity have been attacked and successfully attacked, and I think that the community does not hold together as much as it could do or should do and I think that will be the key to actually breaking down black people in this country. And not only that, whilst other nationalities such as Europeans, white Americans, Australians, all the rest, are still able to come into this country and in a sense replenish the numbers, in a sense we're cut off and isolated. So I think things will be more serious than they are now. I'm quite pessimistic about the future. The black community's still quite a young community. We're still sorting out a lot of things, especially our identity in this country, so lots of black and even myself, I was born in this country and you know you're sorting that out and – I think, I think we're uneasy because we don't fully – we haven't fully accepted our situation and explained it and accepted it to ourselves. So I

think that kind of restricts your full involvement in the society, and like when I compare it to, say, black Americans, they feel a part of America and that they have a history there and they're going to fight for everything there. That doesn't exist here in the same way.

Another issue to consider is the extent to which minority ethnic groups possess organizing memories, heroes and heroines. It has been suggested that in the 1960s and 1970s white working-class involvement in community groups was sustained by 'class memories' of previous actions both in the community and at the work-place. Until these kinds of memories have developed for black people (in separatist ethnic movements) then there may be little basis for their participation in general community groups. In this vein Rex, for example, has argued that black movements are to black people what the labour movement has been to white working-class people (1979).

Ward has suggested that there is a narrow basis for interaction between black people and the white working class because the former are 'recent arrivals', are keen to keep their distinctiveness, and are concentrated in a narrow sector of the housing and labour markets so that the 'situations in which they have, recognise and act upon political interests in common with white British are less evident' (1979).

These issues have been graphically summarized by Donnelly and Ohri:

Recent writers on community work have argued that community groups should form alliances with the trade unions because this 'strategy recognises that only the working class, through its collective action, is in a position to defend its class interests against the operations of capital and that the role of community workers in a local area should be to support and encourage this action'. The argument goes further and suggests that 'traditional forms of community work are dangerous in that they tend to socialise working-class areas into existing economic systems, and community workers who are developing such strategies must be challenged about their attempt to control and dispel working-class actions and protest on behalf of the state'. This analysis views the working class as the key to social justice. The experience of black people in Britain does not support this strategy. The march of London dockers in support of Enoch Powell, the resistance of trade unions to involve black workers and to fight for the rights of black workers (with the exception of a few cases), the rise of the National Front and everyday experience in the streets and factories raises a very fundamental issue – is the working class ready to form an alliance with black groups? It seems that they are not and black groups certainly cannot 'wait' for them. It is the black groups that need to help the working class along in the direction of 'social justice'. If the resources available to improve the quality of life of black people and the white working class stay the same, then any joint action might not be possible. It is essential that the resources available are increased, so that there is some hope for collaboration. (*1982*)

But as we shall discern later, the possibilities for such collaboration are vitiated by other factors. For example, many black people find themselves living in public housing with the most disadvantaged of the working class. Phillips has pointed out how blacks resent being lumped together with the deprived working class and this works against their participation in community activities. Many blacks, particularly amongst some Asian groups, do not see themselves as working class, even though they may share the same economic predicament. For them, class is determined by other factors such as religion, parental status, resources owned in the home country and by their vision of what they, or their children, wish to become:

> I will move out, but to a private house, nowhere else. We are nearly retiring and the children are growing up. But again there is a mortgage problem for us, otherwise we would have bought a house of our own. We can't do this as yet, so we live and wait. But our friends who own their home think that we are no different from dirty white people who live on this estate. We say to them give us a proof and they can't, but it's a fact.

Carmichael and Hamilton (1967) suggest that there are a number of conditions for success in black and white people working together in community organizations, conditions that the community worker can help to sustain. These are that each ethnic group develops its own power base; outlines its respective self-interests; comes to a rational assessment that each will gain by allying with others; and decides that goals to be pursued are specific and identifiable, not vague and general.

What writers like Carmichael and Hamilton neglect in their analysis of anglo-conformity and the domination of the white norm is, paradoxically, the sheer moribundity of many working-class community groups that makes them unattractive to black and white alike. Many groups lack vitality and purpose and are locked into a low level of enjoyment and activity. Harrison has pointed to the moribund nature of much working-class organ-ization in his portrait of groups in Hackney:

> As the meeting wears on, the personal interactions become clearer and one begins to see another sort of reason why council tenants don't turn out to meetings. Chairman Gordon Theobald is energetic and articulate and puts in a lot of work. But he tends to dominate the tenants' side of the meeting, and the officials reinforce that domination. They all address their comments to him, the district manager shows the plans for a new estate office to him alone and does not pass it round. Gordon talks the same language as the officers, he understands the big words. His presence saves the officers the difficult task of learning to express themselves in the language of the manual working class, to rephrase intellec-tualized or Latinate remarks into concrete Anglo-Saxon. The language, the length of time taken, the lack of oppor-tunity for most people to say much, the remote prospects of more than marginal change, all conspire to deter most tenants from attending meetings. (*1983*)

But it is not only the stylized formality and language of meetings, and the kind of allusive language and idiom through which business is often conducted, that deters people from participation; as important for black participants is the fact that what occurs in a meeting is often less important than the pre- and post-meetings (often in someone's home), and the exclusion from these of black people would be inevitable in many working-class areas. It would be foolish to ignore the real gap between white working-class culture, language, education and ways of communication and those of some ethnic groups; it is easy for both white middle-class and black working-class people to be mystified and excluded by the 'street talk' of the white working class (exemplified humorously by Smiley Culture's *Cockney Translation*) leading to inhibitions about participation in community affairs.

The ways in which differences of thinking, procedure, and language conspire to enforce white leadership and induce the drop-out of blacks from community groups is complex. The difficulties of getting people to join groups are small compared to those of helping them to remain as members. The ways in which people talk and banter with each other in a group often define their togetherness, and convey to the newcomer that there is a history of which they have no part. Consciousness of differences in language, both in fluency and idiom, contributes to self-image and thus to the confidence with which people will work with others in community activities:

> The whole issue of language and class came up and it was pointed out that control of language is a factor in prejudice: pupils at Acland Burghley most persecuted are those who have least control of language. The importance of self-image and role-models comes in here. Lack of control of language leads directly to poor self-image and ultimately to frustration and aggression. We need to be aware of our use of language, of the terms of abuse, or mockery, many of which are a deeply ingrained part of our language and culture. (*Acland Burghley School*, 1985)

We note in passing that these difficulties about language and procedure are not confined to groups dominated by the white working class; similar problems have been identified by Ellis in the committees of voluntary agencies, and she sees them as a major obstacle to furthering black participation within the voluntary sector:

> One black member talks of the difficulty he experienced in entering the discussion, recalling that other people would cut across what he was saying, or even finish his sentences. He

also realised the need to gain access to a certain type of knowledge, and to learn a certain way of expressing things 'in a series of complete units' in order to be heard.

The problem can be more basic than one of hidden language. The formal use of English itself, and of sophisticated terminology, is brought from the sphere of middle class professions into voluntary sector management. But when combined with committee jargon – 'points of order', 'tabled resolutions', 'AOB', and so on – committee meetings can be both confusing and intimidating for the newcomer. When to this is added the difficulty of getting items on the agenda, the extent of the disincentive to participation becomes apparent. (*1985*)

People become isolated not only through the language and body gestures of others, but because language itself can no longer be relied upon to develop relationships with others in a tentative and incremental way. Suttles has observed this in his own field research, and his comments are perceptive:

The most obvious restriction on communication between the ethnic groups in the Addams area is their differences of language and dialect. For many of the older residents, Spanish and Italian are still the working languages for everyday life. Even within each of these speech communities, however, the dialects are often so far apart that they lead to grave misunderstandings, invidious comparisons, and mutual avoidance. Where English is spoken, the range of common understanding is not much greater. With the older Italians, Mexicans and Puerto Ricans, their English is often badly broken and is either a source of embarrassment or a tool by which only the bare rudiments of communication can take place. All the subtleties that are usually incorporated into speech are suddenly lost. Thus persons are left adrift without the ordinary innuendos, graces, overtones, and insinuations that play such a critical part in the constant reassurances they furnish one another.

Lacking these essentials, verbal behaviour often loses the easy continuity that we call spontaneity and takes on a halting and rehearsed manner that is usually attributed to calculation. At the same time, the participants are reduced to presenting only the most mundane and blatant information about themselves and their intentions. It becomes almost impossible to hint at one's objectives before fully broaching them, to use circumlocutions or idioms that evade overt admission of vulgarity, and to employ metaphors that protect the participants from the full light of social exposure. A more subtle but no less important deficiency is that inflection and intonation cease to be dependable indices that persons can use to judge the appropriateness of their own reactions. (*1968*)

It will be of no surprise to community workers that the problems with language, moribundity and anglo-conformity are more evident among tenants' associations on public housing estates, although tenants' associations, of course, are only one of several kinds of groups on estates. They are not, on the whole, attractive organizations for black people to join, not least because most do little to take positive action to recruit and maintain black members. Black members are shunned or patronized, and not made welcome. Venues for meetings are changed at the last minute, and the responses to suggestions from black participants are such that they sap the morale and self-confidence of the individual (for example, 'We've been here for thirty years and we know'; or 'We've done that before and it didn't work'). Worst of all, black people often report how ignored or neglected they feel and some give up going – 'why bother to go into that hall and be treated like that?' Why bother to venture out on a dark evening across a desolate estate to the tenants' hall, for what is there to find? Beer and bingo, loud music and pool, activities that define the hall or the association as an embodiment of white working-class solidarity.

Many tenants' associations exist only to run a bar and bingo, and to offer a narrow range of social facilities that usually conform to the white norm. Tenants' associations that provide social services may also hold little for ethnic minority tenants; many associations, for example, offer services to the elderly and on the whole this must be an excluding activity for black people given their younger age structure.

There was little said in our reconnaissance interviews about tenants' associations that was good or positive. The following quotations sum up the general mood amongst Asian and Afro-Caribbean respondents:

The tenants' association people only know how to play bingo, that's all.

The neighbourhood association is not helping the tenants at all, they are only clinging to their chairs.

They're a load of wind. Waffling . . . a jolly old group.

A: It's not really useful but they do hold meetings and discuss children's behaviour, and their activities on this estate; but if we complain about the caretaker or about the dustbin men not clearing all the rubbish, or about any social problem, they ignore us . . .
Q: Don't they even discuss major problems on the estate?
A: No, they don't. They say it is not their job.

The last two comments illuminate, first, how the tenants' association is perceived as a kind of friendship group, a clique of established white friends running the organization more for their personal satisfaction than for service to tenants; and, secondly, that where a neighbourhood organization is not effective in helping black people with improving livelihood it will not attract their interest (nor, it should be added, the interests of white tenants). The overall impression from our interviews was that people had tried time and time again to use a tenants' association to discuss matters of livelihood, but had given up. As one interviewee said rather despairingly of her white neighbours, 'you can't clap with one hand'.

For white and black tenants, support of, and membership in, a tenants' association may be related to the concern of that association in defining and enforcing agreements about common property and behaviour in public places; and in achieving a standard of repairs that strikes tenants as an appreciable contribution to the material side of their livelihood. The link of participation to livelihood is seen in the following extract from an interview which clearly shows the task or instrumental goals of the interviewee:

Maybe my husband knows [the tenants' association]. He goes to work at 9 a.m. and comes back at 5.30 p.m. We do the shopping on Saturdays and on Sundays we mostly have guests in the house, our life is very busy. That is why my husband cannot join these associations, at least once a month or even weekly. But if there is only talking involved, you go to the meetings, sit and talk and talk, and then come back home without having done anything practical. So it is no good attending these meetings, it is a waste of time.

Q: Can you tell me if your husband's friends are involved in these association meetings?

A: No, I don't know. But recently the neighbourhood centre has started teaching English classes and health education classes. This is quite useful, to know about the English language and to find out more about health education once or twice a week, when there is not a lot to do at home, when the children are at school, for instance.

Q: Do you participate in your children's activities in school?

A: Yes, we do. I know many families here. If there is a letter from the school I deal with it and attend parents' meetings regularly. I also teach my children regularly at home for two hours a day when they get back from school. But I don't have the time to attend plays and functions at school. I do go to school to discuss my children's education and behaviour with their teachers.

Q: There is a parent and teachers' association at school, are you a member of it?

A: Yes, I do take part in discussions and meetings.

Q: Do you attend their meeting at the end of each term?

A: Yes, I do.

Some respondents thought that the ineffectiveness of their tenants' associations was related to their dependence on the goodwill and patronage of the local council:

They're very artificial forums in my view that are generally created through the instigation of the housing authority, who will send along sophisticated pseudo-social worker types who will do their best to manipulate the meeting in a way that is beneficial to them and the people from the estate, who are by and large inarticulate and a very unsophisticated group, who forever . . . fail to be together and consequently the whole thing becomes more a puppet exercise than any kind of realistic attempt to develop full-time participation on how the housing stock is managed.

The failure of tenants' associations to recruit black members may be seen as yet another nail in the tenants' association coffin. For many years, community workers have been debating their usefulness and suggesting that their effectiveness, if such it was, was based on a certain homogeneity on estates of race and class which no longer exists. On the other hand, tenants' associations cannot be lightly dismissed, not least because of the growing proportion of some black groups in public housing. Tenants' associations were, and may still become, 'training grounds' for local government councillors; they may become more important as local government offices are decentralized and as schemes for tenant management develop in the public housing sector. As one of our interviewees put it:

The groups don't satisfy my aspirations for a better society, but I don't think you always sit around and wait for the perfect group to come along as you'd never do anything. I think you have to get involved in groups no matter how inept they might appear, no matter how amateurish they might appear, because that is the way people gain experience and develop to reach a stage where they can honestly go forward with the knowledge that they'll have done their apprenticeship at the grass roots and have an understanding of people's problems and can go forward and articulate those problems. But it's only at a very petty level; I see dealing with little repairs of housing and the odd petty legal problem here and there as being neither here nor there. I think that the time has come for government actually to allow the local authorities to encourage the local people to put their views more forcefully, and if you want to put their views more forcefully to have access to the decision-making process with the local authorities.

To the extent that tenants' associations are, or will become, elements of influence in local politics, then they cannot be ignored by black tenants or community workers trying to support them. They are the immediate means of dealing with issues of livelihood; the existence of borough or city-wide associations of black tenants is an important development but, almost by definition, can do little to help black tenants on the immediate issues of livelihood that affect black and white tenants alike. But such occasions do have a potentially powerful role in influencing policy, not least in affecting allocation policy and pressing for more extensive multi-racial management. Their existence may also be supportive of individual groups of black tenants attempting to join tenants' associations. Borough or city-wide associations of black people will almost inevitably attract a majority of participants from amongst the most able and confident; that on its own is no criticism so long as community workers continue to support the participation of the not-so-confident and skilled in their local groups.

Participation in such groups will in most parts of the country mean participation with white neighbours, because the neighbourhoods or estates where black people form the major part of the population are still the exception and not the rule.[1] This is a matter for discussion in the next chapter; the point to be made here is that the community worker who works in a multi-racial area where black people have successfully formed and joined groups where they find themselves in the majority and in leadership can have no grounds for satisfaction or complacency; that community worker has still not resolved the actual problem of helping black and white neighbours to manage their livelihood together, and must therefore address the problem of how to help white people take part in community activities. The development of black groups, whether to carry out political campaigns or provide support and personal development for individuals, is not simply to be seen as a good in itself but also a means to helping individual blacks to have greater mastery in their day-to-day dealings with whites as they seek to manage livelihood together. It is only in situations of the neighbourhood segregation of ethnic groups that blacks and whites do not, on the whole, have to come together for the purpose of work, living together, shopping, recreation and so on. As the PSI study shows, whites and blacks in the UK still live together and share the same residential spaces and facilities, and thus interact with each other in a number of locally based roles and relationships (Brown, 1984). These points were reflected by a number of our interviewees; for example, when asked if whites and blacks should work together on common issues:

> Oh yes, because it's the only way, because it's not gonna be – England's not going to become like South Africa or anything like that. So therefore we're here, we're gonna be here to stay so we might as well contribute more, or you can have your segregation but out of that you can have integration.

> Well – like in St Pauls they had black people now trying to go united together to solve their problems because black and black, you understand what I mean, they're more better; but if the white want to join in it's good for them as well ain't it, 'cos we have a different culture from them, so it's good for them if they want to join us – they all live on the estate there and you know they have to go to the same council house, join the same post office, meeting together in the shops and all that, so it's good for them.

Thus the community worker must confront the question of how white and black working-class people manage their living together, and of how individual blacks, albeit supported by their membership of, or knowledge about, all-black groups, extend their authority in respect of white in a number of roles they play as participants in community activities. On this analysis, a national political strategy about how resources (in housing, jobs, education and so on) are managed and equitably distributed must be complemented by a different kind of local strategy about how whites and blacks manage their relationships together in their joint concerns about neighbourhood issues affecting livelihood.

It is of course true that the persistence of gross inequalities in the distribution of resources and opportunity, and the effects of institutional racism, have a major effect on how whites and blacks living together in the same neighbourhood work together in local roles that they have in common, such as tenant or parent, and work together in establishing 'agreements' between themselves as neighbours.

Agreements about Living Together

We saw in the last chapter how the ability to define and enforce shared agreements about social tasks and responsibilities was an important feature of an interacting community that has developed capability in its relations with the 'outside world' and in evolving a *modus vivendi* amongst its inhabitants. We noted that some of the essential areas in which shared agreements were needed were in respect of noise, personal safety, children and the maintenance of common property. It is naive to think that these agreements are reached satisfactorily only through rules and regulations established by a housing authority, through policing or vigilante activity, or just through understanding between individuals, though each of these might be important. It is equally useful to see that making agreements about living together is achieved through participation in informal and formal groups, and a range of forums and meetings called between neighbours to discuss common issues of livelihood, and between neighbours and those in organizations, such as local government, whose decisions affect an area. The evolution of these group-based mechanisms for making contracts between people is illustrated in the following account from a report of a black tenants' conference.

Broadwater Farm Tenants' Association and Youth Associations was represented by Joanne George who gave an inspiring account of how black tenants had successfully organised to change the atmosphere and fortunes of their estate. The estate is a large estate built in the early 1970s and containing about 1000 units. It began to decline in the late 1970s mainly because of Haringey policy to make one offer only to homeless families and this was usually to Broadwater Farm. It became, in fact, a dumping ground for problem families with the attendant problems of crime, police/youth tensions etc. By organising themselves into a tenants' association, youth association and mothers' group, the residents have secured much of the resources necessary to make the estate a decent place to live. The T.A. is mainly made up of young black women, with a few white members. They hold regular meetings with Housing Officers to talk about new contracts, building works, repairs, tenant problems etc., and also take part in choosing staff for positions on the estate – such as staff for the play building. They are currently working with a consultant from the Priority Estate Project. They also hold meetings with small groups from each block, so tenants can talk openly about their housing problems without Council Officers being there. (*LTO, 1984*)

We are in no doubt that amongst most blacks there is acceptance of the need to work with whites in resolving issues that affect livelihood. Table 5.1 shows the support for the idea of whites and blacks living and working together on common issues. Is the main

Table 5.1. Asians and West Indians: Attitudes towards Multi-Racial Life in Britain (percentages)

	West Indian	Asian
'People of Asian/West Indian origin should have white friends they see outside the work-place'		
Agree	88	87
Disagree	3	3
'People of Asian/West Indian origin should join political organizations alongside white people'		
Agree	80	84
Disagree	7	4
'People of Asian/West Indian origin should join trade unions alongside white people'		
Agree	86	85
Disagree	4	3
'People of Asian/West Indian origin should keep themselves apart from white people'		
Agree	4	5
Disagree	92	83
'People of Asian/West Indian origin should avoid living in mainly white areas'		
Agree	8	7
Disagree	92	83
Base: adults		
Weighted	1,843	3,471
Unweighted	894	1,688

Source: PSI study, Brown, 1984.

Table 5.2. Whites: Attitudes to Life in Multi-Racial Britain (percentages)

'People of Asian/West Indian origin should keep themselves apart from white people'	
Agree	8
Disagree	87
'People of Asian/West Indian origin should avoid living in mainly white areas'	
Agree	18
Disagree	72
'People of Asian/West Indian origin should try to preserve as much of their own culture as possible'	
Agree	50
Disagree	40
Base: adults	
Weighted	5,375
Unweighted	2,265

Source: PSI study, Brown, 1984.

obstacle rather the attitude of whites? Table 5.2 indicates that an overwhelming majority of whites also support the policy of whites and blacks living together and, implicitly, of working together to manage their joint livelihood. (The PSI study, from which these tables are taken, does not break down these white/black responses by class or any other variable.)

The support for the idea that whites and blacks should manage livelihood together emerged from our small number of reconnaissance interviews with black residents. Respondents viewed the task of living together in a highly differentiated way, according to role, interests and purpose. For example, blacks and whites should work together on issues, interests and roles they had in common (e.g. that of tenant) but should pursue a number of other interests, e.g. recreation, separately:

> I'm not a racist even though I've seen many of them display racist factions. I think it's more out of ignorance rather than them be deliberately racist and I think they have been manipulated by elements in whose interest it is to propagate the types of views that are held by some of the white people on the estate. But at the same time I don't think that the whites getting better conditions for the whites on the estate

or the blacks getting better conditions for the blacks on the estate is a beneficial thing because it can reinforce the divisions. I think it has to be a consensus development and a consensus policy and a consensus of the type of life and the type of development we want to see on this estate, which could possibly be a model for other estates . . .

Q: Are you a member of this association?
A: No.
Q: Have you ever complained to them about refuse on the estate?
A: They do not care. They do not want to know what is happening on the estate.
Q: Have you ever met committee members?
A: I used to attend their meetings before but there are no meetings now, and if there were, they did not invite us.
Q: Do you feel that white people and Asians should get together and organize themselves to do something about the welfare of the estate?
A: Yes, I'd like that very much. But there is no action, I tried once.
Q: Don't you think that there is something wrong, somewhere, that your actions are not forceful?
A: Maybe, it is up to the leaders, but again, we are Asians.

Two points emerge from our interviews that need further consideration. First, the livelihood of blacks is seen by them to be affected not only by the police or the authorities or by the discrimination they receive in the job and housing markets, but also by the extent and quality of their daily interactions with neighbours. Their lives, they report, are as impoverished by the nominal community as that of the white working class, and their livelihood as adversely affected by the failure of blacks and whites to manage many of the material and social tasks needed to produce viable communities.

Secondly, our interviewers seemed better able in their dealings with whites to maintain a highly functional distinction between role and person, between public responsibilities and private lives; this is evident, for example, in the differentiated view of participation with whites – it is necessary for some purposes and not for others to do with recreation, culture, religion and so forth. In other words, there are a number of *personal* areas where blacks will want to be with blacks, and other more *public* areas where roles and responsibilities need to be shared with whites if common interests are to be effectively pursued. Our *intuition* is that many whites are unable to employ these distinctions in ordering their relations with blacks, partly because their perceptions of blacks are mediated through myth and stereotype, and partly because their fears of contamination are often so gross that boundaries and distinctions are violated. In addition, their view of blacks as persons is often so degraded through the white norm of cultural and economic superiority, and the psycho-sexual fears and fantasies about blacks, that the involvement and effectiveness of blacks in public roles then becomes a matter of ridicule. We say 'intuition' because we did no interviews with whites; this is clearly an area for further investigation.

It is now a truism of our report that the nominal community is one which offers few opportunities for whites and blacks to develop skills and confidence in public roles, and for whites to re-appraise their valuations of the role effectiveness of blacks. Although blacks may be better able to use the role–person distinction, it is also one that enables them to express their dislike of whites, while at the same time allowing them to accept that both groups have to work together in some areas of livelihood. The dislike or disapproval of the white working class is particularly apparent amongst some Asian groups; it is true that a good measure of this disapproval is self-protective and based on the hostility expressed by white neighbours.

There's people living opposite my house now, they don't have the time in the world to even stand there and smile at you. I mean, if you're putting the clothes out and just sort of wave to them they'll ignore you and go by. And yet if you see a white neighbour coming to them they'll stand there and chat for hours with them, so it makes you wonder, you know. You say to yourself, well what's wrong with me, you know. So this is why you respond to them as they respond to you . . . I mean, if they don't respond to you then I'm sure that you're not gonna go and force them to come and talk to you and be friendly with you. You do try on your own part yourself, but then if there's no response . . .

But there may be other factors that impede the development of shared agreements about community life. Amongst the Asians we interviewed, there was often disapproval of a generalized sort about white Western values; but there were also very specific criticisms and distress about how white neighbours carried out their daily lives. These were mainly to do with the behaviour of children and the lack of interest of white parents in their discipline and education; the attitude to, and treatment of the elderly, the inferior cleanliness and hygiene of white neighbours, and their different values and morality in both private and public life, including the absence of spirituality and the lack of value attached to family life and goals. Working-class whites were seen as 'snobs and low-caste' at the same time; some Asian interviewees saw themselves as higher caste though humbled by the circumstances (for example, of being in public housing) in which they found themselves:

> White people always think that they are somebody special, inside and outside. They want to keep the pace, so we feel that we are Asians and keep to ourselves.

> We do say hello to English people. Some say hello back, some don't. Most of them hate us and pretend to be superior, but in fact they are not. Because of our different background we say hello and are friendly.

It would be foolish to ignore that some Asian households may often define their class position not by job or type of housing but by the visions of improvement they have for themselves and their children, and by reference to family and possessions in the home country. Some Asian families who find themselves in council housing may feel 'de-classed' – with lowered status in their own eyes and those of their family and friends, a loss that could affect their social and religious life and matters such as the marriage prospects of daughters. In this situation, it is perceived class differences that work against the development of shared agree-ments for community life, as well as the fact that such Asian tenants may believe that only individual initiatives and not collective action will deal with immediate housing problems and provide a rung on the ladder of upward mobility. These perceived class differences work not only against solidarity with fellow white tenants, but also impede the development of black groups when both Afro-Caribbeans and other Asians are seen as being of lower social class. Community workers need to recognize these class cleavages between whites and blacks, and within the black community, rather than to construct strategies based on fantasies about either class solidarity or black unity. The realizable goals in neighbourhoods seem rather more to do with helping people who live together (but who are distanced by a number of class, cultural or other differences) to work out the basis of shared agreements about how they will manage their relationships with one another and with the outside world. The management of differences is a key to the construction of viable communities.

Some Asian interviewees realized that the existence of a white superiority complex in poor working-class families itself led to hate and envy: 'Many Indian families live on this estate and the white people become jealous when they see a coloured person doing all right for himself, especially Pakistanis and Indians. So they hate us.' And, of course, others, including the following Afro-Caribbean interviewee, recognized the divisive nature of the 'snob–low caste' syndrome that made it difficult to define shared agreements between neighbours.

I think all the tenants are basically in the same position but there are people who would suggest to the white tenants that they're better off because they're white and that they should frown on their black neighbours or black residents simply because they are white. And this kind of weird racism that is being bred into white people in this country over centuries forces them even within their poverty-striken circumstances to consider themselves superior to people who are living in exactly the same circumstances as themselves. And because they've adopted that position it helps to divide rather than unite them and ultimately the people who should be doing things about their conditions aren't being pressurized to do so because the poor black and the poor whites end up fighting each other.

Another difficulty in the way of neighbours working together
to re-construct relationships was the considerable evidence daily
presented to black families that whites were untrustworthy and
two-faced:

Well you know you don't know how to take them because
today them for you and tomorrow they's not.

My neighbour will stand outside in the garden and say to me,
'Oh, see that party they had last night, I was up till 4 o'clock
at night, you know, because of the music and I phoned the
police up', and this, that and the other and yet her daughter
goes to the girl's party, you know, and the mother's talking
this way. The mother and the daughter will stand outside and
say to me, 'See their curtains, they're horrible', and that sort
of thing, you know, and yet they're going to the party for
free booze and spirit, know what I mean, on a Saturday
evening, which I find totally two-faced. I mean they could be
doing the same with Asian people . . . 'cos I know I make
curries and she likes curries and I pop them over if I've got
anything good made, I'll sort of say 'Would you like a taste
of it?' and pass it over. And yet I know she goes round saying
that Indian people are smelly because they cook curries and
this sort of thing, you know. So it's a totally prejudiced view
by them. But I say to myself people like that are ignorant.

The perceived duplicity of whites affects relationships between
black people and other institutions in the neighbourhood that
affect livelihood:

Before Christmas my oldest boy had a fight with a Japanese
boy. The headmaster punished them both. He made them sit
in his office half a day and asked them to come back after the
interval. Then he let the Japanese boy go, but kept my son
behind. He pushed him around and my son had to sit there
for the whole day. I complained the next day but the
headmaster wouldn't see me. I met his secretary but he
ignored me. It is very difficult when you don't speak the
language. You don't know where to go, who to ask for your
rights. They know the language is your weakness and they
poke fun at you. These white people are not fair at all towards

us. They talk with two tongues. Last year there was a
vacancy for a foreman at the place where my husband works.
They brought a white man from another department in to fill
the vacancy, though my husband was next in line, he was not
given a chance because of his colour and his language.

Such grounds[2] for the dislike of whites may seem unimportant
compared to the experience of overt white racism. But they
cannot be discounted by the community worker as a hindrance to
her efforts to help blacks and whites come together to identify
where issues affect their joint livelihoods. It is highly likely that
when Asians and Afro-Caribbeans answered the PSI study questions about living and collaborating with whites, the picture in the
mind was of whites of a comparable class and education to
themselves, not the kind of white family they found themselves
living next to on a down-at-heel housing estate.

Such perceptions of whites have to be understood in relation to
the residues of anger and hate about whites that remain in the
heart and mind; part of the black person's burden is to carry these
feelings for want of an effective vehicle of expressing them, save
through the public speeches of national figures such as Malcolm
X: 'How can I love the man who raped my mother, killed my
father, and enslaved my ancestors, dropped atom bombs on
Japan, killed off the Indians, and keeps me cooped up in the
slums?' Writing of the blues, Oliver has written of music 'as an
emotional safety-valve, canalising the feelings of anger and resentment' (1969).

To describe such perceptions of white people amongst some
black groups is not simply to state the factor of class as an
inhibitor of the joint management of livelihood; it also invokes
the process of *compadrazzo* – a process described by Miller *et al.*
as one which will 'widen and enhance the individual's primary
groups by either transforming outsiders into family members or
more distant relatives into particularly close associates' (quoted in
Delgado and Humm-Delgado, 1982). Seeing someone like family
(*como familia*) is a process of identification present within some
Asian groups (and not unknown amongst the British working
class, where familiar outsiders are known as 'uncle' or 'auntie'),
and the ability to treat outsiders 'as family' determines the kind of

relationship possible with them. It is self-evident that there are many factors that will prevent white working-class neighbours being seen 'as family', and this will constrain relationships needed to establish shared agreements about community living.

So far we have tried to indicate that there are a range of perceptions held by black and white people of each other that affect their motivation and stamina to work together in community activities – and we have noted in earlier chapters that these perceptions are not necessarily derived from direct contact and communication, but from stereotype, myth and so forth. There are a number of other factors that we can only draw attention to in this limited study: two of the most salient in affecting participation seem to be the attitudes amongst black residents about how they see the future of black people in this country: and secondly, their judgements about how much worse-off they are than whites in housing, employment and so forth, and the extent to which they ascribe these deficits to racist attitudes and procedures. This last is a point we have made several times in this report: that the extent to which blacks and whites will work together in managing those aspects of livelihood that are amenable to collective action will be determined by the privileged access of most whites to those fundamental elements of livelihood such as housing and work.

Conclusions

Simply to ascribe the difficulties present in the participation of blacks and whites in community activities to 'racism' is an unhelpful form of reductionism. To say this is not to deny the existence of racism but to argue that it cannot be properly understood and dealt with if we ignore the complex ways in which it both affects the material livelihood of blacks and mediates the daily relations between black and white residents. We have asserted that racial collaboration is dependent in large part on racial justice, and, of course, the case for racial justice in the distribution of benefits and opportunities is irrefutable on a range of ethical and political grounds. But it would be naive to suggest that the achievement of justice for the black British would on its own resolve the large number of difficulties in the relationships between them and the white British. Indeed, such difficulties that are derived from quite legitimate and valued differences in outlook, values, culture, religion and so forth may be intensified, rather than reduced, through the achievement of racial justice. It has yet to be demonstrated that differences in ethnicity amongst the black British and between them and the white British are likely to disappear when the white British cease to have a privileged position in the housing and employment markets.

Matters about black and white relationships are not simple, black and white issues; they are a tangled web which ensnares those with deterministic explanations which purport to identify single causes or reasons. Such explanations, be they economic, biological or environmental, are inimical to understanding how people manage their relations with one another as they go about their daily round. To reject determinism is to search for more differentiated and complex analyses of black and white relations that develop within, but are not subject only to, major economic or psychological constraints. To describe the cause of something (such as non-participation in community groups) as 'racism', and to further describe racism *only* as a set of class-bound exploitative relationships, or *only* as a white psycho-sexual problem, is to demean the complexity with which the black person experiences his position in a white community. To use such simple analyses is also to distort the nature of the black person's search for livelihood, for such analyses produce rhetoric that slides into the language and games of 'campaigns', 'fights' and 'battles'. The search of the black person for livelihood is more aptly described as 'struggle', for this word catches the reality of a continuing process rather than a once-and-for-all effort or campaign, a process that every black person knows will endure, in different forms and on different issues, no matter what changes take place in the structure of society and in the improvement of the material bases of their livelihood. And the search for livelihood is one of struggle not just to eliminate deficits in housing, employment and so forth but also to develop relations with white people to enhance the material side of livelihood and to manage social tasks and resources.

The notion of 'struggle' captures the fact not only of a continuing process but one which affects black people in the realities of everyday life. This much is self-evident – not just because of racial harassment but in the way black people have learnt to anticipate and defend themselves against hostile, prejudiced or simply patronizing whites in day-to-day encounters. But if it is self-evident, why has so little attention been given to finding out how relations between blacks and whites are managed at the neighbourhood level? Sivanandan (1985) asks a somewhat similar question when he analyses the separation of race from class and community. The flight into ethnicity and ethnic development is a flight from understanding how ordinary black and white working-class people manage their relations with one another. In effect, the concern with racial justice (the right and proper concern), as well as the attention to only *some* aspects of everyday life (such as harassment) have somehow been divorced from what might be called the sociology of everyday life between blacks and whites, as if the issues about day-to-day contact between neighbours were so trivial that they, too, degraded the black struggle. One of our conclusions from this study is that the management of daily life between blacks and whites is of great importance, and is part of the struggle of black people, a struggle that includes, but is not confined to, the achievement of racial justice. The consequences of such a statement may be hard to swallow by white professionals because they will have to confront the realities of white working-class racism, xenophobia, narrowness and so forth. This has been something that both white and black professionals have, for different reasons, found difficult to face and to talk about. Indeed, one of Sivanandan's criticisms of racism awareness training is that it 'eschews the more violent, virulent form of racism, the seed bed of fascism, that of the white working-class which . . . is racist precisely because it is powerless, economically and politically, and violent because the only power it has is personal power' (1985).

But it is not only racism awareness training that has allowed white and black professionals to divert their attention from white working-class racism, and thus from the day-to-day happenings between whites and blacks that sustain or erode hostility. We might also conclude that one of the unhelpful consequences of the concern with institutional racism has been to remove the spotlight from the phenomenon of personal racism in everyday life. Of course, it would not be too cynical to acknowledge that combating institutional racism in one's agency or owning up to one's own racism through racism awareness training (RAT) are probably more attainable and comfortable objectives for white professionals than changing the material conditions of the white working class that are conducive to both racism and the development of fascism. Gurnah has made a similar point:

> after the summer 1981 black rebellions, we cannot over-estimate the appeal of practical solutions to institutional and personal racism. Such solutions attract many interests. Firstly, they attract black people because to some of them, RAT seems to force the recognition of their oppression on the establishment and on the professional middle class; but more importantly, it appears to constitute a concrete programme against that oppression. Secondly, RAT solutions allure parts of the liberal establishment because they provide an answer to their moral opposition to racism. Thirdly, various individuals too are drawn to these solutions because they promise to clear up their confusions and uncertainties about racism. For many, RAT appears to reveal in them extremely important facts about themselves and about their racist society. Finally, even the racist state is persuaded that such training and better trained police force is bound to increase law and order. (*1984*)

There are further difficulties to be considered: is the relationship between institutional and personal racism inverse or direct? Does a decrease in institutional help to lower personal racism? Or does it increase it (through, for example, the white backlash)? And if it does, through what mechanism and in what conditions? What forms of institutional racism do most to sanction and encourage personal racism? What should we thus concentrate on in our agenda about institutional racism in order to have the most effect on personal racism? These are questions that are rarely asked, let alone answered.

It may be that combating institutional racism has little effect on personal racism, not simply because of the 'white backlash' but also because personal racism is sustained by factors outside the scope of campaigns against institutional racism – factors such as the media, the economic plight of many white working-class people and the degree to which negative stereotypes about blacks and blackness have been rooted in the white psyche. But if it is true that the fight against institutional racism will have little or counterproductive effects on personal racism, then all the more reason to put forward as an additional strategy the struggle against personal racism, and the personal racism of the white working class at that.

There are other difficulties in confining the involvement of white professionals in the black struggle to dealing with just their own racism and with that of institutions. Much of the concern with institutional racism is with some of the material bases of livelihood – with jobs, housing, education and so forth. The emphasis on positive discrimination in jobs and housing, or positive action in access to benefits and services, is part of the campaign against institutional racism that stresses the *access* of blacks to some of the material bases of livelihood. This is right and proper, but access is only part of the picture in managing livelihood; *consumption* or *enjoyment* of opportunities is equally important and thus the benefits of gaining access to, for example, decent housing can be vitiated or constrained by the existence of a local social order that inhibits enjoyment of these benefits. Thus again we are forced to confront the reality of white working-class racism in its effect not only on the consumption of improved benefits and services, but also on the total management of the material and social aspects of livelihood.

These comments are not to be misconstrued as a dismissal of the work against intitutional racism, although Sivanandan (1985) and others have begun to look critically at what has been taking place. He argues that what has been achieved has resulted not in the dismantling of institutionally racist structures, but in the institutionalization of ethnicity itself through affirmative employment policies, ethnic advisers and committees, and ethnic projects. Ethnic groups fight against each other for money, position and influence and, while white attitudes are changed in awareness training, the new spiralist ethnics are on the move – a thousand black flowers blooming in the interstices of the white structure, says Sivanandan, a paroxysm of activity which he says has made not the blindest bit of difference to the 'material conditions of the workless, homeless, school-less, welfare-less blacks of slum city'.

Our criticism of the work against institutional racism is that it, too, has reproduced the laissez-faire attitude towards the neighbourhood and has thus neglected the nature of everyday life between white and black working-class neighbours; to say this is to say more than just that access to benefits has been regarded as separate from a struggle to consume and enjoy them. The work against institutional racism has been rightly concerned with legal, policy and funding changes, but neglectful of human relationships. What has been created, in effect, is an objective, quasi-legal framework (stressing 'access to') governing institutional behaviour within which the black and white actors of the urban areas live out their lives; where institutions do intervene to regulate interactions between people, it is mostly, again, at the legal or policy level, usually in the event of a crisis rather than for the purposes of sponsoring the development of relationships. Examples of such crisis-management are policies against racial harassment by tenants (and sometimes their eviction) or proceedings by environmental health departments about the noise and vibration caused by sound-systems and all-night parties.

No one can doubt that it is important for institutions both to define acceptable codes of practice for others (for example, tenants) and to change themselves in order to indicate their values about racial justice and to provide more effective services. The indicative or modelling value of the work against institutional racism is not commented on by Sivanandan but it must be taken seriously in the benefits it may produce. However, indicative policies that signal an institution's values and expectations are always necessary but never enough; much the same can be said about crisis-intervention in helping blacks and whites to manage their relations together. It is just as necessary to treat the neighbourhood as a proper element of social structure and to sponsor development programmes whose objectives would include helping people to come out as neighbours, and thus to put black and white people into contact and communication with each other. Sponsored neighbourhood development would be based on two fundamental assumptions about working-class urban life. The first is that the quality of relationships between people is far too important to be left to chance, or to the efficacy of the 'invisible hand'; in other words, the extent and quality of relations between people in a neighbourhood have to be managed, just as we need to manage relationships in other small and large collectivities if they are not to be wasted or become destructive.

The second assumption is that both in the inner city and in peripheral housing estates conflicts and cleavages between people are often so gross, and the skills, confidence and resources of individuals so depleted, that little will be achieved in helping people better manage their livelihood together without an adequate level of specialist support for people to form and sustain relationships with each other.

It is clear from our own interviews, and from the research of others, that both black and white people recognize how crucially their livelihood is affected by those who live around them, and how helpless they feel as individuals in finding the time, energy, legitimacy and skills better to manage the daily routines and obligations of living together. We have said the objectives of a programme of sponsored development would be to put people in touch with one another; this would be achievable through the growth of formal and informal networks, and through people:

- taking action together on issues that affect their common livelihood;
- working together in common roles that cut across other divisions between people, for example, as parents in the running of a local PTA;
- working together on matters to do with social care and social control;
- working together in a range of groups and forums clustering around identified leadership, in order to talk about and reach agreement on public responsibilities and behaviour that affect each other's livelihood, including matters such as personal safety, the behaviour of children, noise, and the upkeep (on public housing estates) of common property.

It is thus our suggestion that programmes to manage the social structure of a neighbourhood will provide a strategy for dealing with the personal side of the relationships between black and

white people in the daily routines of their lives. If such relationships are to be changed, if we wish to see the end of conflict and
racism between neighbours, then we have to accept that these
relationships are 'live'; that is, dislike, prejudice, racism and so
forth are not simply to be seen as residues of a colonial past
nurtured by ethnocentric education and a right-wing media.
They also have an interactive quality in that they are sustained,
confirmed or eroded by people's everyday experience at work
and in the neighbourhood. Thus the distance and conflict between
blacks and whites, the withdrawal of each into safe physical and
emotional enclosures within the nominal community, the consolidation or dispelling of myths and stereotypes – such matters
are determined in part by how people deal with each other, and in
part by how they show regard and respect for the way others are
trying to pursue and enjoy livelihood in their home and neighbourhood.

In the inner city personal dislike and racism between blacks and
whites is sustained by the expectation of each group that they will
be attacked or robbed by young people from the other group; the
behaviour of each other's children; and the noise and vibration of
people's music. As well as trying to limit the effect of such factors
through design modification, better surveillance and policing,
tenancy conditions, and better resources and services, they must
also be the subject of agreements between people themselves, who
in the last resort may need institutions to help to enforce them.

Will such agreements be forged in urban areas unless working-
class people communicate with each other, and are given the
resources and expert help to sustain co-operative relationships,
and in so doing learn what it takes to manage social networks and
resources? Those urban neighbourhoods where the need is
greatest to manage social relationships and to agree upon public
roles and responsibilities are also those neighbourhoods where
the capacity to do so is often at its lowest. Community capability
in the management of the local social structure, particularly the
relations between whites and blacks, may only be achieved as the
outcome of a sustained process of community development.

There is no reason to dismiss out of hand Sivanandan's claim
(1985) that racism and fascism are a product of the desperate and
dispossessed state of the white working class. Indeed, the fluctuat-

ing and declining fortunes of this class form part of the interactive, 'live' culture of personal racism; the poor and the powerless not only seek scapegoats but do not have the energy and motivation in the struggle for survival to give much heed to the management of the local social structure. But it is outside the remit and power of the welfare professional or policy-maker wholly to change the material conditions of the white working class. What they *can* do is to find local interpretations of the global that are more amenable to intervention. The feelings of helplessness and powerlessness in many working-class communities, for example, are made manifest through people's daily lives; it is powerlessness about getting repairs done, about play facilities for young people, about curtailing the anti-social behaviour of neighbours, about who will occupy the empty flat next door; in short, about managing, either by oneself or through combining with others, all those factors in the environment that affect livelihood. Combining with others gives to the dispossessed a form of personal power that is an alternative to violence and coercion; thus those involved in sponsoring the development of communities must (1) help to facilitate groups and forums in which people can air grievances, provide mutual support and influence, and work together to enhance their common livelihood; and (2) work for forms of neighbourhood government (especially on public housing estates) that give people access to genuine authority over resources and decisions that affect neighbourhood life.

Notes

1 Even though black people tend to be grouped together, most live in enumeration districts (about 165 households each) in which a majority of the households are white, nearly all live in electoral wards where the majority are white, and all live in local authority areas where white people are overwhelmingly in the majority (PSI Study, Brown, 1984, Chapter 4).
2 See also Stopes-Roe and Cochrane (1985).

6
And What Should Community Developers be Doing?

> Trying, as we all are, to be cool and balanced about racial problems, we are, in fact, appearing to be so balanced as to be static. Trying to play it cool, we are actually playing it stone cold.
> (*D. R. Prem*)

Chris's response to the last two chapters was rather mixed: 'It angers and enlightens me, perplexes me and makes me feel pretty useless, all at the same time.'

'Anger?'

'Yes. It reads as if you have set the agenda already. You know you want to drive towards neighbourhood development and to put into it some kind of meaningful role for community workers on black–white relations. It becomes a scratched record. You get stuck, trying to justify a position which appears to have already been adopted. When you decode the fundamental message it could easily be read as, "Oh, the book is saying that so long as black and white neighbours talk to each other everything else will be all right."'

We wanted to protest but Chris was unstoppable: 'Ironically, neighbour relations as a basis for social change are nowhere more acutely fragile than in race relations. How many conversations have gone "Yes, they're OK, they live next door . . . it's the rest." This is white-to-white communication but very widespread locally. It doesn't change a thing . . . So you take a social-science-type look at an ugly brutal reality and try to draw social-science-type conclusions about it. Well, you miss two very important parts of the reality. First, you give no indication of the background to today in terms of race. So you discount the reality of a very potent ideology of race which fuels the racism pouring out of white people. What is happening today exists as a result of a past which is virulent, a highly charged, living reality. That history is portrayed as being about black people but actually it has always been about white institutions, power, decisions and the underlying meanings to support what white people have, by and large, taken on as their view about black people. That is not something it makes any sense to be able to claim to *manage* out of existence. I don't think there is a problem borrowing each other's ladders (white people can be very pleasantly racist) or leaving keys with each other. We could all do this, and still have a highly racist society.

'Furthermore, you talk about class, but where is the analysis of black people as "underclass"? There is no analysis of why the working class turn on black people with powerful physical responses. It *is* a very physical response. Why is that? If you are sending community workers out to take on working-class racism in the name of management give us some proper boxing gloves. We are liable to come back in a bad state.'

'Is there anything else?'

'There's a lack of balance in the discussion – too much on neighbourhood development and not enough on institutional change . . . Frankly I am damned if I am going to be told that to be OK in community work I must sort out black–white neighbour relations when it is quite obvious to me that the town hall is a fairly powerful place, that the health services transmit all kinds of messages, that schools are in profound crisis, that the church has, to say the least, on race lost its way and that employers in the commercial sector are, as ever, getting off scot free. Your analysis narrows me down to neighbour relations and within that the council estate. It literally boxes us in in community work. Why can't we have linked intervention with workers in neighbourhoods linking up with workers inside the institutions?'

'Well, tell us what was enlightening', we asked, looking for some reassurance, as, outside, the thunder rang out across Bloomsbury on a humid afternoon at the beginning of summer.

'It has made me think that you can't reduce the black experience to one only of race or colour, even though they are the most dominant aspects. The chapter has helped me to re-connect race to class and community. Blacks don't experience race or colour in a vacuum – it's lived out through class, and through the community (or lack of it) in which they live.'

'And what is more', we added, alluding to some of Sivanandan's criticisms, 'ethnicity has been distilled from race, class and community in yet further reductionism.'

'Meaning what?'

'Reductionism is a desire to make the complex manageable.'

'And to avoid facing up to the unpalatable.'

'Yes, it's more manageable (both emotionally and financially) to define something as an ethnic problem – a problem about identity, about special services, about preserving language and culture, about complementary schooling . . .'

'. . . than to define it as an issue about the black working class who are subordinated both by colour and class, and who are unable at a political or neighbourhood level to gain support from their peers in the white working class.'

'That's a bit like what Manning and Ohri (1982) have said about the community worker not assuming that the levels of deprivation in an area are the same for all':

> Community workers fail to take into account the additional factor of racism when organising around an issue. Add racism to classism to understand the double oppression of the black working class; add racism to adultism to understand the double oppression of young black people; add racism to sexism to understand the double oppression of black women. In reality it is necessary when considering any oppression or indicator of deprivation to add the factor of racism, if any initiative is to avoid marginalising the needs of the black community and in so doing collude with racism itself.

'And that's really why we use the idea of livelihood such a lot. For blacks (and for whites too, I think), managing livelihood is not just about colour or just about class or just about community . . . it's about all three. We need to know much more about the circumstances in which each of the three is seen as a liability or a resource in managing livelihood. And when do people choose to emphasize ethnicity rather than colour, or the experience of racism they share with other blacks?'

'Let me change tack a bit, and tell you what I found perplexing. I understand that bit about the "live" character of racism, and how it's sustained by what goes on in daily lives between blacks and whites – though you'd better be careful when you write that otherwise people will think you are saying that blacks themselves "cause" racism, that it's their fault because they play loud music or cook curry . . .'

Chris's sentence petered out into silence. Language was becoming a minefield: 'I know that's silly but people do do things that not just aggravate one another but cut across each other's values about living together. I mean, it's all right for you two to go on about "living together, but living differently" but differences on a high-density, badly designed housing estate where people are living on top of one another can intrude on other people's lives in a drastic way. There are very few domestic pleasures any more that are private, that don't intrude into the flats around you.'

'But the extent to which people are indifferent to those around them, the extent to which they regulate their own activities so as not to cause a nuisance to others – that's influenced by how far people feel part of a community and tied to others in a set of common responsibilities for managing livelihood together. All right, so some people who disturb others all the time might just be "pig-ignorant" – but a lot of it is to do with being marginal in the neighbourhood in which you live, and – yes – marginal in the society in which you live. That's why the nominal community is an illusion – you cannot escape from others these days simply by staying behind the front door. Withdrawal is no longer a functional response to the presence of others who are different and living differently – the management of neighbourhood life has in such circumstances to be achieved by mutual influence – and that means engagement, contact, communication, shared agreements, transforming an estate (for example) from simply being a place where people just "lay their head" to a pattern of interactions that have to be managed as a necessary part of managing their livelihood.

'Managing livelihood – I'll scream if I hear that phrase again. It seems to me that a lot of your language in the last chapter was a bit woolly and grand – as if you realized you were trying to convey something important but could not quite get a language that was detailed and specific and practical enough. I suspect you are too evangelical about helping policy-makers to recognize the neighbourhood, and getting them to grasp the notion that relations and social resources have to be managed.'

That was a bit below the belt. We braced ourselves to reply. 'When people have been laissez-faire about something . . .'

'. . . in this case the neighbourhood and the management of social resources and relationships . . .'

'. . . then you can't expect a vocabulary to have developed, or a differential set of concepts. So we get stuck with a limited range of words and ideas – in short, there hasn't been an acceleration in language and concepts to match the complexity of the phenomena we're trying to discuss.'

'And there's no better indication of that than the way in which the word "community" is used in such an elastic and indiscriminate way. It's not that people are necessarily sloppy in their thinking – it's just that our tools for communicating in this area are still very rudimentary.'

'Of course your other big omission', continued Chris, 'is religion, ideology, life philosophies swirling through society but which crucially determine the inability of individuals and institutions to respond. Since you take a social-science-type glimpse at the horror of it all, why don't you widen it to embrace Christianity, Islam, Marxism and so on? Let's face it, if you were examining "Catholic and Protestant in Northern Ireland; Participation in Neighbourhood Roles and Activities" you just wouldn't leave that out, would you? You would want to summarize the impact of that "belief system" on the problem, and on the ability of individuals and institutions to respond. The fear which makes countless city dwellers hide behind multiple locks and huge dogs is real. You can't tell me that the scenes you depict are divorced from the decline of the church as living reality. Ask the question: what will make a fundamental difference? Ultimately, it has to be the views, beliefs, attitudes that individuals hold in their hearts.'

'All right, let's leave that for now, and look at the implications for community development practice of what's been emerging from the project. That is a whole range of people engaged in developing communities, not just full-time community workers with that job title but also many more in voluntary and statutory agencies who are beginning to apply community development principles in their work.'

'So when we talk about community workers it is important to remember that second category of people above.'

'Clearly, community workers have got to start thinking horizontally, about social structure and relations in their neighbourhood, though not forgetting the need for institutional change. They have to give attention to developing community capability as a precondition for an improvement in relationships between various groups in a neighbourhood. They must see the job of helping people to make contact and communicate with each other as fundamental – not as a goal in its own right but as one step in a very long journey of working together to influence each other, as well as resource-holders, in order to make their neighbourhood work. And presumably white community workers have to be organizing more and more with white working-class people, on the assumption that the more they get involved with each other in exercising influence and so on, the less likely they are to be racist. I'm not sure yet about that assumption, but I do know that the more a group of people feels displaced and helpless, the more likely it is to be punitive to others. So on that basis it makes sense to work with them more intensively.'

'And working with blacks?'

'As long as we're discriminating in what we do', replied Chris, enjoying the *double-entendre*. 'Clearly you need black workers, not white, in working with some black groups – for example, with Muslim women, or with groups who don't have much English, or have got a strong religious base. But I wonder if co-working is going to be a more important model in the future.'

'And what made you feel useless?'

'I find the complexity of managing the neighbourhood so vast that I am tempted to "shut my door" simply because the whole thing is so difficult. Managing an organization is only a microcosm of the neighbourhood and you never do it right, and it's pretty uncomfortable at times, so isolated community workers are going to have hell. I suppose it's a question of setting some clear goals for yourself in your role as worker which are about improving the opportunities that people have to manage their own livelihood in ways that give them satisfaction and improve the situation of their neighbours.'

Chris didn't explore that further but talked about white community workers in the UK. 'I'm not sure they understand about the role of social networks in organizing in some black communities, and I'm sceptical about their ability to stay around for long enough, and to pick up on relevant languages, and cultural norms and activities. And then there's the problem of perception. On the one hand, I know some colleagues of mine who don't "see" blacks in the neighbourhood either because they say they're "colour-blind", and they see only "people", neither black nor white, or because they actually haven't noticed them at all. On the other hand, I know white workers who see *only* people's colour, and don't see other factors that might be more relevant to organizing – for example, religion or economic position in the community. And there's their training – if they had any, that is: there are only a handful of training courses that give practical skills for organizing in black communities. Most of what is offered is still at the level of "understanding racial disadvantage" or "introduction to ethnic cultures and values", rather than more central issues to do with racism in institutions and in people, issues which are addressed by few if any of the standard reports or texts on British community work. I also think a lot of white workers have a magical belief in "the issue" – when the "right" issue comes along (or a street party on a fine day to celebrate something or other) that will bring people together. That's not just a kind of sentimental magic – there's a hard-line radical magic around too – some white workers believe that class interests will unite whites and blacks, or that different ethnic minorities will become united on the basis of their blackness.'

In this rough-and-ready assessment of 'white community workers', Chris expressed how ideas and practice skills had not kept pace with the level of concern in community work with racism. The interest amongst national organizations such as ACW had not done much to draw out (beyond the obligatory racism awareness weekend) workers and trainers from behind the safety of the white stockade. We asked what Chris had discovered by way of practice theory in this area, or guidelines for the white community worker, but there was little to point to except the advice produced by Manning and Ohri.[1] Their universal answer is racism awareness training, and more racism awareness training, both for community workers and for members of local community groups. But they do suggest some guidelines for white community workers which are reproduced in full below:

(1) Start from the point of recognition that racism is a reality in British society. It is accurate to assume that no institution, group or organisation you work for/with is free of racism.

(2) Be clear that racism is a white problem in Britain. It is a problem about white people, for which white people must take full responsibility.

(3) Do not abdicate responsibility for racism in your work; it is not the sole task of the 'specialist' self-help black projects. Do not confuse the issues; appointment of black staff is essential to give effect to equal opportunities policies in employment, not to relieve white staff of the responsibility of anti-racist work or demonstrate racial harmony at work.

(4) Recognise that the more you collude with racism (the overt expressions of it in your group, the all-white tenants' association of a multi-racial housing estate), the less likely you will be to intervene in future. Whilst you and other white people may want to resist the notion that Britain is a racist society, monitor the extent to which you intuitively act *in the clear knowledge that it is*, for fear of lack of support from other white people, colleagues, possible isolation and being accused of being 'over sensitive' or 'too passionate' about race.

(5) Do not be misled by 'declarations' of commitment to 'equal opportunity' in organisational statements and constitutions: more importantly, monitor the actions of the group: are its make-up, decision-making, and use of resources genuinely anti-racist, or subtly colluding with racism and largely marginalising, excluding, or abdicating responsibility for the needs of some residents.

(6) Do not confuse 'picking up the pieces' with combating white racism itself. It may be necessary and easier to support a black self-help initiative, but your primary role as a white worker is to challenge white groups and institutions; to attack the

racism which necessitates the growth of such self-help initiatives, with little or no resources.

(7) Resist the temptation to confuse relationships with black workers/people with anti-racism (male relationships with women are no proof of anti-sexism) and be clear that racial harmony is no useful indicator of racial justice.

(8) Encourage other white community workers to focus on and to share anxieties, fears, confusion about white racism, and develop support for each other and strategies for combating it in the area of work where each has responsibility, influence and power.

(9) Community workers need to recognise the need to be familiar with the issues of concern to the black community. This knowledge and sensitivity, if sensibly used, could, in some instances and with hard work, provide a basis for collective action and solidarity among the white and black groups. (1982)

While the guidelines are helpful in providing a general code of practice for the white worker, they amount only to the rudiments of a theory of practice for helping whites and blacks manage livelihood together. One of the conclusions from this brief, exploratory study is that skills and knowledge about practice need to be better articulated and disseminated, both for community workers and other staff in statutory and voluntary agencies working in the community. Otherwise, the concern amongst such professionals, policy-makers and politicians about race relations will be hypocritical because it will not be matched by the ability amongst fieldworkers actually to do something.

This discussion with Chris helped us to see more clearly that we would have to cover three major topics in this chapter: first, the role of the white worker in supporting both black groups and the membership of black people in neighbourhood groups. This would require a critical appraisal of the extent and functioning of black groups in relation to issues of livelihood at the neighbourhood level. Secondly, we would have to cover the role of the black community worker, including that of co-working with a white colleague; and thirdly, the context for community work in multi-racial areas created by the actions, or lack of them, of authorities such as the local council.

But this puts us in a bind: we have developed ideas earlier in the book about fairly broad issues of community capability and the management of livelihood. Yet in searching the literature and other sources for practice guidelines we would invariably find material (if we were lucky) about the *partial* issue of the partici- pation of blacks in both black groups and other neighbourhood organizations. Bearing in mind that difficulty, we have decided to order the rest of this chapter around two major questions: how does the community worker help to develop the community in a way which is supportive of black people who wish to join general neighbourhood, that is non-sectional, groups? And how does the community worker support the formation of black or ethnic groups as a way of representing the personal and collective interests of black people?

Clearly, there is a further question which connects these two: how far is the development of black/ethnic groups a precondition for black residents to succeed in entering, and to function effec- tively within, non-sectional neighbourhood groups?

How Does the Community Worker Develop the Community in a Way which is Supportive of Black People Who Wish to Join Neighbourhood Groups?

At heart, this question is about how white community workers work with neighbourhood groups that are dominated by white members so that they become open to, and supportive of, black people who wish to join them. We have reviewed in preceding chapters the factors that work against black residents taking up membership in neighbourhood groups; not only do we find that a low level of involvement is predicted by matters such as class, employment and home-ownership, but the limited accounts published by community workers are more often about failures than about successes. They also indicate that the involvement of blacks in neighbourhood groups cannot be considered separately from the existence of black or ethnic groups; this is certainly indicated in the three accounts of successful multi-racial organizing (all of which took place in the north-west of England) that are to be found in the British literature, and which offer something akin to practical advice to community workers.

Robin Ward (1979) in writing about his work in Moss Side in the late 1960s suggests the following guidelines:

- there must be no overt competition between ethnic groups for scarce resources;
- in order for neighbourhood groups to be multi-racial they must be seen to be overtly and publicly anti-racist through, for example, statements made in their literature, the press and those made in public meetings by their leadership;
- there must be a settled and long-standing multi-racial community, with a relatively homogeneous social base in terms of class and status;
- a range of different organizational forms emerge to represent different issues;
- new organizations are more likely to become multi-racial rather than established, existing ones. The creation of new groups is more effective than trying to adapt old ones.

All of these points are useful and some address the perennial dilemma of the community worker about whether to by-pass moribund groups, particularly those on housing estates. Ward's comments about a variety of organizational forms echo the experience of many American organizations: the more issues you have, the more people will get involved if they can find the right vehicle for themselves. His comments about competition are intriguing to the extent that community action is one of the areas of livelihood where conflict and competition between groups (in one neighbourhood, or between neighbourhoods) is played out.

Ensor and his colleagues (1982) also write from their experience in Manchester. They began by listing seven factors that ought to influence the strategies of a worker in organizing in multi-ethnic areas:

- the nature of the community;
- the organizations promoted by the workers;
- the worker's ethnic background and experience;
- the nature of the employing agency and the role played by the local state in the area;

- the implication for the worker's role and function of being employed by the local state;
- wider ideological issues to do with racism and feminism.

But much like Ward, their paper is concerned only with the first two factors, and they offer the following advice at the conclusion to their case-study:

- Be wary of assuming any community of interest based on a broad ethnic category or particular locality. Consider differences between groups, and how these are increased or reduced by wider economic and political pressures.
- In most cases give priority to separate ethnic organization and provision.
- Be sparing in your encouragement of links between groups on a formal organizational basis.
- Collective forms of class or black unity are not likely to be effective without:

  (i) prior work on the level of separate ethnic groups;
  (ii) the kinds of issues which will be perceived across all groups as significant;
  (iii) an issue that is capable of being tackled effectively at a local level through joint action.

There is a way in which these last two points about 'the issue' reflect the comment made by Ward about competition over resources. There is a skill here in helping groups and individuals to work together over non-divisible public benefits, or for multi-purpose facilities; other than this, it is hard to deduce what the criteria are for an issue that will be perceived by all as significant *and* be capable of being worked at through joint action at a local level. Part of the real difficulty for the white community worker is how he ever finds out how people in other ethnic groups perceive and rank what is significant to their livelihood. How do they rank issues of livelihood that are amenable to collective *local* action against (1) issues of livelihood (for example, racial harassment) more amenable to collective (usually ethnic) city-wide or national action; and (2) issues that the individual can deal with on his or her own, or does not want to make public, such as legal status, unemployment, political or family problems in the home country, cultural and religious values and so forth. The PSI study tells us that the issues of major importance to black informants were racial discrimination in employment and housing, their treatment by the police, and the quality of their own or their children's education (Brown, 1984). In general, a half of West Indian and Asian informants said that life in Britain had become worse for their ethnic group; while a large part of this evaluation was explained by the effects of the country's economic decline, 'a substantial proportion of informants volunteered an explanation in terms of a worsening of their position relative to white people, under the heading of differential unemployment, racial discrimination, racialism and racialist organisations, or racial attacks'. We can see from this range of responses by the informants in Brown's study that many of the most important areas of dissatisfaction for black people do not easily, if at all, lend themselves to the kind of locally based forms of action with which community workers are mainly concerned.

Part of our learning from experiences in Holland with ethnic minority organizing is that issues have *both* to be close to the imperatives of daily life *and* to offer very few possibilities for individual solution. Since many of these imperatives are to do with survival – with legal status, racism, employment, finding a roof and so on – then not even issues such as play facilities or pollution of the environment are seen as being sufficiently close to daily life. Thus shared agendas between whites and blacks may be non-existent or limited where the material conditions of whites are better because they will already have secured those necessities that are imperative to a decent livelihood, but which remain unattained, or seem unattainable, to members of ethnic minorities.

The third north-west case-study that is courageous enough to draw conclusions and offer advice is that of Alan Barr (1980) based on his experience in Oldham Community Development Project. His advice to workers is as follows:

- Recognize regional and national differences, and those between states, and those between smaller areas like islands.
- Work with younger people because there will be fewer problems about language, education and sex roles. They are less

acquiescent, and more likely to judge their material standards and civil rights by those of this country; for similar reasons work with people with an urban and not a rural background.

- The worker may have to work with elites, that is, those with enough worldliness and sophistication to be comfortable with people from other ethnic groups.
- Foster cultural identification with the agents of change through ethnic workers or co-workers, translation, use of social networks and so on.
- Organize Asians through offering an individual advice and information service.
- Find a common self-interest across ethnic groups by

  (i) a detailed community analysis;
  (ii) looking at the needs of each ethnic group, and helping them to solve these first through an ethnic group approach;
  (iii) a careful educational process that involves working frankly on internal divisions and stereotypes, and in looking at the effects of immigration and causes of poverty outside the neighbourhood.

- Both groups and the community workers must see multi-ethnic groups as ways to build co-operative activity, not because integration as such is a goal, but because only co-operative behaviour can lead to mutual information and education which might foster a greater degree of mutual tolerance.
- The level of participation will be affected by whether ethnic groups are, or see themselves as, a minority; this depends on which variable the worker chooses to highlight – colour, nationality, language, religion or age.

Barr has produced a useful chart which shows for the area of Oldham in which he was working 'the way in which groups may, under different circumstances in relation to different variables, move in and out of minority status on the basis of the range of groups with whom they are able to associate or feel affinity as a result of common interests'. For example, a small group of Indian Christians in a town will become part of the majority if the organization is around religion. Community workers can thus

Table 6.1

Variable	Majority	Minority
Colour	Non-white Pakistani, Bangladeshi, West Indian	White British, Irish, East European
Nationality	Immigrant Pakistani, Bangladeshi, West Indian, East European, Irish	Non-immigrant British
Language	English speaking British, West Indian, Irish	Non-English speaking Pakistani, Bangladeshi, East European
Religion	Christian British, West Indian, Irish, East European	Muslim Pakistani, Bangladeshi
Age	Youthful West Indian, Pakistani, Bangladeshi, Irish	Elderly British, East European

Source: Barr, 1980.

influence which variable around which to organize, and so determine whether a particular ethnic group is a minority or not. Table 6.1 shows Barr's data.

There are accounts in the American literature that support the 'Manchester–Oldham guidelines'. Morrison (1983), for example, lists the following factors that influence 'bi-racial interaction' in community activities:

- equal status of the participants;
- the development of a numer of different organizational forms;
- work on small-scale problems, not large-scale remedial goals, that are essentially neighbourhood-based concerns, and amenable to local action;
- the existence of informal networks and neighbouring between black and white residents (this, of course, reinforces our point about basing community action on community interaction, and the link between the quality of the overall social structure and the character of sectional relations in a neighbourhood, for example, between black and white);

- a positive community self-image, particularly based on the type and tenure of housing and neighbourhood facilities;
- that the opportunities for working together offer blacks and whites genuine possibilities for self-determination.

Like other writers, Morrison also indicates that black and white co-operation in the neighbourhood is more likely to occur and be sustained when it is focused on task-achievement, rather than on social goals, and where blacks and whites are engaged together in a problem-solving process that involves learning, self-training and evaluation. Ethnic minorities are more likely to look to their own groups and extended families for social and recreational needs and, given a scarcity of time and energy, may give priority to realizable tasks that will directly and immediately affect livelihood, and which do not seem achievable by individual means.

But the primacy of task is two-edged for the community worker. Ethnic minorities may be more attuned to specific, task-focused neighbourhood groups. But such groups may be so preoccupied with task that they may be unwilling or unable to change in order to make membership possible for ethnic minorities. Task-dominated groups may not have the time or sensitivity for the expressive and maintenance sides of group life. Another consideration is that neighbourhood groups who are focused on providing advice, advocacy and services are almost inevitably excluding (both of blacks and whites), because the nature of their work requires expertise and leadership, rather than participation, and this will inevitably be located in a small group of experienced people. Moreover, such people may 'cling to their seats' to continue to enjoy the personal satisfaction and power that such expertise and leadership brings.

The fact that such task- or expert-dominated groups contain a small number of participants may be an added inhibition to blacks who wish to join them; Davies (1979), for example, has indicated from research that in joining and staying in groups blacks are influenced by the intimacy and size of the group: the smaller the group, the more black people wanted other blacks as members, and the less comfortable they felt about working with whites.

Intimacy is related not only to the size of a group but to the formality and structure with which it carries out its work. It may be, then, that some blacks may be more attracted to neighbourhood groups with clear, explicit and unambiguous goals, and which stress formality and convention in conducting business. (However, the inhibiting effect of formal procedure has been noted by Ellis, 1985). Groups that know how to use nominal and other structured exercises for discussion and decision-making (Delbecq and Van de Ven 1971, 1981) may also be successful in reducing the 'intimacy deterrent'. Intimacy is, of course, an issue for whites that we have discussed in different ways throughout this book.

The notion of intimacy provides us with a convenient bridge between the community group and another matter: the 'nature' of the agency employing a white community worker in a multi-racial neighbourhood. It appears from some research (for example, Jenkins, 1980) that the more 'intimate' an agency the more success its staff will have in working with minority groups. In this context, we use the word intimate differently, to stress how far minority groups will feel comfortable in using an agency, how welcome, safe and at home they will feel. Thus community workers from a locally based agency that is culturally in tune with ethnic minorities may be more effective in their work; for Jenkins the 'cultural content' of an agency's presence is connected with its use of ethnic food, art, music and history. (We might assume the same for neighbourhood groups, particularly tenants' associations and community centres, where the worker wants to make these more relevant to ethnic minorities in a neighbourhood.)

The cultural content of a worker's agency is also related to the ethnicity of the director, the ethnic composition of the staff (not least of front-line and receptionist staff) and the colour and ethnicity of the board responsible for the overall running of the agency or project. It is clear that for any of these factors to be salient in organizing, then the agency must have a visible and accessible local base. Furthermore, workers must be prepared to work anywhere and at any time – not just in their local office, but in houses, shops, and work-places, and at times that take note of the local patterns of shift-working amongst ethnic groups in a neighbourhood.

It is clear from both British and American experience that the community worker is more likely to be effective in helping black people to organize amongst themselves, or with whites, only when she is prepared to work through individual cases towards collective action, and to be imaginative in working through different cultural forums that bring people together, such as plays, music, and widely known myths and traditions in a group's religion or folklore. Both these factors may suggest an integrated or multi-disciplinary approach to working with ethnic minorities, so that the community worker and her colleagues are actively seeking out cases and issues, using a mixed team of care workers, advice workers, organizers and para-professionals. To organize effectively, it might be necessary to work simultaneously on a wide range of needs within an ethnic group, building up the standing of the local agency and the credibility of the individual community worker. Community workers adopt a compartmentalized view of need at their peril and this is especially the case in organizing ethnic minorities around local issues to do with livelihood.

The development and active use of community resources and networks by the community worker and other agency staff is another factor to be taken into account in successful organizing. This is both because the legitimacy and resources for community action will derive from these networks, and because they indicate how the (white) worker recognizes and values their function within a black community. In much the same way, the white worker must understand and pay proper attention to culturally prescribed rituals, such as formal greetings at the start or end of an encounter, or expectations about eating, drinking, and hospitality when visiting houses. The worker may not succeed if she fails to understand the differences between ethnic groups, and between blacks and whites, in indicating agreement and disagreement, deference and compliance, respect and admonition.

The most extended treatment of social networks and cultural values that is readily available for British readers is that of Rivera and Erlich (1981). They advise strongly against the traditional style of organizing amongst black communities:

The so-called mobilization style of organizing (set up shop in relation to a particular issue, mobilize around it, win what you can and get out) will not work. Developing the trust necessary to fully understand, appreciate and gain access to social networks is going to take a lot of time and patience, much of it beyond the normal work day. Some activities border on the quasi-legal and involve economic exchanges that keep money in the community rather than flowing to outsiders. One organizing key will be to figure out ways of building up existing social networks rather than generating new structures that will undermine these networks – as some of our community action agencies did during the 'War on Poverty'. Rather than beginning with the problems, weaknesses and inadequacies of these communities, our analysis suggests that strengths are to be noted first and foremost, and looked upon as the basis for organization-building.

They suggest that the community worker must use churches, shops that are centres for information exchange and discussion, and social networks which in many ethnic communities are not only supportive in a hostile environment, but are also tied into the economy of the community and provide for access to information and contacts, the communication of expectations, and an 'orientation to getting things done to improve one's lot'. They warn that:

> the kind of organizing we are talking about cannot be done by anyone simply with the 'proper motivation'. A deep and sensitive cultural awareness is required. Bilinguality is clearly preferred, although supportive roles for English-speaking mono-linguals may well emerge. For certain Black and Native American communities bicultural experience and deep respect may take the place of specific linguistic skills. A full appreciation of a group's culture will most often require thorough knowledge of its historical experience – including traditions, political upheavals and folkways.

Their article analyses ethnic communities as neo-*Gemeinschaft* communities; their chart (Table 6.2) indicates how in such communities the strategy for community organization must adapt to the particular character of seven key structural variables. Such an

Table 6.2. Structural Variables in *Gesellschaft* and neo-*Gemeinschaft* Communities and their Implications for Community Organizing Strategies

Variables	*Gesellschaft* communities	Neo-*Gemeinschaft* communities	Implications for community organizing strategies
Culture (ethnicity)	The dominant society with culture and traditions not having a strong ethnic identification. English – main if only language spoken and no strong ties or identification with another country. Basically anglo population.	Relatively homogeneous. English not spoken much or a street variant of it. Strong traditions from the homeland making for isolated, autonomous pockets of Little Tokyos, Havanas, etc.	Knowledge of culture not enough, should be part of the culture and bilingual. Sensitive to cultural patterns and traditions. An appreciative posture a necessity.
Social structure	Vertical. Limited extended family networks with no experience of oppression or racism.	Horizontal. Shared experience of racism and oppression. Many extended family networks.	Ethnic and cultural membership helps in understanding the complexities of the social structure, helps to provide access to family networks.
Power structure	Mainly externally elite and vertical in nature. Community gives up its power in favour of 'institutional trust'.	Mainly internally pluralistic, decision-making usually by consensus. No trust of outside power blocs and their institutions.	Knowledge of power analysis, the formation of coalitions, 'winnable' issues and knowledge of power blocs inside and outside the community.

Table 6.2. Continued

Variables	Gesellschaft communities	Neo-Gemeinschaft communities	Implications for community organizing strategies
Leadership patterns	Leadership by political culture and party system. Extended influence and authority. Charisma and personalism less important.	Charismatic leaders, *personalismo*, strong feelings of alienation and anomie. Sphere of influence limited to that community.	Knowledge of and respect for the leadership patterns of the culture. An understanding of horizontal and consensual decision-making, and leadership by age and wisdom.
Economics	All levels of economic ladder, but a strong middle class and much vertical mobility. Limited, if any, labour market segmentation.	Marginal to poor level of existence. Strong interdependence. Bartering for survival. Welfare a constant reality and reminder of their situation. Major contributors to labour market segmentation.	A thorough understanding of political economy and the need for a progressive analysis of same. The ability to identify short- and long-term issues so as to lessen failure. Knowledge of employment, housing and community development strategies.
Physical appearance	No unique 'flavour' to the communities. A variety of housing patterns.	Strong ethnic flavour in signs, newspapers, magazines. Smells of different foods unique to the homeland. Run-down tenements and substandard housing.	Ability to understand the language and being part of the culture a necessity.
Social networks	Less formal when present. Usually a 'conscious' decision is made in developing them.	Strong and quite formal. Usually an integral part of the culture.	Ability to understand the language, relate to the culture and respect for network changes.

analysis is less useful in the British situation, where the extent of the residential segregation of whites and blacks is nowhere like that present in the United States; nevertheless, their comments about social networks and institutions have been amplified by British workers such as Ensor *et al.* (1982) and Barr (1980). Such networks are not limited to a particular neighbourhood but literally stretch across the world. They may be latent, or not observable to the white outsider, and may become obvious only through critical events happening in the neighbourhood, in the city or in the home country. Key people in these networks are often shopkeepers and professionals, and, as Barr and others have noted, this obliges the community worker to work with 'elites' in a community, and to understand, particularly within an Asian community, its entrepreneurial fabric and the points of economic influence and leverage.

We can summarize the first section on how to support black people to join neighbourhood groups with the comment of one community worker we interviewed: 'You just have to do good community work even better.' She believed that encouraging black residents to risk membership of community groups demanded extra effort in the jobs that were always necessary to do good community work. Meetings had to be properly publicized in different languages and through existing networks and gatekeepers; the times and venues of meetings were important (certainly not in pubs or centres with bars if Muslims were to be involved); making special efforts to go round and accompany people to meetings; a good deal of time and patience was needed, staying power, and the will not to be rushed into deciding who to work with and on what issues; making sure that (white) cliques didn't hold on to information, or change meetings at the last minute. Being a gatekeeper in a meeting (a traditional non-directive role) meant being extra good in making sure that black voices and demands were heard and understood. And you could not divorce people's membership of a group from the services it was willing to offer to them; if a community centre or tenants' hall was open on Sundays for social events or marriages, and offered facilities for prayer, it was more likely that Asian people in a neighbourhood would be more inclined to go to it for meetings of groups.

How Does the Community Worker Support the Formation of Black/Ethnic Groups as a Way of Representing the Personal and Political Interest of Black People in a Neighbourhood?

The sting in this question is in both the head and the tail. There is a particular question to be addressed in this section about the *white* community worker and her or his role in black groups; and, in the tail, there is an emphasis on how far it is possible for black groups to deal with issues of livelihood that appear as neighbourhood issues, rather than ones that can be addressed at a city, regional or national level. There is, too, the matter of the difference between 'black groups' and 'ethnic groups'; the former occur where black people from different ethnic groups unite in a common cause, whereas the latter phrase refers to the organization of black people within their own separate groupings. The differences between the black unity process, the ethnic organization process, and the class unity process have been discussed by Lawrence (1975) and by Miles and Phizacklea (1977). Ensor and his colleagues (1982) have reviewed practice and have come to the conclusion that 'we have discovered few examples of effective *and* sustained community-level action based on forms of "class" or "black" unity in Britain at a local or wider level'.

True unity of blacks has been more evident in major national events and trade union activities than in collaboration over neighbourhood issues, but much of this national activity did not continue much beyond the late 1970s. Part of Sivanandan's explanation for this was the transition that occurred from the black struggle to the anti-racist struggle, and the 'rise and rise of ethnicity':

And when, after the general election of 1979, the Anti-Nazi League (its mission accomplished) disbanded, the issues of racism and fascism had become separated, and the joint struggles of Asians and Afro-Caribbeans likewise. The black struggle (for community and class) was becoming more narrowly a struggle against racism, and the anti-racist struggle itself was tending to divide into struggles that concerned Asians (mainly) and the struggles that concerned Afro-Caribbeans (mainly) . . .

There was no *black* community. The promotion of cultural separatism (euphemistically known as cultural diversity or multiculturalism) was keeping Asians and Afro-Caribbeans apart; the development of a youth culture and a women's culture were further de-composing forces within the community, without, as yet, realigning them in a new black configuration; and the emergence of an Afro-Caribbean managerial class in the race relations industry (and sub-managers in the nationalised self-help groups), together with the flowering of Ugandan Asian entrepreneurship, were breaking up community into class. (*1985*)

There are considerable difficulties in uniting different ethnic groups within a single black organization. The differences between Afro-Caribbean and Asian populations are based on a range of factors, including those to do with language, religion, culture and, often, class. The existence of prejudice and racialism amongst Asians towards Afro-Caribbeans is not to be disregarded. Within the Afro-Caribbean and Asian populations, there are significant differences based on country and religion, on caste and class, and on island and region, town and countryside. Other cleavages within the black British population are based on age, gender and generation, and differences in the interests of those in, and those out of, work. The common experience of colour, or of class, and of white racism may thus be negated in their potential to unify by a range of factors that make for separation of interests and disunity.

Another factor that must be considered in looking at the processes of black and ethnic unity is the geographical distribution of the black British population. We noted in the previous chapter that most black people still live in areas where the majority of the population is white; indeed, Brown's PSI study also noted some indications of movement of black households (particularly West Indian) into areas that were exclusively white or with low or medium densities of black households. But the process of black unity must be hampered by the fact that the geographical distribution of Asians and West Indians overlaps only to a limited extent; the PSI study indicates that:

Two-thirds of Asian households live in a group of areas in which we find only one third of the West Indian households, and vice versa. Much of the difference can be explained by different regional and inter-urban settlement patterns, but residential segregation of this type also arises within towns and cities. (Brown, 1984)

In London, for example, the Asian group as a whole is less concentrated in the inner boroughs than the West Indian group; however, the Bangladeshi group is concentrated in inner London, African Asians and Sikhs are concentrated in the outer boroughs, while Pakistanis have the same inner–outer mix as the white population. The fact that different Asian groups have chosen to settle in different parts of the United Kingdom must also be taken into account in assessing the process of ethnic unity within the Asian group as a whole.

The white community worker with a focus on a small area is more likely to be involved in supporting separate ethnic organizations, rather than a process of black unity. But in many such areas there are difficult problems of organization if the numbers of people from each ethnic group are not sufficient to sustain the work of an organization, or to give it political influence. Here again we have to consider the effect of the geographical distribution and concentration of ethnic groups. A greater proportion of Asian than West Indian households live in enumeration districts with concentrations of their own ethnic group above 30 per cent (Brown, 1984); this data is suggestive of possible difficulties that Afro-Caribbeans may have in generating at a local level sufficient numbers to sustain community participation based on their own group. But the possibility of similar difficulties is also to be noted within the Asian group as a whole: it is only Pakistanis and Bangladeshis that are particularly likely to be found in enumeration districts with concentrations of their own group above 30 per cent; both Indians and African Asians, on the other hand, are more likely to be found in enumeration districts that contain proportionately few Asians.

In such situations, people from ethnic groups have a number

of alternatives. They can join with whites in organizations. They can work with blacks from other ethnic groups. Experience so far suggests that this might be more effective if different groups work together in an umbrella arrangement rather than the merging of individuals into one large group. Or they can join with people from their ethnic group from other parts of a borough or city so that the action they take together no longer has a neighbourhood dimension. This makes sense on many issues, but not necessarily on issues which are of significance in only one particular area or estate.

Some of the difficulties that come from the numbers of people that are needed to sustain effective action may become more obvious when local authorities decentralize services and decision-making (Ouseley (1985) has discussed some of the issues about racism and decentralization). Where decision-making is at a local level, the possibilities of working through borough or city-wide organizations may be fewer, and black residents will have to look to more local collaboration with whites and other blacks to influence locally based decision-makers. The possibilities of a local ethnic organization are also determined by the overlap of ethnicity with territory within small neighbourhoods; as Chris saw in Holland (and as we observed in some Belgian cities), where particular ethnic groups are present in substantial numbers in certain streets within a neighbourhood, this allows organizations to be established around both ethnicity and territory. The role of the community worker here is to help ethnic groups organize on a street basis and to relate to each other and to 'white' streets; and to help the different ethnic groups and white groups to work together on issues that affect all the streets in the neighbourhood as a whole. The forging of 'contracts' between ethnic groups for specific purposes appears more feasible in this kind of situation than attempts at an all-embracing 'black unity' organization.

The worker has also to recognize that such ethnic groups may be better organized than those of their white neighbours, simply because their cohesion is aided by religious and cultural ties, common origins and relationships in the home country, and by their minority status in a white society. On the other hand, such groups may be divided by internal political rivalries that derive from home-country politics, divisions the worker may find it difficult to detect and understand.

The involvement of black people in their own ethnic groups is important in its own right, as a legitimate part of the local demo-cratic process and as a means to improving matters of livelihood; but such involvement also has another value. It may be seen as a way of giving *individuals* the confidence and support to work with whites and blacks from other ethnic groups in general neighbourhood groups such as tenants' associations. Taking part in a group that is dominated by white people and interests may be less burdensome to a black person who is going, not as an individual, but as a representative from his or her own ethnic organization; and who has already built up skills and confidence in committee and group work through prior membership of an ethnic organization.

In much the same way, the existence of 'black sections' of ten-ants' organizations, or the development of black groups or 'front-room cells' on a housing estate, must be recognized not just in terms of achieving a specific task but also for their part in a process through which the skills, confidence and sense of legitimacy of black people to take up membership in other com-munity activities and local politics are extended.

The Role of the White Community Worker

There are three possible strategies for the white community worker in the development of black/ethnic organizations.

First, there is the *'avoidance' strategy*, through which the white worker avoids working with groups in ways which col-onize or disrupt them, or which impede the emergence of organizational abilities, and the willingness to act. The avoi-dance strategy implies that the worker 'de-colonizes' his previ-ous training and work experience so that ways of working that are based on assumptions about the white working class are not carried over unthinkingly to work with ethnic minorities. Avoiding insensitive judgements about sex role, religion, and so forth, and about culturally derived ways of thinking and work-ing, are part of this strategy.

Secondly, the *indirect strategy*. This strategy is based on the question: what is the relationship between the effective functioning of ethnic organizations and the general social construction of a locality? Workers who pursue this strategy do so because they believe that neighbourhoods which contain a flourishing number of organizations and networks are more likely to give rise to active ethnic organizations. The strategy implies the development of social networks and groups in a locality because this will indirectly facilitate the emergence of ethnic organizations. This strategy is attractive to white workers because it enables them to work with white residents and groups rather than, or as well as, working directly with ethnic minorities. In other words, the indirect strategy assumes that an interacting community produces a more supportive environment for the work of ethnic organizations than a nominal community.

Thirdly, the *direct strategy*, in which the white worker works on a face-to-face basis with black people and with ethnic organizations. The basis of this strategy involves both 'doing good community work better', and recognizing and acting upon (1) the cultural limitations of a white worker with an ethnic organization and (2) the different needs and ways of working with which an ethnic organization might expect help. To do good community work better is necessary but not sufficient because different cultural expectations about need and about organizing will require that the white worker adapts *his* expectations and ways of working. Problems about language and about knowledge of religion and culture; lack of information about how dynamics in a group are affected by events and relationships in the whole ethnic community; difficulties with expectation about roles, authority and leadership – all these and many more may mean that the white worker is limited in his usefulness. One consequence of this is that he may have to set a much lower level of performance or competence for himself. For instance, the white worker may have to focus on task rather than on process and, in particular, may have to do far more practical tasks than he might have expected to do with a white working-class group. One worker in our study expressed this as 'not only doing more but leading more', particularly in making relationships between members of ethnic groups and key people in, for example, the local authority.

Other white workers have commented on how their contribution has been more significant in helping to set up ethnic organizations, rather than in the later stage of sustaining them in their work. Roles in this formative stage include acting as a consultant on resources, helping to design a committee structure and procedures, assisting with grant applications, spreading information around the group, and trying to ensure, not always with success, that as many people as possible participate, not just those who already have leadership status within the ethnic community. There is sometimes a particular problem about the difference in status and class between those who become leaders and those in the rest of the group.

There are three other important tasks for the white community worker as part of the direct strategy for working with ethnic organizations. The first is to ensure that the organization has viable connections to its constituency, and that the group has a meaningful reality to those people whom it claims to represent or provide advice and services to. What matters most is not simply the *existence* of ethnic organizations, but the numbers of people who participate in, or generally understand and support, their activities and purposes.

The second is to ensure the connections of black/ethnic organizations to local political processes, and to influential leaders and organizations in the borough, city or region in which they operate. There seems little point in extolling the virtues of ethnic organizations or, for that matter, in black people joining them, if they either choose or are forced to exist within a political vacuum, lacking or being denied the legitimacy and channels of communication to influence decisions within the sphere of local politics.

The third task is to ensure the connections of ethnic organizations both to each other and to white-dominated groups in the same area. Such communications are necessary in order (1) to work together on issues that affect all neighbourhood residents, and (2) to work out agreements about how livelihood is to be jointly managed. These connections between groups are necessary both to negotiate conflicts and differences, and to give a coherent picture to those outside the neighbourhood about its needs and requirements. The development of relations between groups is part of the vitality of an interacting community and, as such, relations between community organizations need to be approached not as once-off or crisis-inspired events but as part of a continuing process liable to considerable difficulties and setbacks.

The effectiveness of ethnic organizations in local politics, their connections to other ethnic organizations and to other white or multi-ethnic neighbourhood groups, and the extent to which they are supported by black people are major concerns to the white community worker. He or she must be interested in whether ethnic organizations give ordinary people a grip on locality-based issues that affect their livelihood. Workers cannot be content with the symbolic value that is sometimes attached to the mere existence of ethnic groups by both black activists and white politicians and administrators; or with the fact that some ethnic groups may be extremely useful in pursuing broader issues of social policy and racial justice but have little relevance to the day-to-day concerns of black people about issues around them that effect their well-being.

It is necessary to say this because well-intentioned white administrators and politicians are often so desperate to find an easily negotiated means of access to 'the black community' that they force, or collude with, ethnic groups to become spokespeople for the 'whole black community', rather than recognizing them as but one voice amongst various ethnic minority communities. This speaking for the whole black community is inevitably a process of detachment from ordinary people and their interests; black oligarchies can form and rigidify and, in these circumstances, the community worker must confront both white politicians and black leaders with questions about constituencies and representation. There is not much evidence available to support a view that ordinary black people are any more involved in local ethnic groups than they are in general community groups; extravagant claims about the organization of the black community are another degradation of the black struggle, for they provide yet further opportunities for white and black organizers to escape their responsibility for organizing ordinary black people around locality-relevant issues of livelihood.

Gurnah provides an example of such extravagance that spoils

an otherwise penetrating article on racism awareness training. He writes of the period after the '1981 rebellions' and refers to 'the evident black unity'. He compounds this trifling extravagance by writing further of 'the black community' (whatever and wherever that is):

> The most sustained and the most effective initiatives against racism are already taking place in the black community. Most black communities have set up advice centres, work associations . . . and social clubs. There are also a number of formal and informal black political organisations such as the *Asian Youth Movement* and *Rastafarian* collectives . . .
>
> (1984)

Such claims are an example of 'black speak', and they wilfully ignore the painful fact that, with few exceptions, the majority of ordinary black people are not involved in local forms of collective action that are either ethnically or multi-ethnically based.

It is often said that the spread and effectiveness of black organizations cannot be apparent to white observers and that, in any case, much organization in black communities is based around much looser networks, ties, and patterns of mutual aid and obligation. Such networks and mutual aid systems are, of course, a substantial element of life in many Afro-Caribbean and Asian communities. Criticisms of the lack of involvement of ordinary black people in organized forms of local collective action are often deflected by pointing to the preference amongst many ethnic groups for working through networks and unstructured forms of co-operation and help. Such criticisms are also deflected by pointing out that religious and cultural activities in some Asian groups have a significant political content that should not be disregarded by the white community worker. We have already pointed out that effective organizing must be based on knowledge and use of these networks; but what is equally important for the worker is not whether these networks exist (for they do) but whether or not they give people an influence on those factors that bear on livelihood (such as inadequate housing) and that may be amenable to local forms of problem-solving. In other words, the community worker must not be complacent about assurances concerning ethnic minority networks but must ask such questions as:

- how many people are involved in, and can expect support from, these networks?
- are they more relevant to some age groups and some parts of the life-cycle than others?
- do they support people in marginal positions such as the unemployed?
- in which ethnic groups are networks and co-operative systems at their strongest and weakest?
- do these networks touch upon all, or only some, aspects of livelihood?
- are these networks diffuse or are they highly concentrated in particular parts of a city or neighbourhood?

These kinds of question will help the worker better to understand the numbers of people likely to be excluded from networks or informal forms of co-operation, and the kinds of issues with which such networks might be less or more effective than organized forms of collective action.

A number of issues and opportunities have been identified in this chapter about the role of the white worker in supporting black individuals and black organizations. There is no doubt that the difficulties facing white community workers are complex, particularly in areas or at times when factors outside their control (rising unemployment, police activities and so forth) have worsened black–white relationships. The experience of some practitioners also suggests that white workers find Asian groups more receptive to offers to help than Afro-Caribbean ones. Some of these difficulties point to the need for co-working with community workers from ethnic minority groups, and there are many useful examples of co-working: the Rochdale Community Project, for instance.

The appointment of black community workers (who comprise some 13 per cent of UK community workers; see Francis *et al.*, 1984) ought to be a major part of a strategy to support the development of black/ethnic groups and the participation of black people in other kinds of community activities. The feasibility of co-working depends in part on how far college and field-based training opportunities are being made available to black trainees, and in part on how far in-service training is available for both white and black workers. There seems to be little point in appointing black people to community work posts if they have been denied opportunities to acquire the necessary skills and support to be effective in their work.

The benefits to be derived from having more black community workers in post would likewise be vitiated by placing them in agencies that remained, in the eyes of ethnic minorities, 'white agencies' serving white interests. The appointment of a single black community worker in a white agency is often a recipe for frustration and conflict, not least because of the amount and range of work to be done; if black community workers are to be an effective part of an overall strategy of support to black people then their appointment must be considered as part of a more radical change in the way their agency is staffed, and its overall services delivered. This will help to avoid situations in which black workers or black projects are expected to be the only ones who take on work with black people and 'black issues', and in which they are not expected by white colleagues to work at all with white groups or on general issues that cut across ethnic lines. Another consequence of seeing black workers only as resources to black groups, is that it allows white staff to escape from their responsibilities for work on white racism, and for challenging institutional forms of racism in their own and other organizations.

The problems and issues facing black workers have been described in a number of articles (see, for example, Lambat, 1980). Such a worker is seen by authorities as an 'insider' but because of his employment (particularly within a state agency) he may be seen by ethnic groups as an 'outsider'. There is the risk that he or she will be treated only as a go-between, a messenger-boy and translator, and as the fount of all knowledge on 'ethnic issues'. The black community worker faces, too, the difficulty of being cast in opposition to established leadership within an ethnic community. As with white community workers, much of his or her role will be basic and task-centred – reading and writing letters, translating, making appointments, providing advice and information on who and how to influence, and working through individual cases towards organized action.

There is little doubt that a black community worker is a considerable asset in many specific situations, where, for example, a knowledge of language, culture, religion and the boundaries of sex roles is essential. In relating to the black community, the worker will be judged not just by his/her sex, but by age, qualifications, experience and the status of the employer. No single black worker could be acceptable to all ethnic communities, and the acceptance of a black worker even within her own ethnic group would be influenced in part by the extent of religious and political factionalism within the group. Because of these and other factors, the appointment of ethnic community workers must not be regarded as an easy and straightforward solution to organizing with black people. Indeed, if one of the objectives of an agency is to promote an interacting community (and to aid black organization indirectly by developing networks and groups in general) then it has to be recognized that the black worker will face similar (and other) problems in relating to the white population to those that other white colleagues face in respect of the black.

The efforts of both white and black community workers to support black people in their participation in community activities are more likely to be successful when local authorities have changed their own attitudes and procedures, and when they have worked with neighbourhood groups to develop a code of practice for anti-racism. The public statements and practices of local authorities, and of large voluntary organizations, can be crucial in defining what is expected of neighbourhood groups, and in setting a climate which is supportive of black people's attempts to take up public roles and responsibilities in their locality.

Local authorities are in a position to encourage an anti-racist code of practice amongst neighbourhood groups (and other voluntary organizations) who are in receipt of grants and the secondment of staff, and which require other services from a council such as the attendance of officers at meetings. The elements of this code of practice for tenants' associations and other neighbourhood groups would include

- a requirement to make public statements about anti-racism both in meetings and in the publications of a group, including explicit statements on its letter-heads of an anti-racist position;
- equal opportunities in the employment and training of any staff;
- a refutation of racial harassment, and a public statement of intention to work with the council in identifying and dealing with racist individuals and families;
- the adoption of a model constitution.

Neighbourhood groups who do not satisfy a local authority in elaborating and adhering to such a code of practice would be at risk of sanctions. Some of these are outlined in a paper on racial harassment by one London borough:

> There are several remedies open to the Council if it wants to take action against TA's which do not adopt the new model constitution. Some of these (or a combination of all or some of them) are:
>
>   (i) not to accept a TA as the recognised body for consultation on matters of housing management as outlined by the Housing Act 1980;
> (ii) not to allow them rent free use of a hall or room;
> (iii) not to allow them use of any Council facilities even at a commercial rent;
> (iv) not to allow them to decide on how environmental improvement money should be spent, as at present, and not to make any other grants of money from the Council.

It would be a matter of judgement whether the existence of such sanctions would force groups into adopting an anti-racist constitution, or whether they would turn their back on the council and become isolated. Of course, the mere adoption of such a constitution is only a necessary and not a sufficient step, as Manning and Ohri indicate.

> A further anti-racist position with which community workers collude is that of assisting community groups and tenants' associations to adopt constitutions which make declarations

of intent not to discriminate on the grounds of race. Both the community worker and the group then delude themselves that they are not racist because the constitution says so. On the other hand, there is no effort to monitor what positive action is being taken to ensure equal access to all. (*1982*)

The monitoring of neighbourhood groups could become a built-in part of a council's relationship with the voluntary sector; this would include the monitoring of groups for the ethnicity of their members, committee and staff. Such monitoring could be done through sample surveys or through insisting that such information be routinely provided as part of grant applications. Such applications might also include a requirement to say how specific services or projects would benefit ethnic minority groups.

Not only do the anti-racist statements and practices of groups have to be monitored, but time and expertise must be made available to explain the purposes and value of anti-racist constitutions to members of neighbourhood groups; it is just as important to help groups think through how their usual practices might have to change, and to support these groups as they experiment with ways of implementing their code of practice. This implies that extra resources have to be made available, and that relevant staff in local authorities and voluntary agencies must be encouraged to examine their own attitudes and practices. The development of a multi-racial housing staff and the application of an appropriate lettings policy would also help to create an environment where black participation in groups was encouraged. Some local authorities are also considering the appointment of specialist workers to help black tenants to participate in tenants' associations, and to set up borough-wide organizations of black tenants.

Perhaps the single important factor affecting participation and other matters relating to livelihood is a council's practices on racial harassment. Appropriate action includes the following elements:

– the modification of tenancy agreements to define racial harassment as a cause for action against a tenant;

- the re-possession of accommodation, and the prosecution of offending families;
- support for victims in taking court proceedings;
- immediate repairs to property damaged in attacks;
- the removal of graffiti and other signs of racial abuse;
- the provision to each tenants' association of facts about the incidence of racist attacks on its estate;
- regular monitoring and improvement of both police and council staff activities on estates;
- the appointment of racial harassment officers.

These are only some considerations; there are many other facets of a council's work that need to be considered, not least how a lettings policy can either expose individual families to harassment, or create conditions in which it might occur (for example, the ratio of children to adults on an estate). Other issues concern the importance of resident caretakers, the opening of estate offices on large estates, and the modification of those design features of estates that encourage crime and deviancy, and which work against positive interaction between residents.

We hope this chapter has given an indication of how community workers might develop their practice, and the kinds of changes that are necessary in the environment created for their work by their agencies and local authorities. The consolidation of more relevant pre- and in-service training is important, not least because what has emerged in this chapter is that supporting black participation is partly, though not wholly, a matter of 'doing good community work better'. There seems to us to be a clear need to re-think practice theory in community work in order to give a particular focus on work with ethnic minority groups; this must proceed alongside creating opportunities through training, publications and conferences for the dissemination of good practice, and the chance to examine critically cases of success and failure in organizing with black people. Our own experiences in this project have suggested that part of this learning process must include access to comparative experiences in other countries where community work has developed with ethnic minority groups – particularly Holland, France and Norway.

It is also clear that helping workers to prepare for successful practice with ethnic minority groups implies a programme that goes far beyond basic training in racism awareness. We hope this chapter has been suggestive of the ways in which roles and functions have to change, and how these are dependent on change in the agency of the fieldworker. The ability to induce parallel change in person, role and organization (as well as the environment in which they work) has emerged as an important feature of more effective work with ethnic minority groups.

Our last task in this chapter is to draw attention to how the roots of modern community work in Britain are to be found in the development of modern housing estates both inside and on the edges of cities. These roots are apparent, for example, in the work of Len White and the Pacifist Services Unit, and that of Muriel Smith and the initiation of the Association of London Housing Estates. The impetus for much of the early practice and theory of community work was to turn the new housing estates that were being built into viable communities. It seems to us that this particular aspect of community work history is about to be repeated, as housing tenure becomes more ethnically polarized. To the extent that some ethnic minority groups are becoming concentrated in the public housing sector (and whites in the private rented and home-ownership sector) then much community work that is concerned with ethnic minorities will be centred on public housing estates. Thus the challenge for practitioners and trainers is not just about modernizing community work to take account of work with ethnic minorities, but also to reappraise how competent it is to work effectively on the housing estates of the 1980s and 1990s. We strongly urge that resources are made available to review existing experience and theory in relation to housing estates, and to provide a comprehensive framework for community work practice on these estates.

Notes

1 The seriousness confronting practitioners and trainers of the absence of practical responses to issues of racism has also been noted in youth work. See Ritchie and Marken (1984).

7

Out of the Paper Bag

> You pose no end of questions, problems and conflicts and
> then leave Chris and friends very much in the dark. She could
> easily be tempted to shut her eyes and believe that it would
> be more worthwhile not to see the issues or to work on
> something else. (*A reader's comment*)

The writing of this study has come to an end amidst street fighting
in Handsworth, Brixton and Tottenham. It is not without reason,
therefore, that our attempts to conclude this book are unbalanced
by a sense of helplessness, and feelings of anguish and anger. It is
clear to us that the deterioration in social relationships in urban
areas, and specifically those between black and white, is partly a
function of economic policies, and of other macro-factors such as
the design of much modern public housing. On this point, there
is ample evidence of the experience and views of black people
themselves in the two reports from the Policy Studies Institute
(Brown, 1984; Smith *et al.*, 1983).

The de-resourcing of urban areas has resulted in the
impoverishment not just of individual lives but of group relationships, and in the decay of social responsibilities and resources. As
we said at the very start of the book, people are socio-degradable.
On the other hand, social reconstruction is not something that
will follow in an automatic or simple way from material reconstruction; nor do we believe that the achievement of racial justice
will on its own produce a change for the better in the relations
between black and white British, though no one can doubt that
the removal brick by brick of the invisible wall of white racism
must be a paramount consideration in the re-building of urban
neighbourhoods.

220

How do we rise above our own helplessness to affect such macro-factors to make suggestions for further developments that sound realistic and credible? One answer is to be very single-minded in our interest in the community worker (and others working in the community) as an agent – as one agent – of the sponsored development of communities. This was Chris's reasonable suggestion to us, and she drew a comparison with the dedicated entomologist trying to learn more about, say, various types of butterflies. He knows that the habitat and food supplies of the butterflies are adversely affected by industrial and governmental decisions far removed from his influence; he can draw attention in his reports and papers to those policies that destroy the environment, but can do little, even when combining with others, to effect major changes in policy. Despite this, he pursues his identification and study of the butterflies as best he can, but always conscious of the wider frames that impinge on the day-to-day behaviour and adaptations in which he is interested.

Following this analogy, one can comment on community workers, and all those others in voluntary and statutory agencies who are, or might be, involved in developing networks and groups within a locality. This study has revealed how bare the emperor is: there is a danger that community work will bring itself into disrepute by failing to deliver on the issue that it feels most strongly about: personal and institutional racism. There is a good deal of work to be done in producing a more effective theory of practice in multi-ethnic areas and, just as fundamentally, in providing workers with the insights and skills for helping to sponsor community interaction as well as action. The blind spot in the vision of many community workers is that which they share with the laissez-faire policy-maker: they seem slow to appreciate that the effectiveness of particular actions and of particular relationships (such as black and white) is related to the quality of the general social infrastructure of a locality. The removal of this blind spot is dependent in part on changes in pre- and in-service training, though here again helplessness intrudes because both are still dependent on 'host' occupations such as social work and youth work. On the other hand, these host occupations do have substantial training programmes and the arguments for change are just as strong for them as for community work training.

But the community worker is not just a community worker: the majority of them are employees in the voluntary sector, as, too, are the vast majority of other professionals concerned with community development (for example, staff in Community Relations Committees, Councils of Voluntary Service and Rural Community Councils). All these employees are, in the main, products of particular pre-service training opportunities that equipped them (or not) for work in the voluntary sector. Thus it is the voluntary sector as a whole which must inquire how far training provided by social work, youth work and so forth equips their future employees to work in multi-ethnic localities. Likewise, the increase in the number of ethnic community workers, the development and monitoring of co-working and the appearance of more locally based and culturally attuned services are also major issues for the voluntary sector as a whole to take up. In this respect, it would be useful to explore the feasibility of establishing a national development unit whose brief would be to help the voluntary sector become more effective in its work in multi-ethnic localities. The work of this unit would include advice, research, organizational development and training; as far as the last two functions are concerned, there would be a major task in offering forms of training that produced changes in person, role and organization and which would thus be a substantial extension of training beyond the current scope of racism awareness workshops. An important lesson from the project is the present crudity of training, and of learning theories about racism and attitude change, and it would be a priority to devise ways of bringing black and white professionals together that helped them to communicate honestly and to demonstrate models of learning that they could use with other colleagues and local people. It might be possible not only to explore the desirability of a national development unit, but, at the same time, to organize a period of innovatory training workshops to identify productive forms of learning between black and white workers in the voluntary sector.

The kinds of further research that might be contemplated have been identified as the book has proceeded. There is a clear need for a regular source of data about participation in voluntary activities, with a greater differentiation of activities and participants than was present in the 1981 General Household Survey. We cannot go very far in adopting a more interventionist, rather than laissez-faire, approach to the development of communities until further work has been carried out to clarify the notions of community capability, as well as the central idea in livelihood that social resources and social tasks have to be managed if they are to flourish and not atrophy. There is much to do in defining more precisely which social resources are salient in managing livelihood, and how they relate to collective forms of endeavour between people (action groups, community businesses and so on) to improve the material basis of livelihood. Part of the work in overcoming the laissez-faire attitude to the development of communities is to carry out studies that accelerate the production of the concepts and language available to us in thinking about, and intervening in, local neighbourhoods. Unless we produce this acceleration towards ideas with a sharper differentiation and analytic power, we will be exposed to the scepticism of policy-makers who understandably find the present vocabulary of 'community' flabby, jaded and often metaphysical. We hope this study has indicated the range of further work that is possible around core ideas such as livelihood, social resources, community capability and the nominal and interacting community.

We have also tried to make evident the need for greater differentiation in the analysis of black–white relationships, because greater clarity and refinement in the way we think will help us to be more effective in the work that we do. The way in which blacks and whites see each other as uniformly hostile and homogeneous groups is mirrored in the reductionist concepts and language that is common amongst white and black professionals. Just as the richness and variety of individuals have been reduced to stereotype and group homogeneity, so too have absolutist theories about race been used to strip everyday encounters and perceptions between blacks and whites of their complexity. Perhaps the culprit is the professional's search for the easy, the comfortable, the predictable, or the containable – racism awareness training, positive action in funding projects, positive discrimination in employment and so forth are necessary but limited, and, above all, safe responses to the evils of institutional racism rather than to the perilous task of intervening in the often raw and turbulent everyday world of the white and black working class. This search for the safe and the containable must of necessity produce a level of blandness and caution in analysing black–white relations, a caution that encouraged generalizations and blanket analyses. It is a caution that is also born of the danger that both black and white professionals feel when they try to talk openly and honestly with each other, especially when they try to move beyond giving each other assurances about their own good intentions and liberated attitudes. There is, too, a mistaken belief that to add differentiation and refinement to our analysis of black–white relations is somehow to blur the moral outrage of racism, and to degrade the black struggle. Our experience in this project has told us the opposite is true; the black struggle is degraded through rhetoric and self-deceit, inflated language and exaggerated claims, and by the difficulty experienced by white and black professionals to endow their diagnoses and prescriptions with some of the complexity that is present in the everyday world that they hope to influence.

And it is to this world of the everyday interactions of people that social researchers must bring their imagination, and funders their resources. Neither economic nor social policies are likely to alter overnight in a way that will produce changes for the better in social relationships; indeed, who can feel confident that policy-makers would have the means of intervention at hand that would be reliable in producing the kinds of changes that are needed in the relationships between people in urban neighbourhoods? The role of government and trust funders in the future should thus be to stimulate and monitor alternative ways to put people in contact with each other at the local level; small-scale experiments in the creation of networks, groups, forums and a whole range of devices for bringing people together to manage their social tasks and resources are what is now required on housing estates in many inner-city areas, as well as on peripheral estates. There is a need to experiment in such areas with ways of putting people in touch with one another, so they are able to communicate and begin to take responsibility for the area in which they live. It has always been, and still is, a goal of social policy to aid the process of people associating with one another in support and self-help groups of different kinds. What is being stressed here, however, is the importance of putting people in touch with one another not in the role of client or in some special category of need but in the role of neighbour. Helping to develop the role of neighbour is a requirement if people in poor urban localities are to feel they are safe and able to manage and contribute towards the evolution of a local social order. Schoenberg and Rosenbaum have reviewed the legacy of research that indicates

> that residents who report that there are people in the neighbourhood who know each other also report that they have a sense of control. In neighbourhoods where neighbouring indices record both a speaking acquaintance among neighbours and some knowledge of the organisational and institutional leadership in the neighbourhood, residents have a greater sense of safety and control. (*1980*)

They indicate from their own and others' research that 'controlling the social order of neighbourhood life and affecting the decisions about one's neighbourhood in working-class and poor areas require social network formation, organisational development and political exchange'. Of course, knowing others and being known oneself determine how significant an individual feels within the place he lives, and this sense of mattering is linked both to self-image and to the positive valuation of the neighbourhood; both in turn are determinants of the predisposition of people to invest time and energy in social networks and community organizations, and thus in the evolution of a neighbourhood as a viable social unit. No matter which way one twists and turns the diagnostic scalpel, one always comes back to the recognition that the construction of viable neighbourhoods in urban areas is dependent on people being able to identify each other, make contact and communicate.

From one viewpoint, it might seem impossible to convince policy-makers that the contrivance of neighbour roles and relations is both a legitimate and achievable task. But from another position, we can see that the development of the role of neighbour is already an aspect of some areas of policy innovation: for example, it is implicit in neighbourhood watch schemes and in programmes to develop community care, self-help and locally based economic initiatives. These innovations and programmes represent partial and sometimes tangential attempts to give help to people to develop neighbour roles, relations and responsibilities. We hope we have been successful in this brief study in indicating some of the difficulties, as well as the opportunities, in helping black and white residents develop their neighbourhood roles and relations. We now need to abstract the partial and tangential and give the development of the role of neighbour a central, explicit place in policy formulation about urban areas.

As a society, we are struggling with major issues that affect the social order; while some politicians and policy-makers create and worsen numerous conflicts and cleavages, others seek desperately for the means to resolve them. There are a number of tools at their disposal, including allocating more and more resources to policing and other forms of surveillance, though both the cost and the efficacy of such a policy is already in question. The revitalization of urban neighbourhoods is an alternative tool in constructing a meaningful social order. We must stress that such revitalization requires the allocation of much-needed resources (for example, £20 million for urgent council house repairs).

At one level, such an allocation of resources must reflect a change in the priorities of political leadership in this country; specifically, what is required is a leadership that can articulate, and win support for, a sense of national purpose based on social values and goals, to which are subordinated *as means* the narrow economic objectives (e.g. 'keeping inflation down') of 'housekeeping politics' that have for so long obscured the vision of those entrusted with the authority and resources of government. At another level, the material side of reconstruction needs to occur as part of a strategy that accepts that the locality is a valued and proper part of social structure and, as such, attention is given to the development of its social assets and responsibilities. The role of neighbour has been thrust on people by economic events such as unemployment; the development of this role within a strategy of providing jobs, decent housing and reform in police behaviour towards young black people is now something that should be taken seriously within social policy if people in urban neighbourhoods are not to tear themselves apart, and if these neighbourhoods are not to disintegrate and burn.

And what of Chris and her colleagues? They remain out there

supporting the morale and competence of hard-pressed residents in the deteriorating structure of the inner city, using largely their own personal skills and energy with few externally provided resources. They cannot compel people to communicate, nor induce them through financial incentives to join in groups; they offer only the possibility of change – and perhaps marginal change at that – if people pool and capitalize the assets they have most doubts about: their own skills and energies. They have an optimism about people's capacities that has often long since deserted the people themselves. We wondered whether studies such as this helped or hindered fieldworkers? Chris's reply was to read one of her poems to us:

> I am the prisoner released
> Blinking into painful sunlight
> Only a small bundle of belongings
> To be with me in a new world.
>
> I am the one who was blind:
> My sight restored, I understand little
> I see, but long to shut my eyes again
> For the sake of familiar sensation.
>
> Funny, I always imagined
> That once I'd fought my way out
> Of my paper bag, I'd be able to see
> Which way to go.

Her involvement, she said, had been stimulating and rewarding but the study did rather remind her of something Lennie Henry had said on television: 'It was so dark you could see better with your eyes closed.' Hence the poem. We had provided some illumination so that she could now better see what she was doing and where she was going. But at the same time, the study had revealed the complexity of the issues about the neighbourhood and black–white relations, as well as the darkness in people's hearts and minds about each other. She knew more but understood less. The effect of a torch, she said, was to make it harder to see what was in the darkness outside its beam; and, furthermore, there wasn't much point in illuminating something if those who should take notice firmly keep their eyes closed: 'You can lead us all to your study, but you can't make us think, let alone act.'

'That sounds very pessimistic, as if you are going to give up.'

'Not at all. I'm going to stick with it however much parts of me might not want to bother, because "bothering" – in fact, making a 180 degree difference to very negative circumstances – is what my work is about.'

8

And Tomorrow's Stockades . . . ?

'Look, you don't know how lucky you are! If you'd been born in days gone by instead of now your life would be very different, I can tell you!

'In those days *everyone* had to go outside – even the inside classes! People lived in one place, and worked in another. And to get from the house where they lived to the house where they worked they had to go out in the air – thousands of them, millions of them, all brushing against each other and breathing in each other's faces! And they packed together in communal travelling houses – shoulder to shoulder, chest to chest!

'They did almost everything communally. They ate in crowds, worked in crowds, relaxed in crowds. Almost everywhere you went, you found yourself in the actual physical presence of other human beings. That's the literal truth. Cumby, I'm not telling you stories.

'Well, of course they were rained on. And burnt by the sun – which was very strong in those days. And they were struck by lightning. And, of course, the contaminated air outside carried diseases; in those days people used to breathe in disease with every breath. And then naturally they'd pass the disease on to everyone around them, by touching them, or breathing over them. Everyone was diseased then, for at least a part of every year – diseased in the nose, so they couldn't breathe properly; diseased in the throat, so they couldn't swallow; diseased in the stomach, so they couldn't digest; diseased in the head, so they couldn't think.

'And they were minced up by their travelling houses – crushed to death by the dozen inside them, ground up beneath them. You have to learn these things, Cumby. That's what it was like then. Even small children had to go outside, and breathe the unfiltered air, and mix with people they didn't like.

229

'They lived like animals – they behaved like animals. There was anarchy! But the reaction to anarchy was even worse. The most stringent order had to be imposed upon people, just so that they could survive their proximity. Society had to be arranged in strict hierarchical patterns, with powerful controls and sanctions. So that when people looked into the future all they could foresee was the necessity for stricter and stricter social order imposed by ever more powerful central authorities, through ever more far-reaching controls. One day, they feared, every aspect of human behaviour would be controlled by some central authority. Nothing would be private – not even people's thoughts. The whole of life would become public and communal. Freedom would vanish entirely.

'Well, of course, what in fact happened was exactly the opposite. *Everything* became private. People recognized the corruption of indiscriminate human contact, and one by one they withdrew from it. Whoever could afford it built a wall around himself and his family to keep out society and its demands. Gradually, as people's technological skills improved, the walls they built became more and more impenetrable. One by one the chinks which they were forced to leave in the fortifications in order to export their skills and import the necessities of life were closed up. All over the world each family with the intelligence and energy to manage it gradually created its own individual controlled environment. Each family built its own castle, into which nothing, whether food, air, information or emotion, was admitted until it had been purified and sterilized to suit the occupier's needs.

'So we built the outer walls of our castles. And inside them we built inner walls to protect each member of the family from the proximity of the others.

'But, as we discovered, there were certain unwelcome intruders which seeped through all these defences. Uncertainty, discontent, anger, melancholy – neither filters nor electronic devices could keep them out. So we learnt to construct certain chemical screens inside our own bodies, and to retire behind them to an inner keep where *everything* was under our control.

'And in that inner keep, Cumby, we enjoy the perfect freedom which men have always dreamt of. What crippled and cut short all man's earlier experiments in freedom is that they were public; and the public freedom of one man must necessarily impinge upon the public freedom of others; so that public freedoms inevitably limit and destroy each other. But our modern *private* freedoms impinge upon no one and nothing. And no one and nothing can impinge upon them. Even death, the last and most inexorable invader of our privacy, is being driven back step by step.

'And that, Cumby, is why you've got to do what you're told, and wear your dark glasses and take your pills – so that you can preserve the precious liberty that mankind has so slowly and so laboriously evolved.'

Uncumber will listen to all this is silence – scowling, no doubt, but attentive. One small point, however, will worry her.

'What about the outside people?' she will object. 'How are they perfectly free, if they're outside this controlled environment?'

Aelfric will sigh with exasperation.

'For heaven's sake, Cumby! They're not the same as us at all. They're entirely different!'

Michael Frayn,
A Very Private Life (1981)

References

Abraham, R. D. (1970), *Positively Black* (New York: Prentice Hall).

Acland Burghley School (1985), *Report on a Conference on Race* (London: Acland Burghley School).

Annamanthodo, P. (1985), *Racism Awareness Training and CVS*, in Circulation 89, Council of Voluntary Service, National Association, 15 March.

Archbishop of Canterbury's Commission (1985), *Faith in the City: A Call for Action by Church and Nation* (London: Church House Publishing).

Banton, M. (1983), 'The influence of colonial status upon black–white relations in England 1948–58, *Sociology*, November.

Barr, A. (1980), 'Community development and minorities: problems and feasible strategies', *Community Development Journal*, October.

Blee, K. (1984), 'Family ties and class conflict: the politics of immigrant communities in the Great Lakes region, 1890–1920', *Social Problems*, February.

Bolger, S., and Scott, D. (1984), *Starting from Strengths: The Report of the Panel to Promote the Continuing Development of Part-Time and Voluntary Youth and Community Workers* (Leicester: NYB).

Booth, H. (1985), 'Which "ethnic question"? The development of questions identifying ethnic origin in official statistics', *Sociological Review*, vol. 33, no. 2.

Bridges, L., and Fekete, L. (1985), 'Victims, the "urban jungle" and the new realism', *Race and Class* (summer).

Brown, C. (1984), *Black and White Britain: The Third PSI survey* (London: PSI).

Bryan, B., *et al.* (1985), 'Chain reactions: black women organising', *Race and Class*, Summer.

Carmichael, S., and Hamilton, C. V. (1967), *Black Power: The Politics of Liberation in America* (New York: Random House).

Cashmore, E. E. (1984), *Dictionary of Race and Ethnic Relations* (London: Routledge & Kegan Paul).

Central Statistical Office (1983, 1985), *Social Trends* (London: HMSO).

Cheetham, J. (1982), *Social Work and Ethnicity* (London: Allen & Unwin).

Cheetham, J. (1985), 'Race and research in social services departments', *Research, Policy and Planning*, vol. 3, no. 1.

Cheetham, J., *et al.* (1981), *Social and Community Work in a Multi-Racial Society* (London: Harper & Row).

Coleman, A. (1985), *Utopia on Trial* (London: Shipman).

Commission For Racial Equality (1985), *Race and Mortgage Lending* (London: CRE).

Cowan, J. (1982), *Many Cultures, One Community?* (London), mimeo.

Cross, C. (1978), *Ethnic Minorities in the Inner City* (London: CRE).

Davies, L. (1979), 'Racial composition of groups', *Social Work*, May.

Davis, A. (1982), *Women, Race and Class* (London: Women's Press).

Delbecq, A. L., and Van de Ven, A. (1971), 'Nominal versus interacting group processes for community decision-making', *Journal of the Academy of Management*, vol. 14, no. 2.

Delbecq, A. L., and Van de Ven, A. (1981), A group process model for problem identification and programme planning', in Henderson and Thomas, op. cit.

Delgado, M., and Humm-Delgado, D. (1982), 'Natural support systems: a source of strength in Hispanic communities', *Social Work*, January.

Department of the Environment (1985), *An Inquiry into the Condition of the Local Authority Housing Stock in England* (London: Department of the Environment).

Dolores, Gerry and Sunita (1983), 'Three black women talk about sexuality and racism', *Spare Rib*, no. 135 (October).

Donnelly, L., and Ohri, A. (1982), 'Alliances and coalitions in the struggle for racial equality', in Ohri *et al.*, op cit.

Dryden, J. (1982), 'A social services department and the Bengali community', in Cheetham, op. cit.

Dungate, M. (1984), *A multi-racial society: the role of national voluntary organisations* (London: Bedford Square Press).

Ellis, J. (1985) 'Management committees and race equality', *Management Development Unit Bulletin* (NCVO), no. 5 (June).

Ensor, C., *et al.* (1982), 'Organising in a multi-ethnic society', *Community Development Journal*, April.

Field, J., and Hedges, B. (1984), *A National Survey of Volunteering* (London: SCPR).

Fleming, J., and Harrison, M. (1984/5), 'Anti-racist youth work – a review', *Youth and Policy*, no. 11 (winter).

Francis, D. (1982), 'The scope for community initiatives and voluntary action in rural areas, Phd thesis, London University.

Francis, D., *et al.* (1984), *A Survey of Community Workers in the United Kingdom* (London: NISW).

Frayn, M. (1981), *A Very Private Life* (London: Fontana).

Fryer, P. (1984), *Staying Power: The History of Black People in Britain* (London: Pluto Press).

Gilbert, N., *et al.* (1974), 'Demographic correlates of citizen participation: an analysis of race, community size and citizen influence', *Social Services Review*, December.

Glasgow, D. (1973), 'Black power through community control', in Goodman, op. cit.

Goodman, J. A. (1973), *Dynamics of Racism in Social Work Practice* (New York: NASW).

Greater London Council (1984), *Racial Harassment in London* (London: GLC).

Grier, W. H., and Cobbs, P. M. (1969), *Black Rage* (London: Cape).

Gurnah, A. (1984), 'The politics of racism awareness training', *Critical Social Policy*, no. 11 (winter).

Harrison, P. (1983), *Inside the Inner City* (Harmondsworth: Penguin).

Hechter, M. (1977), 'The political economy of ethnic change', *American Journal of Sociology*, vol. 79, no. 5.

Henderson, P., and Thomas, D. N. (1981), *Readings in Community Work* (London: Allen & Unwin).

Hernton, C. C. (1969), *Sex and Racism* (London: Deutsch).

HMSO (1982), *The Brixton Disorders 10–12 April 1981*, Report of an Inquiry by the Rt. Hon. The Lord Scarman OBE (London: HMSO).

Hoch, P. (1979), *White Hero, Black Beast: Racism, Sexism and the Mask of Masculinity* (London: Pluto Press).

Home Office (1981), *Racial Attacks, Report of a Home Office Study* (London: HMSO).

Jahoda, M. (1982), *Employment and Unemployment: A Social-Psychological Analysis* (Cambridge: CUP).

Jenkins, S. (1980), 'The ethnic agency defined', *Social Service Review*, June.

John, G. (1984), 'Projects versus politics', *Talking Point* (ACW), December.

John, G., and Parkes, N. (1984), *Working with Black Youth: Complementary or Competing Resources?*, Extension Report 2 (Leicester: NYB).

Keneally, T. (1982), *Schindler's Ark* (London: Hodder).

Knight, B., and Hayes, R. (1981), *Self-Help in the Inner City* (London: LVSC).

Kohfeld, C. W., *et al.* (1981), 'Neighbourhood associations and urban crime', *Journal of Community Action*, no. 2.

Kosinski, J. (1972), *The Painted Bird* (London: Corgi).

Kosmin, B. (1982), 'Political identity in Battersea', in Wallman, op. cit.

Lambat, I. (1980), 'Community work with an Asian community', in P. Henderson *et al.* (eds), *Boundaries of Change in Community Work* (London: Allen & Unwin).

Lawrence, D. (1975), *Black Migrants, White Natives* (Cambridge: CUP).

Ley D. (1970), *The Black Inner City as Frontier Outpost* (Washington, DC: Association of American Geographers).

Little, A. (1982), *Adult Education and the Black Communities* (Leicester: Advisory Centre for Adult and Continuing Education).

London Tenants Organisation (1984), *Report on a Black Tenants' Conference* (London: LTO).

Longres, J. F. (1982), 'Minority groups: an interest-group perspective', *Social Work*, January.

Malcolm X (1967), 'Afro-American history', *International Socialist Review*, March–April.

Manning, B., and Ohri, A. (1982), 'Racism – the response of community work', in Ohri *et al.*, op. cit.

Miles, R., and Phizacklea, A. (1977), 'Class, race, ethnicity and political action', *Political Studies*, vol. 25, no. 4.

Miles, R., and Phizacklea, A. (1979), *Racism and Political Action in Britain* (London: RKP).

Morris, L. (1985), 'Local social networks and domestic organisation: a study of redundant steel workers and their wives', *Sociological Review*, vol. 33, no. 2.

Morrison, J. D. (1983), 'Racial change or racial stabilisation: policy and progress at neighbourhood level', *Journal of Sociology and Social Welfare*, March.

Mukherjee, T. (n.d.), *I'm Not Blaming You: An Anti-Racist Analysis* (London: URJIT).

Mullard, C. (1973), *Black Britain* (London: Allen & Unwin).

Nederlandse organisatie van Welzijuswerkers (1983), *Opbouwwerk en racisme/ fascisme* (Netherlands: NOW).

O'Brien, D. (1975), *Neighbourhood Organisation and Interest-Group Processes* (Princeton: Princeton University Press).

O'Brien, D. (1981), 'The public goods dilemma and the "apathy" of the poor toward neighbourhood organisation', in P. Henderson and D. N. Thomas, op. cit.

Office of Population Census and Surveys (1981) *General Household Survey* (London: HMSO).

Ohri, A., *et al.* (1982), *Community Work and Racism* (London: RKP).

Oliver, P. (1969), *The Meaning of the Blues* (Ontario: Macmillan).

Ouseley, H. (1985), '"Treating them all the same" decentralising institutional racism', *Going Local?* no. 2 (April).

Owusu-Bempah, J. (1985), *Racism: A White Problem*, in Circulation 100, Council of Voluntary Service, National Association, 16 August.

Page, M. (1983), 'Language and community politics – or exorcising the old ideal', *Talking Point* (ACW), March.

Parkes, N. (1984), 'Part-time work with black youth' in John and Parkes, op. cit.

Phillips, M. (1982), 'Separatism or black control?', in Ohri *et al.*, op. cit.

Plant, R. (1974), *Community and Ideology* (London: RKP).

Prem, D. R. (1966), *The Parliamentary Leper* (Delhi: Everest Press).

Rex, J. (1979), 'Black militancy and class conflict', in Miles and Phizacklea, op. cit.

Richardson, A. (1983), *Participation* (London: RKP).

Ritchie, N., and Marken, M. (1984), *Anti-Racist Youth Work* (Leicester: NYB).

Rivera, F. G., and Erlich, J. L. (1981), 'Neo-*Gemeinschaft* minority communities: implications for community organisation in the United States', *Community Development Journal*, October.

Robertson, C. (1984), 'Do we listen to what local people really want?' *Talking Point* (ACW), October.

Rothman, J. (1977), *Issues in Race and Ethnic Relations* (Itasca: Peacock).

Rushdie, S. (1982), 'The new empire within Britain', *New Society*, 9 December.

Satow, A. (1982), 'Racism awareness training: training to make a difference', in Ohri *et al.*, op. cit.

Saunders, M. S. (1973), 'The Ghetto: Some Perceptions of a Black Social Worker', in Goodman, op. cit.

Sayer, B. D. (1985), 'The critique of politics and political economy: capitalism, communism and the state in Marx's writings of the mid-1840s', *Sociological Review*, vol. 33, no. 2.

Schoenberg, S. P. (1979), 'Criteria for evaluation of neighbourhood vitality in working-class and poor areas in core cities', *Social Problems*, October.

Schoenberg, S. P. (1980), 'Community stability and decay in St Louis: the ethnic factor in two urban neighbourhoods', *Ethnicity*, vol. 7.

Schoenberg, S. P., and Rosenbaum, P. L. (1977), *Prerequisites to Participation by the Poor in an Urban Neighborhood*, paper presented at the convention of the American Sociological Association (Chicago).

Schoenberg, S. P., and Rosenbaum, P. L. (1980), *Neighbourhoods that Work* (New Jersey: Rutgers University Press).

Scott, D., *et al.* (n.d.), 'Strategies for community work in multi-ethnic areas', unpublished mimeo.

Seabrook, J. (1984), *The Idea of Neighbourhood* (London: Pluto Press).

Sills, P. (1974/5), 'Community work: the action dimension', *New Community*, vol. 4, no. 1.

Sinclair, T. (1984), 'The turning point approach to multi-ethnic fieldwork supervision', *Journal of Community Education*, vol. 3, no. 3.

Sivanandan, A. (1985), 'RAT and the degradation of black struggle', *Race and Class*, vol. 26, no. 4.

Small, S. (1983), *Police and People in London*, Vol. 2: *A Group of Young Black People* (London: PSI).

Smith, D. J. *et al.* (1983), *People and Police in London*, 4 vols (London: PSI).

Soloman, B. B. (1976), *Black Empowerment: Social Work in Oppressed Communities* (New York: Columbia University Press).

Sondhi, R. (1982), 'The Asian Resource Centre – Birmingham', in Ohri *et al.*, op. cit.

Stopes-Roe, M., and Cochrane, R. (1985), 'As others see us . . .', *New Society*, 1 November.

Suttles, G. D. (1968), *The Social Order of the Slum* (Chicago: Chicago University Press).

Suttles, G. D. (1972), *The Social Construction of Communities* (Chicago: Chicago University Press).

Tamney, J. (1975), *Solidarity in a Slum* (New York: Wiley).

Television History Workshop (1981), *The Brixton Tapes*, 34-minute video tape, with user pack (42 Queen Square, London WC1).

Thomas, D. N. (1971a), 'Taking care of the estate', *Race Today*, April.

Thomas, D. N. (1971b), 'Community relations and community work', *Race Today*, August.

Thomas, D. N. (1985), 'State and neighbourhood' and 'Private Lives', *Community Care*, 31 January and 1 February.

Unell, J. (1983), *Reaching Out to the Asian Community* (London: COPE).

Wallman, S. (1975/6), 'A street in Waterloo', *New Community*, vol. 4, no. 4.

Wallman, S. (1979), *Ethnicity at Work* (London: Macmillan).

Wallman, S. (1982), *Living in South London* (London: Gower).

Ward, R. (1979), 'Where race didn't divide: some reflections on slum clearance in Moss Side', in Miles and Phizacklea, op. cit.

Warren, R. L. (1963), *The Community in America* (Chicago: Rand McNally).

Watkins, T. R., and Gonzales, R. (1982), 'Outreach to Mexican Americans', *Social Work*, January.

Willmot, P., and Thomas, D. N. (1984), *The Significance of Community* (London: PSI).

Wilson, A. (1978), *Finding a Voice: Asian Women in Britain* (London: Virago).

Wiseman, P. (1979), 'Community work in a multi-racial area', in M. Dungate *et al. Collective Action* (London: ACW).

Yancey, W. L., *et al.* (1976), 'Emergent ethnicity: a review and reformulation', *American Sociological Review*, vol. 41, no. 3.

Young, J. and Lea, J. (1982), 'Race and crime', *Marxism Today*, August.

Zinn, M. B. (1979), 'Field research in minority communities: political, ethical and methodological observations by an insider', *Social Problems*, December.

Appendix 1

Consultation Before the Six-Month Project

Our initial thoughts on the project were distributed in June 1983 to a number of colleagues and organizations. Their responses helped us to reappraise our proposals and design the present project. The following were involved in this initial consultation:

The Runnymede Trust
National Association of Community Relations Councils
Commission for Racial Equality
National Federation of Community Organisations
Voluntary Services Unit
Research Unit on Ethnic Relations, University of Aston in Birmingham
Race Relations Officer, London Borough of Camden SSD
Camden Council of Social Service

The paper was also circulated to members of the London Council of Community Work Training, the London Tenants' Organization, and to several charitable trusts with an interest in this area.

The gist of our proposal for this project is reproduced below, although we present it with diffidence because, as one of our readers noted, the proposal makes assumptions 'upon which a whole number of stereotypes are built and the proposal is made within the framework of these stereotypes . . . I hope you can see this and that future proposals will not become encased in this framework, which merely reproduces racism'. Bearing these comments in mind, the proposal was as follows:

This proposal is about the participation of black people in community organizations. These organizations (such as tenants' associations, playground committees, neighbourhood care groups etc.) have become an important part of our civic life. It is becoming clear that in multi-ethnic urban areas many of these community groups have few black members, and are often indifferent to the needs of black constituents or at least unsure how best to respond to them. The exclusion of black people and their interests from community groups is an issue that has to be squarely tackled for it represents the absence of the opportunity to participate in one of the most basic elements of our social and democratic life.

This concern with black participation in community groups does not assume that the emergence of wholly black groups is undesirable; on the contrary these groups have a vital role, and part of our interest in this area is both the extent of participation of black people in black groups, and the relationship between these groups and community organizations.

Our concern with community groups is that they are part of the voluntary sector, and to help enhance the involvement of black people in them is an aspect of a more general effort to assist the white voluntary sector to adjust to being part of a multi-ethnic society. This proposal accepts that there is a growing recognition in the voluntary sector about the need to make this adjustment; amongst community groups, how-ever, the situation is less satisfactory and it is common to encounter racism, ignorance, indifference as well as a sense of helplessness amongst community workers and community leaders who recognise the need to change this situation . . .

As a result of this proposal, the Voluntary Services Unit agreed to support a six-month exploratory project.

Appendix 2

Interviews in the Six-Month Project

Pushpinder Chowdhry and Hugh Morrison undertook a limited number of interviews amongst Asian and Afro-Caribbean residents. The interviews were tape-recorded and then transcribed.

The interviews with Asians, of which there were fifteen, took place in north London, in Barnet, Brent and in Southall. Eleven interviews were with women, and four with men. The home countries of the interviewees were Bangladesh, Pakistan, India and East Africa. The interviewees were from a number of different age groups, although most of the interviewees had teenage or grown-up children. The interviews were done in the language of the interviewee and then translated. It should be noted that these interviews were carried out in the period of turmoil following Mrs Gandhi's assassination.

There were eleven interviews with Afro-Caribbeans, nine of which were done in south London, and one each in Birmingham and Bristol. Six were men and five were women. Most had been born in Britain or came here as children, and had been here for over twenty years; six had families with small children.

The interviewees were located through personal contact and introductions; they do not, of course, represent a 'scientific' sample and nor do they allow us to generalize. The interviews were mainly 'reconnaissance interviews' that gave us some insight into how residents perceived some of the issues we encountered in the literature and in our contacts with community workers. They gave us a 'feel' for the everyday reality of some of these issues and in the book we have tried to use them to illustrate specific points or issues. We have done our best to avoid the trap of using them to generalize about 'all Asians' and 'all Afro-Caribbeans'. The checklist of questions used to provide a flexible guide for the interviews is reproduced below. Most of the interviews were carried out on public housing estates.

David Thomas carried out ten interviews with white community workers based in London. They came from both statutory and voluntary agencies, and were recruited through personal contact and through membership of the workshops held as part of the project. A number of agencies were also visited, for example the National Federation of Community Organizations and the London Tenants' Organization.

Participation in Community Groups: an Exploratory Study

Checklist of Questions

These are provided only to 'guide' the general direction of the interviews.

1 Background

How long on estate?
How did they get on to estate?
Feelings about estate?
What do they do when they have complaints?
Have they used TA/advice centres?
Responsibilities within the (extended) family.

2 Issues

What kind of problems do you have living on this estate?
What are the most important issues facing you as a black person on this estate?
Are the issues which affect black people different from those that affect white people on the estate?
What do you think ought to be done to solve some of these issues?
Do you think black people have more/different problems to other tenants on this estate?
Do you think that black and white people should work together on issues that affect them both?
Do you think you'll live on this estate for a long time?

Do you and your friends get on well with people on this estate?
How optimistic do you feel about the future of black people in
this country?

3 Belonging

Where do most of your family live?
Do you have any friends amongst people on this estate?
What social contacts do you have with white neighbours?
Do you take much interest in what's going on on this estate?
Do you ever discuss any of the problems on this estate with your
neighbours – and with white neighbours?
Do you feel you have anything in common with your neighbours?
And what about English/white people? Are they easy to get on
with?
What are your general feelings about white people on this estate?
Would you join any groups with them?
Would you discuss any of your problems with white neighbours?
What do you like/dislike about people around here?
Are there any particular things that put you off getting to know
your white neighbours better?
Do you feel as if you 'belong' around here?

4 Memberships

We want to find out about:
(a) their knowledge of what groups exist;
(b) how they evaluate these groups;
(c) are they members/participants of groups either on the estate
     or outside?

What groups (give examples) exist on this estate?
Are you a member/do you participate?
What about group/activities outside the estate/neighbourhood?
What do you think about groups on this estate?
What use do these groups on the estate have for you, as a black
person?
Are there any things about these groups that you do not like?
Can you tell me what kind of things stop you taking a greater
interest in these groups?

If you did join the TA/group what would you gain from it?

Do you think people on the TA/group would welcome you if you joined?

How would the TA/group have to change to make you feel that you wanted to join?

What would your family say if you began to take an active interest in groups on this estate?

Do you think black people would get together in their own groups to solve their own problems?

Do you think white and black people should work together in groups?

How do you like to spend your leisure time?

Do you take much of an interest in politics?

What about local politics around here? Have you not got involved in anything?

Remember, these are questions to guide the interview. Do please put in others as they occur to you. The most important thing is to *probe* after these initial questions, encouraging the interviewees to expand on a point, and always trying to find out what is behind a response. Always ask an interviewee to *explain* a reply to one of these questions. Always think about:

If yes, why?
If no, why not?

Appendix 3

Project Workshops

Two one-day workshops were held in January and March 1985 as part of the project. The purpose of the workshops was to share our preliminary thoughts with participants, to test our ideas and to gain further information through discussion. Both workshops were, for different reasons, controversial and often heated occasions; in the event, they provided more insight into the relationships between black and white professionals than the specific issue of black participation in community groups.

The workshops were attended on each occasion by some twenty participants, both black and white, mostly community workers, but also with some social work and probation staff. There was a mix of voluntary and statutory agencies. Just under half of each workshop came from areas outside London.

At the request of the participants, a recall day was arranged for both workshops in September 1985 to discuss the draft report. This was attended by four people.

Appendix 4

The National Survey of Volunteering Shuffle Cards

These shuffle cards are reproduced from the National Survey of Volunteering (Field and Hedges, 1984). They explain the categories that are used in Table 2.1 in Chapter 2.

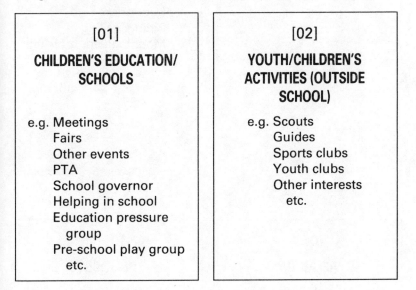

[01]

CHILDREN'S EDUCATION/ SCHOOLS

e.g. Meetings
    Fairs
    Other events
    PTA
    School governor
    Helping in school
    Education pressure
        group
    Pre-school play group
        etc.

[02]

YOUTH/CHILDREN'S ACTIVITIES (OUTSIDE SCHOOL)

e.g. Scouts
    Guides
    Sports clubs
    Youth clubs
    Other interests
        etc.

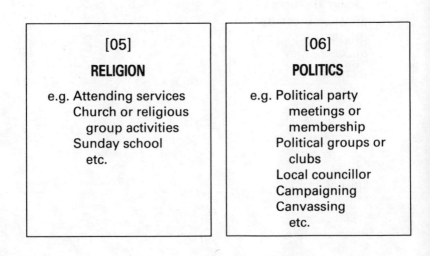

[03]

EDUCATION – YOUR OWN OR GENERAL INTEREST

e.g. Evening or daytime
classes
Teaching (unpaid)
School or college
governor
Students' Union
Education pressure
group
etc.

[04]

SPORTS/EXERCISE (TAKING PART IN OR GOING TO WATCH)

e.g. Football
Swimming
Golf
Badminton
Athletics
Keep fit/dancing
Sports club
Supporters club
Riding, sailing
Mountaineering/hiking

[05]

RELIGION

e.g. Attending services
Church or religious
group activities
Sunday school
etc.

[06]

POLITICS

e.g. Political party
meetings or
membership
Political groups or
clubs
Local councillor
Campaigning
Canvassing
etc.

[07]

SOCIAL WELFARE

e.g. Social Services
Department
Voluntary organiz-
ations such as
Oxfam
Shelter
Samaritans
Citizens (or other)
Advice Bureau
NSPCC
Volunteer Bureau
Save the Children
Fund
etc.

[08]

THE ELDERLY

e.g. Pensioners' clubs
Meals on Wheels
Visiting at home
Voluntary organiz-
ations such as
Age Concern
Help the Aged
etc.

[09]

HEALTH AND SAFETY (OTHER THAN GOING TO DOCTOR, ETC.)

e.g. Red Cross
St John Ambulance
Blood donor
A charity for medical
research
Organizations to help
groups such as
the blind
the deaf
spastics, etc.
Life saving
Mountain rescue
etc.

[10]

THE ENVIRONMENT, CONSERVATION, ANIMALS

e.g. RSPCA
Town or countryside
preservation or
conservation group
etc.

[11]

JUSTICE AND HUMAN RIGHTS

e.g. Legal Advice centre
Magistrate
Prison visiting or
  aftercare
Amnesty International
Community or race
  relations
etc.

[12]

LOCAL COMMUNITY OR NEIGHBOURHOOD GROUPS OR ACTIVITIES

e.g. Tenants' association
Residents' association
Community group
  (formal or informal)
Local conservation or
  pressure group
Self-help group
Consumers' group
Women's group
etc.

[13]

CITIZENSHIP (NATIONAL OR INTERNATIONAL)

e.g. Women's Institute
Freemasons
Rotary
WRVS
etc.

[14]

HOBBY, RECREATION, SOCIAL OR SPECIAL INTEREST GROUPS

e.g. Gardening
Theatre, arts
Cinema
Social club
Bingo
Any special interest
etc.

Index